# FROM SHIFTLESS TO SHIFTY

## My Forty-Six Years as a Public Defender

JOHN WOOD

First Edition

NEWMAN SPRINGS PUBLISHING
830 Park Ave, Suite 155
Meadville, PA 16335

First originally published by Newman Springs Publishing 2025

ISBN 979-8-89308-045-2 (Paperback)
ISBN 979-8-89308-046-9 (Digital)

Printed in the United States of America

To the memory of
John Courtney,
Al Nugent,
and
the redoubtable TJH

# Foreword

**When I first started this** project, I wanted to write something serious—something deep. I wanted it to be about punishment, about justice, about being merciful. Maybe character studies of a few of the many individuals I represented over so many years as a public defender. As I wrote down these ponderous thoughts, I found that what bubbled up instead was a sense of a certain loopiness in the whole thing, which forced itself into my thoughts, and that is what I imagine is reflected in these pages.

Please don't think I didn't take my participation in the criminal justice system seriously because I did. But, somehow, there is a certain craziness that is a large part of the criminal justice world as I experienced it that just kept rising to the surface. Some of this undoubtedly emanated from myself and my own personality, which I admit is a little skewed, and as I mention somewhere in my musings, there is no question that generally I was marching—and continue to march—to a different drummer than most of the rest of humanity.

If my approach offends you, there are many serious works on the subject that somehow fail to treat the goings-on in the criminal courts with any sense of humor whatsoever. If you, the reader, find my discussion of life in the criminal courts in the Commonwealth of Massachusetts offensive and not sufficiently dignified for the subject,

I apologize. If I were to show you my numerous attempts at serious approaches to the subject, you might find yourself laughing just as hard as possibly you might as I recount the odds and ends of the forty-six years I spent practicing, if that's the right word, as a public defender.

# 1

# Beginnings

**As I thought about it,** shortly after my retirement, it occurred to me that this is the story of how I managed to practice law for forty-six years without having the slightest aptitude for the thing. I'm not sure how this happened, but all the early signs were that I had no legal ability whatsoever. Everybody tried to tell me this, but I wouldn't listen.

I was enamored of the *Perry Mason* series on television and had this idea that I was going to be a criminal defense attorney and free innocent people from the evil Hamilton Burgers of the world. This was just a vague idea, and I had no clue what it would be like to be a lawyer or what it would take to become one. My father was a lawyer, but he was a Wall Street type, and that was something quite different from what I imagined I would become. There was, however, a reminiscence from my father that when he graduated from law school, he had a chance to work for a prominent criminal lawyer of the day. He didn't, he told me, because there was no money in it. It was just a story, but I thought there were indications he might have been good as a defense lawyer, and perhaps "like father, like son" would mean something.

As an example, I remember when I was just learning to drive, and I was on Second Avenue in New York City. I was behind the wheel with my father next to me in the passenger seat. There was a cop at an intersection directing traffic. He was waving his arms and blowing his whistle. I was nervous and confused, and I went through the intersection, even though apparently the cop had ordered me to stop. I got whistled over. My father jumped out of the car, went back, and said a few words to the cop. I was sure I was going to get a ticket or arrested or something. My father returned to the car and said I could go ahead. He had given the cop a story—something about how I misunderstood and thought I had been told to go ahead, which I certainly had not been. Some quick thinking and some bullshit had saved me. A small matter, but I was impressed.

I did not at that time realize that quick thinking and bullshit were to become hallmarks of my ersatz law career many years hence. My first brush with the law, and I had been saved. That's probably not the nicest thing my father ever did for me but close. He was a real stern guy.

On my way to becoming the very Perry attorney, I would have to obtain a law degree, and that meant going to law school and, of course, law school tuition. I first had to deal with the paymaster to make sure that would be taken care of. This meant on one of those Sunday afternoon guy get-togethers with my father, I would have to bring up the subject of my interest in the legal profession. Timidly, I broached the subject. The response was characteristic: "Are you *sure* that's what you want to do?"

This meant he disapproved, as he did with many of my projects, but he didn't say no, and I felt I had the green light to take the next step, which would be the Law School Admission Test (LSAT). This test, as far as I knew, was required in order to submit an application for admission to any law school. I was currently on the three-year plan at Harvard College and in my last year. The plan was to take the LSAT that fall, ace the test, apply to a top law school, which meant Harvard, and then go to law school the following fall. I took the test with no preparation and received an un-Perry-like low score. Effectively, this blew my plans apart big time. What did I do? I punted and took the extra year at Harvard College. My three-year plan had now extended into a fourth year.

Time to reconsider the whole law school idea. That grade on the LSAT was the first of many signs that I ought to consider something else. The exam was loaded with questions about reading comprehension, whatever that is, and I struggled with that. One had to read a paragraph and then answer questions about what followed from this and that, logically. This was not my skill set. I was good at visual stuff. I had been enthusiastic about art courses in prep school and had also thought about becoming an architect. Unfortunately, designing buildings required a knowledge of physics, a subject which was a mystery to me.

I was forced to discuss my future with the dean of students after pulling a D in basic physics my first year. Later on, I took a course in architectural sciences. The instructor, an internationally accomplished artist, on the first day held up a paintbrush and said, "This is an emotional object." We painted instead with gum erasers, which were not so emotional.

I didn't do well in that course, so I tried a course that did use the emotional objects—an art course. That killed any thoughts of becoming a starving artist, although I was told I had talent. I was not enamored of the starving part and also the messy cleanup that came with each of my numerous projects. In a quandary, I took something called a preference test, which was supposed to help those of us struggling with career choices, which many of us were. It was page after page of questions asking for our preferences on a wide range of subjects. What did we think about such and such on a scale of one to ten? At the end of the test, all the scores were tabulated and, bingo, one's best career choice was revealed. I'm certain that "lawyer" was one of the possibilities. My most suitable career according to the test? Forest ranger. I was disgusted. At least I had a pair of binoculars and had spent one summer's employment clearing trails in the Catskills. So I was ready.

My mother also weighed in on the subject. She was convinced I should go to business school on account of my success as a summertime entrepreneur. I had run a soda stand on a golf course one year and, in another, made money with a car wash business. My partner and I had flyers that we left on windshields at a local beach club. We charged a dollar a wash. Business was good. Also, prior to these ventures, I had sold packets of vegetable seeds to the apartment dwellers in the high-rise the family lived in in New York. These were seeds that were never going to be planted—no Golden Bantam corn in a window box. This was more of the cute kid endeavor as I was only twelve years old. My mother reasoned that, even so, it all added up to a successful business career.

If this wasn't enough, there was also my head of house at Harvard. He routinely met with each of the seniors in his dorm to discuss their future plans. I disclosed at my meeting with him that I had an interest in law school and a law career. Upon hearing this, he virtually sprang from his chair. "Don't do it! Don't do it!" I was an activist, he said, and activists, in his mind, weren't a good fit for the law. I guessed he knew what an activist was since he was reputed to have been one of the most decorated soldiers who fought in World War II, and he carried the war wound to go with it. I had been involved in several dorm projects and had come to know him well and respected his judgment. Just the same, I was startled by his opinion about my career leaning.

All this left me well into my last year of college with doubts about becoming the next Perry or even becoming the next anything. There was, however, a part of me that did not give up on ideas once I had seized upon them. Call it obstinacy, persistence, or maybe compulsive behavior, if one is inclined to be less kind, and I could not give up on my dream quite that easily. So I ignored all this and forged ahead—sort of against all odds type of nonsense.

During that last year, there was a meeting sponsored by the dean of admissions to Harvard Law for any Harvard students interested in going to Harvard Law School. I attended this meeting along with a large group of seniors. There was obviously going to be a lot of competition for HLS, even though the HLS classes were large, at about five hundred. The dean went on about the law school, and it sounded as if he was discouraging people from applying. After all, although he didn't say this, he would have to look at all the applications and make many tough decisions. And this came out of the meeting, although it's hard to believe that this was actually said: "The thicker the applicant's file, the thicker the applicant." So the school had a paperwork reduction policy, just like the internal revenue. This appealed to me. It was as if there was a commonsense bottom line way of doing things that survived after all the brief writing and hair splitting had ended. Law school might be an interesting place, I thought.

I had also followed a suggestion from my father, which was why not go to an actual courthouse and see what courtroom advocacy was really like. There was at that time a notorious criminal trial in progress at the Federal Courthouse in New York City's Foley Square. I went and took a seat. The courtroom was packed. I had no idea what the case was about. The defense lawyer was definitely not patterned after Mr. Mason. He had a shock of white hair, a florid complexion, and a loud tie. I saw some of his cross-examination of a government witness, whom he attacked with gusto and, I thought, with great effectiveness.

After lunch, I did some exploring to see what else was going on. I found a courtroom on another floor and went in. As energetic as the proceedings were in the criminal case, this was the opposite. The courtroom was moribund. There were two lawyers, a clerk, a bailiff, a judge, and stacks of paper on each end of the counsel table. I was the only spectator. It was a civil case, I guessed. I had no idea who was suing whom for what. My attention must have gone elsewhere because at some point, I looked up, and the courtroom was empty except for the bailiff. He left his seat and went over to the window. The courtroom was high-ceilinged and looked out over a courtyard.

The bailiff threw open one of the large windows at the side of the room. It was December, and a blast of icy air rolled in. He turned to me and said apologetically that he had to "let out all the hot air."

A meaningful moment, I thought. I can do this—the hot air part. I already knew how to open a window. I felt as if I was a prospector that was nearing a gold seam of nuttiness that I suspected lurked underneath the surface of the research and the "may it please the courts" and the legal memos. There just had to be untapped reservoirs waiting to be exploited. And I knew two things: I wanted to be a part of it and, worse, that I would fit right in.

So there I was at the holiday break in my last year of college, anxiously pondering the possibility of becoming a lawyer. My father is unenthusiastic, my mother is against it, my head of house thinks I shouldn't consider it, and the preference people think I'd do better patrolling the Sierra Madre or some other remote patch of the earth. I could certainly just apply to some law schools and let the chips fall. And that would have been okay. But I had my sights set on Harvard Law, and so the wiliness for which I later became well known, perhaps not in a good way, took over, and I hatched a plan. Why not take the LSATs again and see if I could do better?

The question of how the admissions department would treat a second go-round on the LSATs had actually been asked at the meeting with the dean. The answer was that, "Sure, you could retake the exam, but the second test score would be heavily discounted because of the experience in taking it once before." But why not? I couldn't do much worse. Also, it would have been a year and a half since I had taken the first one, so maybe a smaller discount. There was a problem, which was that the results of this second test would not be available until after the applications were due. With my usual devil-may-care attitude, I included letters along with the applications to each of the schools I applied to, notifying them that I would be taking the test a second time and if they could kindly wait for the new score before making a decision. Some nerve.

I had applied to four law schools. Three of them ignored my request and mailed out their decisions. I first heard from two of the three. Unexpectedly, I was accepted by a good school in the Midwest and would have gone there had not things turned out differently.

Another school had me on its wait list. A third school, a small liberal arts school in New Haven, Connecticut, had yet to be heard from. Soon a letter from that school arrived. Upon opening the envelope, I noted there was a check inside. I was the payee. What could this possibly be for? Coincidentally, it was in the amount of fifty dollars, the same amount as my application fee.

I read the accompanying letter with puzzlement. It took me a while to digest its contents, but paraphrased, this is what it said: my application fee was being returned out of kindness because that school had a policy which was they didn't waste time processing applications from dummies such as myself, thank you ever so much. They say that the object of a liberal education is self-knowledge, and I happily added this to my fund of the same, and my fondness for this university and its law school grew in abundance and promised to continue well into the future. I had not yet heard from Harvard and had not yet received the score from my second go-round with the LSAT.

The day of that test had previously arrived, and I resolved to do my best and improve on what I had done before. That would not be difficult, but I was hoping for a substantial improvement. All the test-takers gathered at the exam site and awaited the test materials, which were not to be opened until the gun went off. Soon the okay to start was given, and there was a rustling of paper as the assembled opened their test booklets. I opened mine and was stunned. Gone were those incomprehensible reading comprehension questions with their multiple-choice complexities that I found so perplexing. My test was almost all something called spatial relations. It was squares and circles and triangles and parallelograms and rhombuses and trapezoids and their interrelationship. I had always excelled at plane geometry, so the test was easy and a joy to take.

I finished well within the allotted time and drummed my pencil on my chair arm to let the strivers know I had finished early and what a breeze the test had been. And, yes, I soon received my score, and I was within a few points of perfection. Shortly, I received the joyous letter from Harvard Law that I had been accepted. I imagined that a copy of that acceptance letter now graced what was assuredly my ultra-thin applicant's file. Should an asterisk be placed on this? Maybe. I was about to find out that law school learning was not about geometrics but instead the daunting "Socratic" method.

# 2

# Our Foreign Language

**College life had been enjoyable,** and in many ways, I was reluctant to leave it. An event took place while I was there that was of little importance in the great scheme of things, but in a small way, it had some bearing on the legal world I was about to enter. In one of my years—junior, senior, I don't remember—word spread about an issue of such importance that a large-scale demonstration was planned in order to show student opposition. Was it about the Jim Crow South, about the rights of women, about the proliferation of nuclear weapons, about world hunger? Perish the thought. It was about something far more earth-shaking. It had been learned that after over three hundred years, the college was proposing to no longer issue diplomas inscribed in Latin but rather in common, ordinary English.

Shock waves spread throughout the student body. The thought that the *praeses et socii* of *Collegii Harvardiana* were no longer going to grant a diploma to me, Johannes Franciscus Woodibus Junius, and also countersigned by the *deanus*, filled me with a fury that I could only dimly appreciate. I, along with the other ten thousand men of Harvard, who according to song, only want victory today, prepared to march on the president's lodgings on Quincy Street that very evening. At the appointed hour, the howling mob, demanding that this heinous proposal be rescinded, descended on that residence, watched at a careful distance by members of the Campus, Cambridge, and maybe even the State Police. The din was enormous.

Suddenly, the door to the president's second-floor balcony flew open, and the crowd grew quiet. The president (truly, the *praeses*) himself quickly appeared to address the rabble. In a quavering voice that carried across the now silent mob, this is what he said: "What's chic in Greek and pat in Latin, I always distinguish more clearly in English." As fast as he had appeared, he now disappeared.

The throng was stunned. There were a few boos and catcalls, but slowly the crowd thinned, and within a short time, the streets were emptied, and life went back to normal. Students returned to their dorms and resumed reading Aeschylus or Ovid in the original or maybe the latest men's magazine, depending on one's enthusiasms. And that year, the diplomas were, as promised, issued in the more distinguishable English.

It is worth noting that Harvard Law School is geographically located just north of the college, separated by one narrow road. Formerly, there was a traffic light that allowed pedestrians to cross, but so many zoned-out Harvards met with distress at that intersection, either by accident or intentionally, depending on who was driving, that the road was at some point buried. Now the two campuses are joined only by a walkway. Notwithstanding the ease of going from the college to the law school, the sentiment that English is most distinguished could make no headway northward onto the law school campus, and that school still maintains its medieval heritage from when law students inhabited the Latin Quarter and spoke to each other in a foreign language.

I have attempted to stamp on these Latin words and phrases like so many cockroaches from underneath the baseboards but have not been able to get them all, and I ask to be forgiven if some words or phrases akin to *obiter dicta* or *res adjudicata* occasionally sneak in. Where appropriate, I will provide, as best I can, the distinguished English translation.

# 3

# Law School

**After a summer of traveling** in foreign places and holding fast to my lawyer's dictionary with its Latin terms, I arrived to start my legal education. I began my career with much anticipation. Early days took us new students through some sort of orientation. Eventually, classes began. As first year law students, we took basic courses that would acclimate us to the legal world. The classrooms were of the classic style, semicircular banks of seats on ascending platforms, not so much that we could see the professor, but so that the professor could see us. We wouldn't be able to so easily escape the humiliation which we were sure was awaiting us. There were four sections of one hundred twenty-five students each. The teaching method was, as I mentioned, the Socratic method, which meant we learned our lessons by answering questions from the Socrates who was teaching the course. It wasn't long before the learning through humiliation began, although it occasionally was of the gentler sort.

I can remember one class where the question was what was the basis of a particular case decision. A brave student ventured that it was that the document in question was not under seal, to which the professor replied that that might have been good law in the twelfth century, to great laughter.

I was in an early class, probably my first in that course. An elderly gentleman took the podium and introduced himself. I noticed that the textbook that had been required for this course and which cost a bundle had a name on the spine which coincidentally was the same as the man who had just introduced himself. We were asked to open the book to a certain page and to look at a certain paragraph. The professor started to read to us from the referenced paragraph. So here we were at Harvard Law School, starting off what we hoped would be successful careers in the law—summa cum laudes, Rhodes Scholars, football All-Americas, what have you—and we were now about to be read to as if we were second graders. What happened next takes a bit of explanation.

The text being read concerned a purchase or a sale and spelled out the amount involved. Let's say the amount was $1,567.40. At that part of the paragraph, this was the way it was read by our learned Socrates: "Dollar sign one comma five six seven dot four zero." We were astounded, and yet nobody got up and left, certainly because the price of admission was so high; but I knew just as surely as I knew that passage said fifteen hundred sixty-seven dollars and forty cents that the next three years were not going to be easy. The lesson was, of course, to conclude that the figure was a dollar amount was an assumption and that in law, you can never assume anything. Was that dot just a dot? Or was it a period? Or was it a decimal point or a flyspeck or some imperfection in the paper? To find out, you'd need legal advice, and that involves the bread and butter of the legal profession—billable hours. Next time you see that some large corporation is setting aside billions for legal expenses, you'll know why.

I found that my infrequent forays into class discussion were met with hilarity by my fellows and consternation by the professors. I spent hours upon hours in the library studying and reading cases. I spent long evenings poring over the assigned casebooks. I joined a study group. And still, I was not getting it, and I knew it. Many times I wondered if sitting in some watchtower in some far-off forest scanning the horizon would not be a better use of my time.

Somehow, I managed to stagger through the first year and then through the second. My grades were pathetic, but I was determined to finish and obtain the degree. I began to doubt that I would ever practice law. The Perry dream was still alive, but just barely. In my last year, I took a course taught by a famous professor. In that subject, he was the last word. He was reputed to have been before the Supreme Court an uncountable number of times and never lost. His class was run on a rigorous schedule. He would call on students not at random but by going down the row. One class would end, and he would then pick up where he left off, so I knew when my time was coming. I thought I was safe for a while and that I could deal with whatever came my way until this happened. The professor was doing the Socratic method and had a student desperately trying to answer his questions. The student wasn't doing well and found himself out of his seat and in the well of the classroom in front of the chalkboard.

The professor had one thousand plus one thousand on the board and was demanding the student add this up. This unfortunate man was so rattled he couldn't do it. The professor was incredulous. This was the easy part of the exercise, and the student was screwing it up. The student was being yelled at, and we all knew what we hoped we were not seeing—a mental event right in front of us. I knew that this was likely me when my turn came, so when the professor neared my place in the row, I was nowhere to be found. Soon I cut more classes, and sooner than I had wished, I was in the dean's office with a short discussion about my future. A leave of absence was agreed upon, and thankfully, I was out of there, and for how long, I had no idea. A lot of tears were shed, but fortunately, I had an extra hanky for the dean. But it was a relief to be gone. I did leave with a promise that if I felt like coming back at some point, they would give me consideration. For this, I was grateful.

I soon had a job working for a bank, counting stock certificates for a mutual fund the bank was putting together. A dead-end job, but a paycheck was welcome. Somehow, I managed to get fired as a result of some unfortunate impertinence, but I was soon able to find employment in the customer service department of a mutual fund. I managed to hold onto this job and my tongue, even though I was continually harangued by my boss for the manner in which I served the customers. A lot was going on, and it was a breather for sure. After a year and a half, I felt much better about my prospects and thought, Why not? At least get the degree. I reapplied and was admitted into my last year. I was determined to get that diploma at all costs.

I had moved away from the Cambridge scene and was now living in the Roxbury section of Boston, about an hour's subway ride from the school. I made sure I attended all my classes and sat in my assigned seat like the obedient student I had now become. Since this was not my original class, I knew nobody and was not in anyone's study group. After classes, I was off to my apartment at what seemed like the other side of the world. Getting as far away from the law school campus as possible was a tonic. The separation helped, and I was able to keep up with the classwork with no distractions. A good supply of my favorite beverages no doubt helped with the studies and anxieties I might have had about whether I would finally succeed in earning the coveted diploma.

Only one incident ruffled the waters of my existence. In a class I was taking, I volunteered to answer a professor's question, or as it is said in Latin, a *quaere*. Note that in law, one is *quaeried*, not questioned, in keeping with the rubric that whatever we more clearly distinguish in English is much more complex, and therefore legal world worthy in Latin. The way this goes is the professor stands at the front of the class and moves his voice into the back of his throat and then announces "*quaere*!" This means the class discussion is about to begin. English has had some effect over the years, so it is pronounced "queery."

I gave the answer, a satisfactory answer I thought, and I was done. Instead, I was surprised by a follow-up question, which was, how had I arrived at that conclusion? This was because, of course, the Socratic method requires that one question answered is immediately followed by another puzzling question. The word *idiotic* was not stated but was an unspoken modifier to the word *conclusion*. I couldn't think of anything from an ancient language, so I offered an answer that was so silly that I refrain from revealing here what that was. After the laughter subsided, I was curtly told that was a "novel doctrine." Shamed, I avoided class participation whenever possible.

Wonderfully, I managed to pass the exams, and it finally happened that on the steps of Langdell Hall on a warm June day I received my diploma awarded *ad gradum baccalaurei in legibus* from *Universitas Harvardiana*. It's law school after all, and so the sheepskin was in lovely Latin. The diploma may have been more distinguishable in English, but the silly Latin pedigree still held sway. And I didn't care what language the diploma was in. At long last, that ordeal was over, and I was now on my way to what? I had no idea.

# 4

## Shiftless

**Nothing was going on at** this point. I had no job. I had not done what many had done, which was to intern at law firms during the summer and thereby have a job secured upon graduation. And I had not gone through the rigorous hiring practice that took place during the year when firms were looking for recruits. I didn't know quite what to do, so for lack of anything else, I took the Massachusetts bar exam. My father and I had already agreed that New York was not big enough for the both of us, so a return to New York was out of the question. I still wasn't sure what was going to happen—whether I was going to practice law or not. I hadn't prepared for the bar exam and promptly was notified I had failed it.

In the meantime, just to keep busy, I did some research and created a list of what I believed to be the top firms in Boston. I came up with a list of twenty-two and proceeded to apply for employment. I am unable to recall whether the fact of the bar exam failure was something that had happened before I went looking for a job or not. In any case, I was not admitted to practice at the time I started the arduous process of trying to convince somebody or anybody that I was worthy of their employ.

So look at it this way. I am applying to the top firms in Boston. I have not passed the bar, and I graduated somewhere near the bottom of a class of five hundred and, in addition, have taken five years to finish law school. But I was determined. If they were going to find me unworthy, they were going to have to say it to my face. Every day, I would call a firm or two and ask to speak to the hiring partner. I was persistent, and I think I was able to get a face-to-face interview with every one of the twenty-two firms on my list.

At the interviews, everybody was very cordial, and things always started out on a high note. I would hand over my résumé, and there would be a moment while the interviewer looked it over. I had been to all the best schools and was Harvard over and under, as it is said. Unfailingly, the fact that the résumé showed that I had graduated from law school five years after graduating from college elicited questions because even those guys could add, subtract, multiply, and divide and knew that it took only three years to matriculate at law school. It was apparent that the thought was this: I'll bet this engaging young man did something interesting for those two years between college graduation and starting law school. They were expecting I had worked with Schweitzer or Cousteau or gone around the world on a freighter. They had doubtless heard of high school dropouts but never imagined there was such a thing as a law school dropout—and from Harvard Law, no less.

It wasn't long before I ran out of explanations for this phenomenon. The one I used most often was that I just got bored with law school and decided to take a breather. This was definitely not working. Apparently, ambitious young men bent on a law career did not, in their minds, decide to take "breathers" midstream. Everyone was very nice. No one said, "Are you nuts?" They didn't have to ask since they had already concluded that I was. And maybe they were right.

Follow-up calls now meant it was their turn to come up with stories. Usually, it was that it sure was wonderful to have met me, but they were not hiring right now. I was wished good luck with a suggestion that maybe I should try looking in another state, maybe west of the Mississippi. Also, I was assured that my résumé would be kept on file, and, no, it was not the circular file. It took me a while, but I struck out at all twenty-two. Quite an experience.

So I plunged into an abyss of despondency. No job, no money, no prospects. I was now truly shiftless. The eventide shadows of a life going nowhere began to gather about me. I had achieved what many people would have given their eye teeth for—a sheepskin from Harvard Law School—and yet I had somehow managed to convert that to a place on the unemployment line. I was determined to get on the road back to something, although I had no idea what, but for starters, I at least needed a paycheck. I began looking in the newspaper for a place to find work—anyplace.

One day, I discovered that the Boston Public Library was looking for help sorting books. I applied and was accepted at the rate of sixty dollars per week. And they did not ask questions about what I had been doing in those extra two years nor ask me to parse the rule in Shelley's case. I was happy to be doing something, even though this might involve heavy lifting. But not the intellectual kind, the physical kind. The Boston Public had something like twenty or thirty branches. Books taken from one branch could be returned to any branch. A van daily picked up books returned to other than their home branches and brought them to the central library in Copley

Square for transshipment. The books were bagged in heavy canvas bags. They had to be hoisted and then emptied onto a large table in the basement of the BPL. Each bag had the name of a branch stenciled on it. Books were sorted and placed in the canvas bags marked with the name of the branch those books belonged to. Truly, an intellectually taxing job. I was working with a rough crowd. Several of the employees thought book sorting was the same as taking three-pointers for the Boston Celtics.

After two or three months of this, I sought to improve my station in life. I contacted a placement agency which, after a while, found me a job with an insurance company. This was a colossus that did business everywhere. I was in the "forms" department, where we redrafted policies according to changes required by amendments to state insurance laws. We to us. Them to him. That sort of thing. Mostly, it was bull sessions, paper airplanes, and memos about nuclear attacks that ended with the familiar "and kiss your ass goodbye." In the meantime, I was solidifying my shiftless status by flunking the bar exam not once more but two more times. This was very "un-Mason-like," but there were other things going on, and I put on my best "What, me worry?" aspect.

After the third fail in a row, I decided to take, for me, an unusual step. Why not take a bar prep course? I asked around and signed up for one that had the best reputation. It met evenings at some hall on Massachusetts Avenue. Regrettably, this was near a place called the Kentucky Tavern, which was a few blocks away on Newbury Street. What the Kentucky part had to do with it, I never knew. It was there that I learned for the first time what a boilermaker was—naturally, nothing to do with the steel business. A group of us, sufficiently boiled, would discuss whatever and then wend our way up to the class. I'm not sure how much I got from the classes, but at least I went to all of them.

The date for the exam arrived, and I dutifully showed up and did the best I could. To my mind, it was no different than the previous times I had taken the test, and I was confident that number four was also a no-pass. I explained this to my bride of a few months. She didn't take it well, and both of us shed many a tear. At least I was employed, as was she, so there was that.

At my insurance job, there was another who was also on his fourth attempt. He knew a thing or two about how to get the results because one day, a few weeks after the test, he stopped by my desk and told me we had both passed. What an unexpected event! This, of course, changed everything in one hell of a hurry. From Mr. Nowhere Man, I was now on a mission. I was somebody, even though I wondered if what had happened was that my exam grader might have had an off day or graded my paper at that same Kentucky Tavern.

Soon I was in the chambers of the Supreme Judicial Court, being sworn in to uphold whatever needed to be upheld and was presented with my shingle. It was a proud moment on a gorgeous warm early spring day such as can only be found in New England. My father was there, and he managed to spirit away my certificate. It took me all of twenty years to get it back. A sidelight to all this was something that I had long forgotten. Years after I had retired, a group from my HLS graduating class occasionally met for lunch. I attended a couple of these luncheons, and at one, there was for some reason a discussion about how there was an interview as part of the bar admission process.

I didn't remember any interview. The man next to me remembered his interview. He mentioned that his interviewer was impressed that he was to be clerking for a well-known Federal Court of Appeals

Judge. The interviewer knew the judge and, in parting, he asked that his regards be passed on to this well-reputed judge. A nice story, I thought. As I was driving home, a memory suddenly floated out of the muck which is a certain segment of my mind. Yes, I now recalled. I did have an interview, but my interviewer didn't wish felicitations to a famous judge as there was no famous judge in my immediate future. Instead, it was a question: "What took you so long?" Boilermakers, for sure.

Now that I was street legal, I didn't fool with those State Street guys whom I referred to as the gang of twenty-two. "Too bad for them" was my attitude. The Mason idea was now revived in all its glory, and instead, I went straight to the classified phone book and searched for a listing for a public defender agency. I discovered a number for an organization entitled the Massachusetts Defenders Committee and I called it. This got me a time and place for an interview. Other than mispronouncing the name of the administrative assistant, the interview went well, and I was offered a job.

The starting salary was $5,900—per year, not month. Okay by me, and I was told that soon that would increase to the munificent sum of $6,900 per year. It's always nice to have a little luck to help out, and the lucky part was that the chief counsel of the Defenders was a Harvard Law man. There was only one other HLS man on the staff, and apparently, more hires from Harvard were sought after. This was back in the day when I'm guessing this type of job was not thought much of by Harvard Law graduates so not many Harvards applied. I had a previously planned vacation, and it would be several weeks before I would be starting, and after the long road forward, it looked as if I would actually be practicing law, something I never thought would happen.

# 5

# I Get to Practice

**At last, the day arrived,** and I reported to the Defenders' office located on Beacon Street in downtown Boston. Here I was, ready to start my career actually practicing law, and it was to be *Perry Mason* law—criminal defense. I was exulted. It was the fulfillment of a dream. It had taken me almost seven years to accomplish what most did in three or four, and I had no experience whatsoever. I expected that there would be something in the way of a training program since it was known I had never practiced. I was introduced to an attorney who took me across the street to the Boston Juvenile Court. This lawyer handled a few cases by going to the bench with what I guessed were clients.

There was a lot of whispering, and then the clients would leave. I had no idea what was going on. This happened two or three times, and then we left and had lunch. That, apparently, was the training program. At lunch, there was some small talk and then, since I was sufficiently trained, I was given a half dozen files and told to report to a suburban court the next day. I examined the files and saw that in each, there was nothing except a list of the charges and the name of the defendant. That's it? I was going to court to represent a half dozen accused about whom I knew nothing? My anxiety level spiked accordingly. And where were the Paul Drakes and Della Streets I was going to need to deal with all the Hamilton Burgers I was going to face? Help!

The next day, with my heart in my throat, I drove to the lovely courthouse in the quiet suburban town that certainly, under all the serenity, had its share of criminal activity. It's important here to explain the setup. The district courts in Massachusetts were colloquially known as police courts. This was because many of them were attached at the hip to police stations, as was the one I went to on my first day.

To emphasize this point, the police station was on the first floor, and the court was on the second floor as if the court were an afterthought. In addition to the stairs that led to the courtroom, there was an interior stairway which went directly from the police lockup to the court's prisoner dock. The cases were all prosecuted by senior police officers, and it was also a well-kept secret that underneath their robes, the judges were wearing police uniforms. The saving grace was that whatever happened in these police courts could easily be appealed to the superior court. Nothing fancy—just say, "I appeal." This process was necessary because the district courts didn't have juries, and the only way to get a jury trial, a guaranteed constitutional right, was to appeal to the superior court where there were juries. This meant that since whatever happened in the district court could be made meaningless just by saying, "I appeal," there was a sort of "whatever" attitude that cloaked the proceedings.

There also was the fact that none of the district court hearings were transcribed. No court stenographers, no tape recorders, no nothing. This meant that people could shoot their mouths off about almost anything and frequently did. The net effect of all this was to envelop the district court proceedings with a sort of weirdness that was hard to appreciate unless you got used to it, something I was about to do.

Anxiously, I climbed the stairs to the second-floor courtroom and prepared to initiate myself into the legal world. It had slipped out that this was my first day on the job, and I could feel the sharks circling to take advantage of me. I was also going to learn about what has now become a total no-no, which is handling cases "on the fly," something that was routine in those halcyon days. There was a part of representation that I haven't mentioned, which was the paperwork. The Defenders had something called a face sheet that was required to be filled out for every client. This was a multi-carboned form with many requests for information and little room to write it all in. The idea was to have information for the superior court attorney in case there was an appeal. If the face sheet wasn't completed, you got yelled at. Filling these things out took forever. Who needed to know how many brothers and sisters a client had and what their names and ages were?

Obediently, on that first fateful day, I went about completing the required forms. The most perplexing part of the form was labeled "story." This seemed to me to be a rather poor word choice—as if whatever was said should be looked at with a jaundiced eye. And some of these stories went on at length and required extra sheets of paper. The judge was most accommodating and took several recesses while I went about completing my forms.

One of my clients was a man who had two charges: receiving stolen goods and assault and battery. I interviewed him and then discussed the cases with the police prosecutor. It seemed my client had been caught trying to sell a hot radio in a bar room and also assaulted and battered a lady friend. The prosecutor offered six months in the county prison in exchange for a plea. I brought this unfortunate news to my client, who, surprisingly, was agreeable. We then went before the judge, who accepted the sentence and then promptly suspended it and imposed probation on the theory we were being too harsh on the young defendant. My client thus, despite my efforts, did not go to jail but walked out a free man. He was most profuse in his thanks but did graciously decline the offer of my business card, which I proffered in case he should have need of legal representation in the future—and kindly, he did not suggest I should not let the door hit me on the way out.

So there it was. I had performed admirably on my first day. Just like the storied public defenders of yore, I had sought to have my client jailed meanwhile accepting a paycheck from the government with a "well done" scrawled across the bottom. But this was not to last because as I went along, I was to gain experience which would stand that perception on its head as I found better ways to deal with the enemy. And something else was happening that first day, which was I sensed that I had found my place and that this was what I would likely be doing until I couldn't move or go nuts, whichever came first. As to the latter, I was probably already halfway there. And there was this feeling that as nutty as any of my clients might be, I was already way beyond them. This gave me an understanding which, as time went on, would put me at a big advantage.

In the unlikely event that I thought I would want to go on to something else, I wanted at least to get some jury experience, and that was not immediately forthcoming. This was because of the way the office was structured. District court lawyers were on the seventh floor, and the superior court lawyers, who were the ones who handled jury matters, were on the third. The two rarely spoke except for reprimands about failures to completely fill out the face sheet. The only way to gain the coveted jury experience was for someone assigned to the superior court to leave, get disbarred, or die. The process was painfully slow. Waiting for my chance would surely mean years in the district courts.

My long-suffering wife wanted to know why, since I was so smart, I wasn't working in a firm and making a pile so she didn't have to bear the bulk of the burden in providing for our just-above-subsistence lifestyle. I assured her that it was just a question of gaining some jury experience, and then I would be on my way to fame and fortune. I lied and I knew it, and that is why, instead, in the end, she was the one who, tired of the waiting, wound up moving on, searching for fame and fortune on her own.

It is worth noting that this first day was a harbinger of things to come. It was as if I was surrounded by some sort of force field of weirdness that infected everything I did. As soon as I became involved in some matter in the courts, it was as if the wheels started to come off and the system began to malfunction. For instance, in that case, there was no reason why the judge could not have accepted the plea bargain. Everyone was for it. The defendant was on board. It had been thought about, and all the parties agreed. There was no reason for the judge to go off on his own tangent. Did I say something out of line? Wasn't my demeanor sufficiently obsequious? I have no reason to offer as to why the judge refused to gracefully jail my client. I had worked so hard to have him incarcerated. But it was a warning that whenever I participated in any criminal matter, there was a good chance that something strange was going to become part of the proceedings.

I didn't deliberately try to engage in bizarre behavior, but a certain something seemed to follow me wherever I went. Part of this stemmed from the fact that, at least initially, I obviously didn't have the faintest idea what I was doing, and people tended to go off in unusual directions when presented with my representational efforts. I was hopeful that this would change as I went along and I became more experienced, even though I recognized there was also the possibility it might only get worse. Time would tell.

There was probably not a lot that is noteworthy of the time I spent in district court practice, but it was a most valuable proving ground for the future. The routine was the same, although the intensity varied from court to court. Some courts, coveted by the slackers, had hardly any business at all. One suspected that connections higher up resulted in excess coverage in some courts and far too little in others. I always wanted the busy in-town courts to gain experience with the heavier cases. Since I was from Harvard and the bulk of the staff was from Suffolk or maybe Boston University, I was regarded as a lightweight and given assignments that were less formidable. I'm not putting these schools down—they are fine schools, and the attitude is understandable. In many ways, they were right, and I was unprepared for the challenges some of the busier courts presented.

Early in my career, and as I was just beginning my work in the district courts, a rather remarkable thing happened. I had stopped smoking and put on a little weight. I was tall and had that stern visage that I was born with. I believed everything the defendants told me, and as a result, I was having a fair number of bench trials. I was having limited success, although it was not for a lack of trying, and

I felt sheepish about my inability to establish my clients' professed innocence.

Soon, and I can't account for how this happened, some people began to liken me to my boyhood hero and started familiarly to call me Perry. It would go this way: I would pass a bailiff in the corridor, and he would say, "Howya doin', Perry?"

This would be accompanied by a guffaw or a smirk because, unlike the TV Perry who won all his cases, I lost almost all of mine. I was the anti-Perry or maybe the bizarro Perry. Still, I appreciated it, and I would swell with pride whenever I was so called.

I continued with my determination to be a real very Perry and assumed it was just a matter of time that with practice and experience, I would be acing out the prosecution and walking my innocent client defendants. On my way to this destination, I began to make a disconcerting discovery, which was that there seemed to be a severe shortage of wrongly accused defendants—the type that my TV hero was vindicating on a weekly basis. I looked high and low and couldn't find any. I continued to buy some of the bogus stories provided by my self-proclaimed "innocent" clients only to go to court to be annihilated by mounds of evidence.

It didn't take me long to realize that I was in an entirely different ball game than I originally had thought. The Mason mirage was slowly fading from view, evanescing as it were, and being replaced by something else. What that was, was not entirely clear in this early stage of my career. It is likely a little cynical to say that my job was to aid my clients in "beating the rap" but maybe not too far off from the truth. This frank appraisal helped explain the attitudes taken by the district court judges, which was to help the government win cases and was an affirmation of the suspicion that those judges were, in fact, ex officio members of the police department.

Looked at in a gentler fashion, the public defender enterprise was to assist clients through the process and to a resolution of their criminal matters. Nonetheless, this involved a huge shifting of gears from my romanticized view of myself as a Perry Mason clone to an assessment of the reality. So it was now the beginning of arrivederci to Perry and slowly the awakening of a new concept—that of the crafty, or dare I say shifty attorney. But I had a long way to go before I would be able to claim either of those descriptions and also be recognized as one or the other of them.

If I was going to do something for my clients, I was going to have to take a different approach—and that I did. I was learning as I went along, which was the best way, and maybe for me the only way. If there was something I was unsure about, I could just appeal, which had the effect of vacating the disposition and sending the case on to the superior court to be handled by one of our superior court attorneys who would presumably have a lot more experience and maybe wisdom than I had. An example of this was a case I had in a district court where my client was charged with molesting two young boys. There was a bench trial and, as usual, I lost. The judge then imposed a sentence of two and a half years in the house of correction, the maximum, but to run concurrent as to each of the charges. I informed the court my client was entering an appeal.

The judge said okay if he wants to do that, then I'm making the sentences from and after, meaning my client would now be appealing a five-year sentence. This horrific outcome threw me for a loop, and I had no idea whether I should accept the two and a half years. Sentences of a year or more by statute had a day's grace for an appeal decision. I went back to the office and anxiously asked for advice. After a brief discussion, it was recommended by the third-floor guys my client should take the two and a half years.

The next day, I went back, withdrew the appeal request, and the concurrent sentences were imposed. I was disappointed. I had wanted to fight the case but felt I needed to defer to those with more experience.

I had a supervisor who was one of the Suffolks, and he didn't like me. He would rag on me for any perceived shortcomings, such as misspelling the name of some defendant's grandfather on the face sheet or some other inconsequential failure. Once—actually, more than once—he got on me because I didn't discuss the defendants' cases with the arresting officers. I explained that I spoke with the prosecutor, and I thought this was enough. I had a reason, which I didn't bother to explain, why I didn't speak with the police, and it was based on experience. Say it was a stolen car case, and you spoke with the officers involved. Generally, but not universally, the police were regular guys. They would take the opportunity to fill me in on the four hundred other things that they knew my client had done but hadn't been able to catch him at. By the time the conversation was over, I would be taking a different view of what was best for my client's and society's future. So that's why I avoided cop conferences.

I was also learning other things—getting a feel for the business, getting a feel of how to present myself and my cases, such as they were. Say I had to argue some sort of motion in front of a judge. It was always a judge in district court. The standard silliness is to start off by saying, "May it please the court"—something I early gave up because most of what I had to say either displeased the court or was ignored. I would give my pitch, and the judge would, after a minute or so, become wildly enthusiastic. He (no women in those ancient times) would shake his head in assent, smile broadly, and all but climb down off the bench to congratulate me on my fine and winning presentation. I'd think that I had won and stop before I was finished.

After a number of these experiences in which, shockingly, my motions were denied, I realized that judicial enthusiasm was just a ruse to get me to shut up and stop wasting the court's time. I learned to counter this by looking at my shoes or staring off into space so I wasn't thrown off by the display of false enthusiasm for my efforts.

I learned quite early that one of the ways to upset the judges that gave me and my clients a hard time was to say that the defendant appealed. Judges, as kings of their courts, assumed that the justice they dispensed was the last word in wisdom and should be accepted by all and sundry. To have some "wet behind the ears" public defender tell the court the judgment was being appealed was extremely irritating and was an interruption in the general activity of paying no attention to this upstart whatsoever. The response to "the defendant appeals, Your Honor" syndrome varied. It was a right that I exercised frequently and with enthusiasm, not the least because I knew that certain judges got buzzed as a result.

Some judges just pulled a face and went on with the usual, which was to pretend that I didn't exist. Others howled at me with something like "What are you appealing for?" This gave me the chance to offer some spurious reason, which thinly showed that the only real reason was to tick off the court. Others would yell that if the defendant was going to appeal, they would give him or her something he or she could really appeal, and the sentence would be doubled or tripled as in the case I just referenced.

Last, I was in a court where cases were frequently disposed of with suspended sentences, which were usually accepted by the defendants. It was only a matter of time before the defendants, now probationers, were surrendered and sent to jail. By then, it was too late to appeal since the disposition could only be appealed at the time it was imposed. Realizing this, I appealed the suspended sentences as they were handed out while the judges stewed. Soon, calls from the presiding judge were in to the main office of the Defenders, demanding that I be replaced with an attorney more compliant to the court's operation. To my surprise, I was backed up, and I went on singing my song of "I appeal."

One of the early courts I was assigned to had a crusty judge right out of central casting. Tall, leathery complexion, gaunt with piercing eyes was the aspect. I had about six months in this court, and it was an education. Each of the district courts was like a small fiefdom. The probation people, the clerks, and at least the police prosecutor, if not the police themselves, formed a tight clique. I was an outsider and generally got nowhere. After a few months of my assignment to his court, this judge would occasionally take me into his lobby and give me a few pointers, like maybe I would do better if I pled everyone guilty, and that's because they are all guilty.

I've mentioned how there was no record of what was said in these courts, and so it was possible to rattle on any way one wanted to. A favorite of this judge was, before sentencing, to declare with enthusiasm, "As the twig is bent, so is the tree." I don't recall anybody ever laughing. Certainly not the defendants.

A frequent criminal complaint was for a charge of non-support of wife and or minor child. Thankfully, this has long since been taken off the books. The welfare department brought complaints whenever, as required, the department was not reimbursed for welfare disbursements. The defendant would have been ordered to make those payments to welfare as part of his probation. The unlucky defendants would have received heavy suspended sentences to enforce those orders—two years to the house of correction was the norm.

I was in the "twig is bent" court one day, and the first half dozen cases were probation violations for failure to make the payments. All went to jail. The judge pounded on his bench with both fists and bellowed, "Bring them in. I'm in the mood today."

Justice on parade and no stenographer. I had a number of these cases on most days. They were indefensible except to plead for more time to get money up or to modify the order. The courts were unrelenting, and violations usually resulted in a prison sentence. On one of these cases, my plea for mercy was ignored, and my client was carted off to serve his time. Later that day, haggard and worn, I was walking up Beacon Hill toward the office when I saw what appeared to be that same client that had earlier been sentenced walking down the street toward me. Asking if it was him, I was told that it was. But hadn't he just that morning been sent away?

His explanation: he had been allowed a phone call and had called his father. His father paid up the arrearage, and he was reprieved. Money talks. Money will always talk.

All the courts were different, and some were more accommodating than others. I was early assigned to a court in the suburbs, which covered a number of the surrounding towns. It was a busy court, and the court personnel were friendly, and the associate justice was a Harvard Law man who took an interest in whatever progress I was making. He saw that I was just starting off and wanted to encourage me in my efforts. Several luncheons with him, which included the police prosecutor, were memorable and amusing. The police prosecutor was always along so as to give balance to these get-togethers and assure there was no funny stuff. The prosecutor was a long-tenured captain on the local force with a great sense of humor, who uniformly maintained that the youths of his town were all "full of pot and pills"—a most engaging viewpoint and maybe not totally wrong.

There was a case I was assigned in that court which was of a routine nature. My defendant was charged with possession of marijuana, a relatively minor offense, although then looked upon more seriously than today. A small amount was involved, and I knew that not much in the way of a penalty would be imposed. What caught my interest was the codefendant who was charged with distribution of a controlled substance, marijuana, a felony. The story was that my client met up with his codefendant, the dealer, in some lonely spot to make the purchase.

The police were wise, and as the deal was "going down," as it is said, the police showed up, and both were arrested. And what was so remarkable about this unremarkable case? The dealer was a student matriculating at that small liberal arts school in New Haven, Connecticut—the school that had summarily dumped on my application to its law school. As I was quick to note, the dealer, our true blue son of Eli, had with him a dictionary when arrested, which, of course, naturally being weak in spelling, he might need in case he met up with a word difficult to spell, such as, let's say, the word *pot*. Except he wouldn't have found that word if he were to consult his dictionary but instead the very thing itself because that word would have been on one of the many pages of the dictionary that had been excised so as to make room for his stash.

On the other hand, on reflection, I had to hand it to him. In order to get out of this scrape, our boy of blue had made a remarkable choice for his counselor. He was being represented by a prominent member of the Massachusetts Senate—the minority leader, in fact—although it was not much of a minority because Republicans in the Massachusetts legislature were few and far between. He was an imposing figure, sort of Daniel Webster-esque, except a lot taller. I couldn't help thinking that the judge sitting on the case would certainly know that this prominent legislator might at some point have a say in future salary increases for the judiciary and that might influence how he saw the case. I felt sure that this kind of maneuver would have been looked upon with favor by the legal wizards at that particular law school.

But looked at in another way, this was a young man ahead of his time. Now that more than 50 percent of the Commonwealth has tried the stuff, its possession has been made legal, making this young man prescient and, in his own way, a force for progress. I am overwhelmed when I think about the whole thing. Nothing of consequence happened to either defendant, and I'm sure that Mr. Boola Boola went on to a successful career. And something else happened as a result of this case, although I am unable to understand why. Any resentment I might have had, and I had some, toward that institution that would not consider me for its law school had miraculously and almost completely disappeared.

# 6

# Courtroom Follies

**As pleasant and reaffirming as** the months I spent in that court were, there were plenty of other activities that reminded me of my place as a fifth wheel in the district courts. One of the features of my early years at the defenders was a thankless duty that the office required. All district courts operated Monday through Friday, with the exception of the Boston Municipal Court (BMC), which had Saturday sessions. The district court lawyers were assigned to this on a rotating basis, and there was no overtime or hazardous pay attached.

My day arrived, and I showed up at the court at the appointed hour as required. Before the session started, I informed the clerk that I was the public defender assigned for the day in the event a public defender was needed. This was one of the busiest courts in the Commonwealth, and I had never been there. What I did not know was how things went in that court, and I did not know that the judge, who one might think was directly descended from Cotton Mather and only a few generations removed, despised the public defenders.

The judge appears, and the first case is called. It is a prisoner in custody and he is charged with the crime of public drunkenness. He is brought out of the lockup and he can hardly stand. He is disheveled and reeks of alcohol. He has a bruise on his forehead where one could guess he fell or walked into a lamppost or whatever. He is clearly still intoxicated. The judge then asks in a loud voice if the public defender is present. Of course, he had been told and knew I was present, and I am beginning to realize I am a part of a humiliation game that I most certainly want to avoid. I stand and identify myself. The judge gleefully assigns me the case and then does this. He leans forward and in a stage whisper that could be heard on the other side of the Boston Common says, "Here's your big chance!"

Guffaws from the audience. Humiliated, I do my thing, which is to shrink into my shoes and wish I had taken up the forest service.

The reason the judge didn't like the Defenders Committee was that it was messing up the little operation he had going in his courtroom. He proceeded on the theory that he was running a theatrical production and, truly, he had an audience of retirees who sat in the back and laughed at his jokes and his ploys. I'm guessing they even had a club—like maybe something called the Backbenchers. The judge, who considered himself wiser than Solomon and appeared almost as old, brooked no interference with his sideshow. The public defenders wanted continuances to interview clients and prepare cases. They thought impossible thoughts like maybe some of the defendants were not guilty.

The way the judge ran it was with a coterie of lawyers who would accept cases to be disposed of on the fly. Softball cross-examination was required, appeals of the judge's sentences forbidden, and the word *continuance* was banished from the courthouse dictionary. These lawyers were paid by chits, which were issued on the spot by the judge and could be cashed at the city treasury. I knew of one lawyer who would save up his pay stubs, then cash them all at once. He would then disappear for a few weeks, and it would be leaked by those in the know that he was on a bender.

Cases were often concluded with an encomium from the judge. I had a case involving an antique firearm which resulted in a rarity—a not guilty—due to a technicality regarding antique firearms. At the conclusion, the judge intoned, "By the time that gun was loaded and fired, the crime wave would be over" to the delight of the watchers. Occasionally, there would be a case involving a liquor law violation at a strip club. The Backbenchers would know in advance and pack the courtroom. When the case was called, the strippers would walk in en masse and occupy the bench at the front provided for potential witnesses. They would sit in half undress, legs daintily crossed, preparing to testify that the violation had not occurred. This was great theater and also great advertising for the accused establishment.

I was not yet quite done with my humiliator. Years later, I was assigned to the court on a full-time basis, and the wrangling began. The judge was already under the gun because among the watchers were spies who were filing complaints with the Supreme Court about some of the judge's activities. I was not one of those and had learned to rock along with the vagaries of the court as best I could. I was there one time when a case was in the process of being resolved. The defendant was charged with the crime of being present where heroin is kept or deposited. Don't ask. Nobody was sure what it meant. Thankfully, it's long gone from the criminal dossier.

The judge was trying to talk the defendant into accepting some long-forgotten disposition and kept telling him, in order to help gain his acquiescence, that it was only a misdemeanor. Finally, the defendant was persuaded, accepted the offered disposition, and the case was over. I did unusual things as a lawyer, which was to read the statutes and keep up on the possible penalties. This was important in case a client was hit with the maximum and complained that you never told him he could get that. So I knew this: being present was a felony, and I also knew the maximum sentence.

A felony in Massachusetts is any crime for which a sentence to the state prison could be imposed. Three and a half years in state's prison was the maximum penalty for the being present charge. Even though I went to Harvard does not mean I couldn't be stupid, and I often was, a burden that I continuously bear. There are also levels of stupidity, and one of them is the category of "utterly."

Later, during the session, I found myself at the sidebar for some reason, and unthinking, I said to the judge, "You know, Judge, being present is a felony."

The judge became quite naturally upset at being corrected by this smart ass who was also one of those despicable public defenders and responded tartly with this: "You show me one person who is serving time in Walpole (the then name for the state prison), and I'll buy you a Cadillac!" And if that wasn't enough, he added this: "And I can afford it!"

This was very clever because, of course, it was extremely unlikely that anyone ever did go to Walpole on a charge of being present, and the probability of finding such a person was essentially zero. But I was right, and it still was a felony, even though I regret to say I didn't win myself a Cadillac. The Cadillac remark was what? A comment on my low pay scale? I've never been able to figure that one out.

In these later days, there were two of us assigned to this court because of the high volume of business. The judge was running into criticism from the higher-ups that he was not using the public defenders the way he should, and cracks were appearing in his long-running operation. No longer was he able to assign one case to the defenders and then appoint his coterie lawyers to the balance of the cases with a note to the docket that the public defender was busy, which I would be since I would be interviewing my client and taking forever to fill out the annoying face sheet. My compadre was a jovial fellow who got along well with the judge. He didn't ask for continuances and didn't appeal, something I did with regularity. A perk for his cooperation was that he was invited to the lobby when the judge had to view a film which had run afoul of the obscenity laws. Guess I missed out.

So what about a judge who makes fun of new lawyers, defies the mandates of the Supreme Court, and offers to buy you cars if you can prove him wrong? Why, of course, he is venerated, and not one but at least two portraits are painted, one would guess at government expense, and hung in the very courtrooms that he used to preside over. The result was that later on, when I was trying cases in that same court, which by then had moved to a new location, I was watched over by his likeness, and I could not help but remember that each one of those later cases was, in some respects, still my big chance.

I was assigned to a number of district courts as I waited for the hoped-for elevation to the superior court staff. I continued to be assigned mostly to the suburban courts as I sought to shake my lightweight status and be sent to the big city courts where there were the heavier cases. Just the same, I was all in and took on every responsibility I could in order to better myself through experience. Slowly, I was advancing in the Defenders organization, and the reproofs of my supervisor had largely subsided. Every day, I was in one court or another, handling a slew of criminal cases. Interspersed with the ongoing frenzied activity, there were moments of levity which served to keep things in perspective even as our clients were being jailed with alarming frequency. Underneath the seriousness, there was an ongoing weirdness which was part of the daily routine. The bizarre was the order of the day.

Take, for instance, a day in a local district court where not much was happening and the lawyers and court personnel were in their respective reveries while one of these boring cases with multiple defendants was being tried. There was an old statute that authorized the arrest of disturbers of the peace and also disorderly persons. Nobody knew how to define either of these crimes, so this statute was the subject of frequent litigation, particularly by legal nitpickers who wanted to know "exactly" what these terms meant. The high court wrote many opinions affirming that the terms were not "unconstitutionally" vague as opposed to vague in a normal common-sense way, demonstrating that it had no idea what the terms meant either.

This is the way many of these cases came up. On warm, early spring days, teenagers would congregate outdoors to enjoy the first signs of the new season. There would be conversation and maybe some beer and maybe some puffing. A crotchety neighbor would hear the noise and call the police. The police would arrive and nicely ask the youths to disperse. This would be met with protests about their rights. Voices would be raised, and the noise would escalate. Soon, a few would be arrested for being disturbers or disorderly. It was a rite of spring in mainly suburban courts, and the dockets were clogged with these cases.

I was in court for a trial on many of them. These charges were frequently litigated since nobody knew what the violation truly was.

The judges would listen and then continue the cases with no finding of guilt, the charges to be dismissed after a period of time. An admonition to behave was followed by a sop that the kindly judge had saved the young man from having a record.

In one of these cases in a local district court, the trial was protracted. Much testimony was elicited, and the defendant's friends were called to testify that nobody had been disorderly. A witness was asked if he had seen the defendant, and he had, and next was he carrying something, and yes, he was, and what was it. Said with the much-parodied New England accent, it was a "beahr." It is the purview of some judges to pay no attention to what is going on in their courtroom, and this was apparently true of this judge whose mind had evidently wandered.

Suddenly, he snapped to and asked incredulously, "He was carrying a what?"

"A beahr."

"A what?" he asked, even more incredulously.

The courtroom dissolved in laughter. *Wake up, Judge. A beer is not a bear, even if it sounds like one.*

Among all the silliness, I was acquiring a most important skill, which was that I could try anything by which I mean that no story was too far-fetched for me to present it on my client's behalf. This was a skill that had to be mastered because many clients simply did not want to plead guilty or had a claim that they were innocent accompanied by a story that was often utter nonsense. This meant that in order for the case to move forward, there had to be a trial, nonsense or not. Since these were district court cases, the trials were in front of judges who just laughed at you and found the defendants guilty. I would have done my job, and the defendant, if aggrieved, would simply "appeal" to the superior court. I was learning by doing and I handled hundreds of cases, at the very least, if not a lot more.

It is with regret that I note that this manner of learning will never be repeated because so much has changed, and attitudes have changed although not necessarily for the better. District courts now have juries and are thus courts of finality, so you can't play Perry Mason and then bail to the superior court if things go wrong.

I also was learning something else important. When I first started out, I used to go to the library (we actually had a small one at the office) and read up on case law. My thought was that if I really knew the law, I would be able to find cases and loopholes that would benefit my client, even if my client's story was, well, just a story. This was the kind of thing they taught at Harvard Law. I would read the cases, and the arguments for the defendants would sound pretty good until I reached the end, and it would say "defendant's appeal dismissed," "judgment for the Commonwealth affirmed," or "defendant's exceptions overruled." I began to realize that reading the law was not going to get me anywhere, nor was knowledge of the same going to get me anywhere. After all, stealing was stealing, robbery was robbery, and assault and battery was, yes, assault and battery. Nothing complicated there.

Further, the government had everything. They had witnesses, they had well-trained lawyers and police. They had research. They had investigators and forensics. Worst of all, they had evidence. And what did the defendant have? Shall I leave a blank space here? What the defendant had was half-crazed people like myself who had long ago lost it and joined the Sancho Panzas of the world, tilting against windmills. There had to be another way to fight for my clients other than reading a bunch of judgment-affirmed-for-the-government-type cases. And I was about to learn that there was. For one fine day, I was told that one of the superior court attorneys had been taken out on a stretcher, or maybe in a straitjacket, and I would be moving on to replace him and, at last, get a chance to try jury cases. A new chapter was about to start, and I was to learn that I now had new weapons at my disposal on my way to becoming a presence in the representation of my clients. In cases before judges, I have already described what happened with them. I was about to take a crack at seeing how juries responded to my "I can try anything" gambit. I was looking forward to the opportunity.

So now I was taking a different view of my role as a defense lawyer, whether as a public defender or privately retained. The mirage of rescuing innocent clients from the maws of justice was, I had finally concluded, just that—a figment of my imagination. Something else had happened, and that was the way I looked at my clients. I saw how the court system treated them. They were scolded, punished, humiliated, and frequently sent away to prison. As this happened, my sense of empathy and even identification with my clients grew. I desperately wanted to help them through the process. I began to discover there was a kind of psychic drama being played out and that I was a part of it and, in my determination to help my clients, I was learning new things.

My elevation to the superior court was going to, I hoped, provide me with an opportunity to develop new tools which I could use to assist my clients through the process and attain for them the best possible disposition of their cases, even if it didn't, as most often happened, result in an acquittal.

# 7

# I Get to Try Jury Cases

**The Defenders Committee had now** become a larger operation and moved to new quarters on Boylston Street. All the offices were on the same floor, so there was no longer the geographical separation between the districts and the superiors. This made for a more congenial atmosphere, at least on the surface. It also meant that the superiors could insult the districts to their face without bothering to get on an elevator to do it. It also meant a change in supervision.

My new supervisor was a strange bird who kept a large Doberman at home and a dead, plexiglass-encased Piranha on his desk. He had a fearsome reputation and was reputed to be an outstanding defendant's attorney. Generally, the other attorneys seemed to be afraid of him but for no apparent reason. Right from the start, we got along rather well. "Hitting it off" as a description might be a stretch, however. My initial go-round with this man was at our first group meeting of the lawyers he was supervising, a half dozen or so. We were to discuss current cases. One attorney was asked to discuss one of his assigned cases. He was also asked what the possible penalties could be. This attorney didn't know. Did anyone know?

Harvard-like, I did and said so. Case files were kept in letter-sized manila folders and were assigned by the supervisor by writing the name of the attorney on the outside of the folder along with the date of the assignment. Our much-loved supervisor grabbed the file, crossed off the name of the currently assigned attorney, and dramatically wrote in my name and the current date and gave me the file.

Later, I looked over the case and wished I had kept my mouth shut. A very serious matter. And this was not the first nor definitely the last time when omertà should have been observed.

Recruits from the district courts were looked upon with skepticism. They were to be given nothing that would require much intelligence to handle. Chief among these "you can't go wrong" cases were the escape charges. These were not going to be trials because these cases were indefensible, and there was thus little chance for a screw-up.

I was initially assigned to the Middlesex Superior Court. The Middlesex County correctional facility was leaking like a sieve. Work releasers were taking off, and inmates were hiding in garbage cans or climbing the walls. It was a scandal. One of my first assignments was to handle four escape cases. This was before the day of rules regarding conflicting representation, so I was able to represent all four at once. I interviewed my clients and conferred with my opposite number. No one wanted extra time, and the DA was agreeable to suspended sentences to begin after their release from their current bids, and thus no new committed time would be added.

We went before the judge and offered the pleas, which were accepted, and stated our agreed recommendation. Even though the superior courts were courts of record with stenographers taking down every word, it didn't mean that they were any less bizarre. One might be limited in what one could say, but this did not rule out sight gags. This judge, who was the son of a former Supreme Court judge, sat on the bench behind a banker's lamp wearing a green eyeshade. It made him look like a recent import from Vegas, and he acted the part on occasion. Upon hearing our recommendation of suspended sentences, the judge bawled, "What happened to the six months I said I was going to give all the escapees?"

And that's what they got: six months to be served from and after their current sentences. So there it was. I had managed to screw up the "unscrewable" and had made a mess of the thing, just as I had in my first foray in the district court. I was relaunched into a new and most wondrous orbit.

I had just experienced one of the dangers of the guilty plea, which was that the judges could do what they wanted. They would bark at the prosecutors and tell them they were too lenient and impose heavier sentences than recommended. The judges had to exercise some caution because if they were too tough, no one would plead guilty, all the defendants would want trials, and the wheels of justice would grind to a halt. Questions among lawyers appearing in the session were, "Do you know this judge? Does he go along with recommendations?"

Eventually, this all changed to a more civilized procedure where a defendant could offer a plea with the realization that if the judge did not accept the defense offer, he would be allowed to withdraw his plea and proceed to trial. That way, the wheels of justice would be greased for case dispositions without the defendants fearing they would get whacked in the process.

Finally, my first trial arrived. The same routine was true with these cases as with the district court—no training, no videotaped instructions, no how-to manuals, no nothing. You just jumped in. I forget the charges and anything about the case except for one thing: I was so nervous I got a bloody nose. And then, after this medical event, the trial began. Somewhere in the middle of the case, there was some evidence that I wanted to object to. Nobody ever told me how to object, so I did this: I raised my hand while seated at the defense table like a fourth-grader with the answer. Everyone stopped speaking, and after a pause, the clerk said to me acidly, "You stand when you want to address the court."

After I had finally risen out of my shoes and the jury had stopped snickering, the case proceeded. I didn't win that one. But an important lesson, perhaps the most important, was learned. I never fail to stand when addressing the court and also to stand when the court addresses me. I may not be hip on other points of courtroom decorum, but this I always do.

More trials followed, and I managed to build myself a losing streak. Four in a row. Four seemed to be a magic number for me. The DAs I faced were all experienced, and they toyed with me. But I watched, and I learned things from them.

In addition to trials, there were also motions to be presented. There was a courtroom in this ancient superior court building which had been added by excavating a piece of abutting land. The windows were high up because the courtroom was half underground. This room was referred to by the locals as "the dugout," but no baseball, except maybe a few defendants who went for extra bases. It was where I had to present and argue my first superior court motion to suppress. This was shortly after my first trial. It was before an experienced and long-tenured superior court judge.

At the close of my presentation, the judge remarked that my argument in support of my motion was the stupidest argument he had ever heard, not one of, but the stupidest, and he had been around for a while. He didn't even ask to go off the record before he said this. At least I stood while he lectured me. That was before I crouched underneath the counsel table, cloaked in fear and loathing.

I am nothing but determined, and I kept my hopes up that sometime, somehow, I would win a trial, and finally, I did. It was a nothing case as cases go, but like these nothing cases, they are extremely important to the client and, of course, to my banged-up ego. The defendant was charged with possession of marijuana. What made this case unusual was that the possession took place inside the county prison. There had been a check for contraband. The prisoners were lined up in the unit and searched one by one. After going through the line and being cleared, the defendant was observed picking something up off the floor. A guard demanded to know what it was in his hand, and at first, the defendant refused to show it to him. It was eventually discovered to be a small baggie with the contraband inside. The defendant's story was that after he went through the checkpoint, he saw the baggie lying on the floor and out of curiosity picked it up. He at first refused to open his hand because he suddenly realized that what he had picked up might be something he shouldn't have.

No matter the improbability of this story, I nevertheless made ready for trial. It was a jury of twelve (six-person juries hadn't been invented yet). The trial was short, and my best memory is the defendant testified. The defendant was acquitted. I was overjoyed. I had won one—finally. What I remember most was that the judge seemed pleased with the case as it was presented and gave us a good charge and even seemed happy with the result.

I rushed back to the office, swollen with pride. I knocked on the door of the office next to mine, where four senior attorneys—those of the old third floor group—were gathered and excitedly uttered, "Not guilty!" I almost got my nose broken when the door was slammed in my face. Another lesson was learned and appreciated. As public defenders, we lose most of our cases. If we win a third of our trials, we have performed above and beyond expectations. The wins and losses are not the most important; it is, of course, how the game is played. And so the lesson was this: always, when returning to the office after a win, I should be sure to act as if a family member just passed away, and if I am asked how the case went, I should say, "What case?" But if pressed, I might say it was a not guilty, and I should act as if it was just another day at the office, even though inside, my spirit would be soaring.

So this was good. I had a win, and I was getting a feel for how things go. I was hopeful that at some point, I would be accepted into the superior court group, and I felt as if I was making some headway in my career. I had vanquished, I thought, the Perry fantasy in its entirety. Some, but not yet all, even referred to me as Mr. Wood as the snickered "Hiya, Perry" receded into the background.

# 8

## An Important Case

**The time sequence over the** next few years I'm not sure about, but a significant case, a truly landmark case in my career, was about to come my way—a landmark case for me and my client but, in the great scheme of things, unnoticed. Still, it was important in what it shows about the operation of the system. I was assigned to represent a man charged with possession of a firearm. He had a codefendant charged with the same thing, or maybe it was carrying a firearm under his control in a motor vehicle. Either one of those charges carries the same penalty. The police had received a tip from an informant that a bank robbery had been planned. A description of the would-be robbers was given as well as the car they were driving. That car was stopped, and the defendants and the car were searched.

Between the feet of my client was found a firearm and a gym-type bag which contained a pair of sunglasses, a shirt, a hat, and a newspaper—arguably, the newspaper to conceal the weapon and the rest to be used as a disguise. My client, plus the codefendant, the driver of the car, were both arrested and charged. The defendants were Muslims and had a half dozen or so supporters who came to court with them. They were similarly dressed—black suits, white shirts, black shoes, black bow ties, and shaved heads. This was before the time of court security—there was none—and perhaps I imagined this, but they all seemed to be sensitive to the contents of their left inside jacket pockets.

The codefendant was represented by one of those lawyers who was in the van of modern thinking. His mantra was that the case was politically motivated and a lot of other things as well. The Chicago Seven or Eight or Half Dozen, whatever, was a recent memory. I don't remember his name, but for convenience, I'll call him Mr. Lefty. There was the usual backing and filling pretrial—conferences, motion hearings, and the like.

The case was in a cavernous old courtroom in a town outside Boston. Each day the case was on the list, it was among a number of others, so the court was crowded with attorneys, clients, and onlookers. The charges were brought under a recently enacted statute that required, upon conviction, a mandatory minimum penalty of one year in the house of correction. This was during the crack years, and this law had been enacted to try and stem the large number of shootings taking place in urban areas. Supposedly, there was no way around the one-year mandatory sentence—do all 365 days. No parole, no good time, no dismissals, and no suspended sentences. Several pretrial conferences were held with a view to concluding the cases short of trial, but nothing could be resolved. The one-year mandatory sentence made it difficult to reach a resolution, even though there was a maximum of two and a half years.

My client was not amenable to a plea in any case. I had informed him that yes, there was the mandatory minimum, but I reminded him of the maximum of two and one-half years which he could receive if he went to trial and lost. He didn't care. He was going to trial. The judge in the case seemed easy to get along with. He had a sense of humor. He was obviously experienced, although not as a trier of jury cases. He was a district court judge sitting in the superior court because of a shortage of superior court judges. He obviously thought the defendants were guilty, but he was a judge, so that was normal and even expected. He was used to the idea that he was the one who decided innocence or guilt and was uncomfortable with the fact that that decision was in the hands of other people—the jury.

What this was going to mean, I was unsure about, but as in any jury case, there are always possibilities—although they appeared to be slim in this case. In discussing the case at length with my supervisor, the general feeling was that it was going to be unwinnable, and I was sent off with a laugh and a "Good luck to you, pal."

None of this, of course, mattered. The important thing was that since the defendant wanted a trial, the case needed to be tried. My "I can try anything" watchword would, as usual, be front and center. Up until this time, I had been keeping a low profile. I was trying my share of cases and doing the things I was supposed to do for my clients. Other than the usual rough-around-the-edges behavior that some found annoying, there had been no truly off-kilter happenings. But as this case progressed, there was a faint stirring of the air and an occasional flash of heat lightning that promised the unusual was about to visit. It took a while, but it most certainly did. And this is how it happened.

The trial day arrived, and the list was lengthy, so there were many people in this large courtroom and a delay in starting the trial. Plenty of time to get nervous. Surprise of surprises, Mr. Lefty had buckled and somehow had found a way around the mandatory one-year minimum, and his client, pretrial, pled guilty with the expectation of a six-months nonmandatory sentence. This was supposed to be an impossibility since the statute had been drafted to foreclose such an eventuality. This was the first rumbling that the unusual was to be the order of the day. The codefendant's sentencing was held in abeyance so that he, the codefendant, didn't testify in my client's trial and try to bail him out. If he did, his promised sentence would be canceled, and he, the codefendant, would be back on the one-year mandatory.

A jury was empaneled, and the case began, and I am flying solo. We had a rarity, a private stenographer who was recording the testimony—I'm guessing hired by Mr. Lefty. I remember little about the trial, but I do recall cross-examining the ballistician as to his test fire of the weapon (to qualify as a firearm under the statute, the weapon must be capable of discharging a projectile).

He had done the usual, which was to load the weapon and then fire it into a tank of water. The bullet would be retrieved as proof of the discharge. On cross-examination, I asked him if he had checked the tank to see that it was empty before the test fire. He had. And then the big score, which was when I asked him if he actually saw the bullet come out of the gun upon firing, and of course, he had to say no. Brilliant. Right out of my HLS trial practice class.

After the Commonwealth rested, the crucial part of the case came up. My client had decided he would testify. He takes the stand and tells his story, which I don't remember what that was, and as he is doing so, the judge starts horning in. He just couldn't control himself. He asks the defendant insinuating questions and essentially takes over the prosecution of the case. One question after another comes from the judge until finally, my client, taken completely aback, spontaneously says, "I don't think I'm getting a fair trial here" (this is all taking place right in front of the jury).

To which the judge unbelievably retorts, "Yeah, all you," and there's a pause, and I'm thinking, *He's not, is he?* But he collects himself and finishes, "All you defendants think that." The case concludes, and the jury retires. I haven't the faintest idea what I argued, but it must have been the usual "I can try anything" dynamite because, after a short wait, the jury returns and, in front of a packed and astounded courtroom, finds the defendant not guilty.

In my excitement, my glasses flew off. And landed where? Halfway across the room? My client and his entourage were roundly pleased. But now came the main event. The judge could not contain his disgust. It is traditional for the judge to thank the jurors for their service, even if he or she disagrees with the verdict, and most judges can do that even if they are surly about it. But there were no thanks from our disgruntled jurist, and instead, the jury got this from the irate judge: "The next time there is a bank robbery in (he named the town), don't blame the stupid judges. Blame the stupid jurors." And off he marched from the bench.

My client and his retinue made ready to leave, while Mr. Lefty had to pack up his kit and re-explain his politics and make his excuses as to how his apolitical stumblebum cocounsel had happened to walk his client while his was going to have to do a very political six months. I was extended an invitation to meet with the local Imam, which I politely declined, and instead had lunch with the stenographer, whom I had come to know during the course of the pretrial and trial proceedings. He revealed to me a part of the action which I had missed. He had been seated just under the right-hand corner of the bench, between the judge and the jury. The judge had leaned over and, with his arm hanging over the side of the bench and within a few inches of his head, had whispered, "Don't take this," just before reminding the jury how stupid it was.

The judge's hand was so close that he could literally have smacked him if he had recorded the statement. And the stenographer, fearing for his own safety, as the police always say before embarking on an illegal frisk, consequently omitted that statement from his transcription.

So there it is. It's the stupid jurors who are screwing up the functioning of the criminal justice system. If only the jury could be gotten rid of and the smart, "unstupid" judges could run the show, defendants could be stuck in jail with impunity. The lesson here: in order to be effective as defense counsel, one must have the ability and the courage to try cases. If the defense lawyer can't try cases or is afraid to try cases, then he or she is at the mercy of the government. This is what all that long district court experience taught me and what this case reinforced. It is not important that the cases be winners or "good" cases to try. It is important to be able to put forward as well as possible the defense that your client has given you.

In this case, one that looked hopeless, I did that, and it worked out spectacularly. I had begun to realize that the jury had opened up new possibilities to do something for my clients. I repeat: in district court, the judges did pretty much what they wanted to, and you, as the defender, were virtually powerless to affect the outcome of any case. Sure, you could cajole and put forward any extenuating circumstances or things about your client that you thought should soften the blow, but that was pretty much it. I had become aware that juries looked at the world a little differently than the functionaries in the legal system did, and results in cases such as this one could be had. It was just an inkling at this point, and I was soon to learn other lessons about how the system worked and to use those lessons for the benefit of my clients.

This case also made me supremely happy because it vindicated my belief that every time I stepped into a courtroom, there was a good chance that something out of the ordinary was going to happen. Pressure was put on the judge because I was audacious enough to try this case, whereas Mr. Lefty did what any normal, level-headed lawyer would have done, which was to make a deal for his client. The fact that I didn't and instead went to work to try a case which, to all intents and purposes, was a loser, resulted in the usual strange occurrence.

I was also learning something about trying jury cases. I heard a lot about how different lawyers had secret sauces that they used to win cases. They had their not-guilty ties and their not-guilty suits. They had special tricks. I heard about one lawyer who, when his client was about to be identified as the perpetrator, would pull back his sleeve and show that he was wearing two watches. The jury would be distracted and miss the crucial ID. A few lawyers in the Defenders were of the opinion that trying cases was one big con job. It seemed to me that the jury couldn't be conned, at least I couldn't con them. My thought was that if the jury thinks you are giving them a con job, the jury will hold it against you and your client.

I used to worry about my appearance before a jury. I tried different ties, shoes, and suits. After a while, and after losing my share or maybe more than my share, I gave up and relaxed and just tried to do the best I could with what I had. The jury would understand and appreciate the effort. I also knew that since HLS had been lost on me and I didn't understand the finer points, I was doing well with juror identification. I didn't know much about cross-examination and thought, and still think, that some of my best crosses were "No questions, Your Honor."

The jury could feel as if one of their own members was the one conducting the case since I would ask the same silly questions that no real lawyer would ever ask, and that meant that the jury and I were working as a team to try and defend my client. Frequent reprimands from the court and an insinuation that I was incompetent would invariably, I hoped, help put the jury on the side of the defense. At this point, this was just a feeling, but it was something that was beginning to influence how I handled jury matters.

And there is another important lesson to be learned from what happened in this case, and that is the function of the judge. I hear lawyers coming back from court shaking their heads. The judge did this and the judge did that, and they can't believe it. They complain mightily at what the judge did that made their efforts on behalf of their clients so difficult. They should relax. Much has been written about the function of judges. There are standards and guidelines and rules and the like. But there is no getting around the true judicial function, which is to help, aid, and do all possible to assure that the Commonwealth gets a conviction. And there is an obvious reason for this in the minds of the judges, and that is you can't let all these utterly guilty defendants get away with this stuff they are pulling. We would have total anarchy.

This attitude can be tolerated or at least understood because the evidence almost always points to guilt. Even the most evenhanded judge is going to try to slant the case if they see you trying to sell some ridiculosity to the jury, and it looks like the jurors might be buying it. No point in getting mad about it. Just expect it and learn to deal with it as best one possibly can. And there are ways. But one should also always be sensitive to the fact there are, on rare occasions, judges that did poorly in judge school who don't understand this and are actually fair, but they are truly scarce. When you find one, it is best to cajole, flatter, and bring him or her coffee and ask if he or she can please hear all your cases.

Back at the office, I put on my best face that a family member had taken ill and said nothing to anybody. As I waited to give the news about the case, I recalled there had been some laughter and remembered the "Good luck" send-off as the trial date approached. A loss on the case had been all but assured, it was assumed. Finally, my supervisor poked his head in my office door and asked, "How did it go?" with that look of "as if he didn't know."

I pretended I didn't know what he was talking about but finally owned up that the defendant had been acquitted. He was appropriately astonished and didn't completely believe me. It was only after calling the court to get verification that the truth was accepted, and of course, I became a big hero for at least that day because I had won this unwinnable case. It didn't take long to get back to reality in a big way, for as impossible as that case had been, I was soon to embark on a new assignment that would require me to handle cases nobody could win.

# 9

# I Am Promoted

**This new assignment was sold** to me by my supervisor as a promotion because of my recent successes on the just-described case and a few others, and it put me into Suffolk County where all the heavy criminal cases were. I was pleased to be at the center of the criminal business, even though I knew I would be taking on a herculean task. I use the word *promotion* loosely since I was being detailed to do a thankless job that no one else wanted. I was now to head up a team to defend the prosecution of so-called "major violators." Initially, this team consisted only of myself but was later expanded to include others as the volume of business increased due to the popularity of the program with the prosecution.

I was awarded this job because I was considered so smart that I would be able to win these unwinnable cases, just as I had in that gun case with the unexpected result. I had another suspicion, which was that this was a covert attempt to get rid of me. That was never going to work. Years later—many years later—I learned that about the time of the gun trial, I had been on a shortlist of attorneys scheduled for the axe. I had apparently offended some members of the staff with my brusque attitude and crossed many judges who were friendly with the chief counsel. In attendance at that gun trial, waiting for his case to be called, was a prominent criminal defense attorney who was looked up to by the chief counsel and was not in on the prevailing view of my future. I learned long after the fact that he sang praises to the chief about my effort in handling that case, and I was saved, at least for the moment. Clearly, my unorthodox approach to my cases was stirring the pot, something which gladdened my heart. What would life be without a certain amount of adversity?

A theory had been developed that most of the crime was being committed by a small number of perpetrators and that if those could be identified, prosecuted, and put away for several lifetimes, crime would be substantially lessened. Money had been lavished on the prosecutor's office to create a unit coincidentally called the "Major Violators Unit" to facilitate those prosecutions. The idea was to select cases where the defendant had a long record and where those cases were an easy win. I was the sacrificial lamb for these prosecutions.

There was a special session set up, and a judge assigned who had no problem doling out telephone-number-type sentences. My initiation was to try a sexual assault case involving a physician who was assaulted while she was out taking a jog in the fens—in broad daylight no less. A top prosecutor was assigned to the case. He had a reputation and an intimidating and threatening style, which made it seem that the jury would have to reckon with him personally if it didn't come back with a verdict of guilty. He would communicate this through a raised voice and by flailing his arms in his excitement in castigating the defendant and, in this case, also his lawyer. It worked. It was a guilty verdict, and I have repressed whatever memory I have of the disposition. Maybe an area code was added to the telephone number.

While the jury was out, I was across the street at a luncheon spot. The prosecutor was sitting at a table nearby. We were separated by a partition, and he didn't know I was there. I overheard someone asking him how the case had gone and something about the defense counsel. He remarked that the defense to the case was somewhat unusual. Music to my ears. I was still swimming upstream and doing the best I could, but I certainly was happy to lay claim to being the attorney with the unusual defenses. As I went along, none of my unusual defenses worked, and my clients were being buried. The cases were just too strong. I had one client who was convicted of a lesser-included charge rather than the main charge and so received only half the time he would have ordinarily. I regarded this as a great victory.

That case involved the burglary of a dorm room in the Harvard Business School. The evidence was that the police had been called and that the officers arrived in time to watch my client and his two codefendants exit a window with the merchandise. These B-School guys were rich. Stereos, TVs, camel hair coats. I was silly enough to think that these latter-day Robin Hoods, emphasis on hoods, might catch a break from the jury in the form of an acquittal. Wrong about that.

In this protean struggle, I was learning other ways in which the deck was stacked in favor of the government. I have already mentioned the function of the judge in criminal cases, but I was finding that the rules of evidence were tilted in the government's favor as well. Here is an example of how this works: the hearsay rule. I probably shouldn't comment because I've already made it clear that most of my legal education was Greek to me or any language other than

English one might name, but as a matter of practice, this is how the hearsay rule is applied in the trial of criminal cases. An out-of-court statement offered to prove the truth of the issue is hearsay. For instance, if the issue is what color a certain auto is, a witness can testify that he saw the car and it was red. The witness can't say, "I know the car is red because Joe, who is not a witness in the case, told me."

There is an exception to the hearsay rule, and that is that an out-of-court statement offered to prove the truth, offered as part of the government's case by a quasi-government official, such as a police officer, is an exception to the hearsay rule, and the testimony may be admitted with defense counsel's objection strongly overruled.

Also in vogue at one time or another was the so-called excited utterance rule. For instance, if someone became unduly excited upon seeing a red car and said, "By crikey, that's a red car, I can't believe it!" That out-of-court statement may be admitted as an exception to the hearsay rule. The excitement inherent in such an event is taken to be of such moment as to provide for the veracity of the statement and allow its admission in evidence. This kind of evidence was most often offered in so-called domestic violence cases but can be offered in any case as long as the requisite excitement can be established.

These two examples are just part of a long list of government-oriented exceptions to the hearsay rule that allow the prosecution to prove cases that might otherwise be lost. It is worth noting that generally, the defense is unable to produce the necessary government officials or requisite excitement to make use of these exceptions, and attempts to establish the same are frowned upon and are usually overruled.

There is also the issue of leading questions. As a rule, on cross-examination, leading questions can be asked, so leading the witness is not a problem, but they must be confined to cross-examination. Suppose as defense counsel you call a witness on behalf of your client. You are now on direct examination and cannot lead. You have the witness on the stand, and you say, "Please give your name to the court," and there is an objection. The ruling will be "Sustained—leading." The use of the leading question objection by the government is to preclude the defense from even thinking about putting on an affirmative defense.

For instance, to even suggest in the question that the witness has a name is leading that witness, and upon objection, that question will be excluded. The leading question objection is an effective tool that saves time and hastens the objective of the trial, which is to have the defendant found guilty and sentenced to a lengthy prison term. There are numerous other ways in which the defense is precluded from mounting any kind of case, and I will discuss them as they occur to me.

So I soldiered on through the valley of the shadow of whatever, where there was no place to hide from the grueling cases I was assigned to handle. I threw everything I could at the government—everything I could think of at this early stage in my career—but nothing worked. Fortunately, my stay with the major violators' cases was a brief one, and much of what happened to my clients has been lost to memory or possibly is contained in a repressed memory capsule. Eventually, I was moved back into the rotation trying the run-of-the-mill felony cases in Suffolk County, where I had now established myself. A relief, and yet the strangeness that relentlessly followed me was about to continue.

# 10

## Back to a Kind of Normality

**Now I was handling cases** which more closely approximated the normality. The judge didn't get seriously out of line, and I did not have a winning evidentiary hand—more like no defense whatsoever—yet these cases were not as formidable as the "violator" cases. They were important to be tried, even though nearly defenseless, because my clients had an aversion to pleading guilty and wanted to exercise their important constitutional right, which was to have their cases decided by a jury. Still, there was a kind of twilight zone atmosphere that permeated these cases in which it was hard to see where reality existed. All that could be done was to hold on tight and hope at the end that one's sanity was still intact.

One of these involved an armed robbery. My client allegedly walked into a barroom as it was being opened for the day, appeared to brandish a weapon, and demanded money. The man at the till, who happened to be the chief probation officer at a local court, complied. He had just counted the register and knew what was in the till—ninety-nine ones. The police were called, a description was given, and shortly the defendant was produced, identified by the victim, arrested, and charged.

I interviewed the defendant. We went over the police affidavit and noted that the description of the assailant was that he was wearing a burgundy-colored leather jacket. When arrested, the defendant happened to have ninety-nine ones in his pocket. No weapon was found. The defendant was incensed. It couldn't be him because he was wearing a jacket that was red, not burgundy. A half-hearted suggestion that burgundy and red were similar was met with hostility. And the ninety-nine ones? He won those gambling behind some establishment called the Shrimp Boat.

With this ironclad defense, we answered, "Ready for trial." It was tried before the only female judge at the time, an imposing woman with an impressive coiffure of white hair. The evidence was presented, and I somehow was able to give one of my "I can try anything" closings, but just barely. A quick verdict of guilty was anticipated. Instead, the jury was out deliberating for an inordinate amount of time. Finally, there was a note from the panel that one of the jurors wanted to speak to the judge. That juror was brought down and, after swearing she was not in any way related to the defendant and that she had not been threatened by any of the other jurors, said she didn't feel well. Over my vociferous objection, she was excused. An alternate was selected and barely made it into the jury room before a verdict of guilty was agreed upon. My client was crestfallen but still maintains his innocence.

I take pride in the work I did on that case and regard it as a success. The defendant was never going to plead guilty, and the case had to be tried. I can't remember whether the defendant testified, but if he did, then it would be part and parcel of my unusual manner of presenting cases. There appeared to be little reason for the jury to have been out for half a day on the case and preliminarily to be deadlocked. Whatever I was doing or not doing was apparently working for the defendant, even in this case where most certainly burgundy and red are at opposite ends of the color spectrum.

If that case was out of the ordinary in how it ran its course, it hardly compares with another case I eventually tried. Of course, if one accepts that there was a general weirdness that surrounded most of what I was doing, then these cases were completely ordinary. Clearly, I was not good at telling clients whatever was necessary to convince them to plead out cases that should be pled.

This case involved a rape and a robbery. The assailant was arrested as a result of a description given by the victim. He was described as fat, about five-foot-eight, 250 pounds, long red hair, missing the upper right front tooth, and having a tattoo of a bird on his left arm. He had made bail, and I set up an office appointment for him. He arrived at the appointed time, and I noticed he was fat, weighed about 250 pounds, had long red hair, was about five-foot-eight, was missing his upper right front tooth, and had a tattoo of a bird on his left arm. So what was his defense? That wasn't a tattoo of a bird; it was a seal. The drawing was so crude it could have been anything—a boat, an elephant, a koala bear.

Obviously, this was a case of mistaken identification. The case went to trial in the Suffolk Superior Court before a twelve-person jury. The judge, who was then the chief judge of the superior court, seemed amused by the proceedings. He gave us a very fair trial. I remember little of the trial itself, except for the moment when the defendant removed his shirt and paraded his torso in front of the jury and pointed to the tattoo which clearly, arguably, was of a seal, not a bird as described by the victim. The case was submitted, and after a time, the jury returned and cleared him of the sexual assault but not the robbery. He was sentenced to a short term in the state's prison.

So how could he have been cleared of the rape charge in what appeared to be a very strong government case? I certainly couldn't take credit for any wizardry because there was little magic in what I did. A clue to what went on was an article that appeared in a local publication. It was an op-ed piece that spared me in its criticism of what went on in the trial. The details of the article are not important, save to again point out that the jury has a different idea of what constitutes guilt or innocence from the smart members of the prosecution and the judiciary. If I was spared criticism, it was the prosecutor who was flayed, to put it mildly. There can be no escaping a conclusion that what I have been saying is true, which is on an everyday basis the criminal justice system operates in unexpected ways and the jury is at the center of it.

And here is another of this type of case where nothing makes little sense, a requirement for my participation in any criminal matter. My client was charged with burglary in the daytime. No one was home, and my client was alleged to have gone inside to help himself to whatever he could find. He was observed in the act by a neighbor, and the police caught up with my client some distance away. What tied him to the house break, among other evidence, was a cut he had allegedly sustained in breaking some glass to gain entry. There was blood at the scene and blood on his hand. And how did he account for the blood on his hand? He had picked a hickey. This was one sizable hickey because a substantial amount of blood was involved.

So here we are in the trial session before a most fearsome judge, and we have a jury, and they are hearing the hickey story. If the jury deliberated more than five minutes, I don't remember. The defendant was quickly sentenced by the mean man judge to the maximum—ten years. Luckily, the crime was committed before sunset or it would have been twenty. The defendant lost track in the confusion and, as he left the courtroom with me at his shoulder on my way up to the dock to receive the expected huzzahs, he asked me, "What'd I get?"

"Ten years," I told him.

He was thoroughly pleased. "Whooee!" he uttered. He could go to the joint and lord it over those with the measly three- and five-year bids. I was proud. Another well-served client, and I had distinguished myself by offering up the hickey story.

So kudos to me. I tried these cases and did not go mental doing it, which was an achievement. I continued to cling to that weakness which was when confronted by stories such as in the three above cases, I found myself unable to rise up and scream something like, "What do you think I am, an idiot?" or "Don't lie to me—you did it!" or "I'll get you a hundred years with that story." Maybe I'm just perverse, but I find myself nodding agreeably that, yes, that clearly is a seal and not a dove or let me see the hickey and readying myself for trial. I tell myself it's the client's case, not mine, and it is embarrassing to tell a client he or she has no chance. This is especially true if, as sometimes happens, one of these cases where there is overwhelming evidence goes to trial and the defendant is acquitted. Maybe the clients know something I don't, so I do it their way.

At this point, I was trying a lot of cases, most of which are lost to memory, but there was a hiatus where the organization made me a supervisor in a number of the district courts. I had come up in the world and now had a number of the newer lawyers in my charge. I took this very seriously. I had frequent team meetings in which cases were discussed, and I sat in court and watched so later I could critique performances. I didn't think I was overly critical, but there was some grumbling about some of my comments.

"Why the fuck did you do that?" was one that was not roundly appreciated. I was required at the end of every six months to write up an evaluation of each of the attorneys in my charge. In hindsight, I recognize that sometimes it is better to take the long view of things—the very long view. I didn't think I was harsh in some of my comments in these evaluations, but let's say there might have been, in a few of these, an unstated suggestion that the criminal element would be better served if this particular person were doing something else.

Now remember, I didn't actually say that, but reading between the lines, it might have been there. Many of these people, an alarmingly large number of them in fact, heeded that suggestion and did find another line of work. They became judges—a staggering number of them. From time to time, I would have to appear in front of one of them. I would search my recollection and try to recall what sort of kindness I had put on his or her evaluation form. If I had a hearing in front of one of them, it would go like this: "You are asking me to do what, Mr. Wood?" This would be followed by a knowing smile. At least I still got the Mister.

At this point, I thought of myself as a sort of tough guy. One morning, we were having one of our team meetings in an anteroom provided by the court when I noticed a rather unassuming individual standing over in a corner listening in on our discussion. This was supposed to be privileged talk, and I didn't know who this person was, so to demonstrate my adept social skills, I asked, "Who the fuck are you?"

He told me who the fuck he was and introduced himself as the newly appointed deputy chief counsel of the Defenders. Oh good. Fortunately, he was a man with a sense of humor, and I was allowed to keep my job.

# 11

## Some Noteworthy Cases

**Here are a few examples** of some courtroom imponderables. I was assigned to represent a defendant charged with assault by means of a dangerous weapon. The defendant was a gem carrier and carried precious stones between various jewelry stores. He wore a turban or some sort of headdress and a long Arab-type coat. I don't know what the name of the garb was. He had an Arab-sounding name, but in reality, he was an Arab in masquerade and had an ordinary name and was born in Roxbury instead of Riyadh.

He was walking down some alley late at night when an elderly woman appeared to put out her trash. It was a bad area, according to her, so when she did this, she took along her dog which, upon seeing the defendant, put up a fuss—like an attack fuss. The defendant drew a sidearm, which he was licensed to carry, and pointed it in the general direction of the animal. My client was this huge guy in this Arab getup, which made him look like Alibaba and an assortment of the forty thieves all rolled into one. He scared the hell out of the woman and maybe also the dog. She was terrified and called the police.

The police arrived shortly, and after some conversation, the defendant was arrested and charged with assault on the woman. In the district court, the defendant had been offered a continuance without a finding of guilt, case to be dismissed after a year, which disposition he had refused. A continuance without requires an admission of guilt, which the defendant would not do. He appealed, and the case stood for trial in the superior court. The day of the trial, we were before a senior judge who, a short time ago, had presided over one of the most closely watched cases of the past decade. He was a highly respected judge. As the parties were dispensing with the preliminaries, he stuck his head out of his lobby and rasped, "Any chance of a resolution?" He could have added, "of this inconsequential little case?" For once, there was not going to be one of these endless series of lobby conferences to try and settle. This was a real trial judge.

Often, cases are held for lobby in the session because the judges want to try and avoid a trial. The lawyers are called into the lobby. The judge wants to hear what the case is about. The DA expounds on the ton of evidence he has, so much evidence that he can hardly fit it in the courtroom. The defense counsel offers up his or her nonsense, and the judge looks at you, the defense counsel, as if to say, "Get off it." There then might be a discussion of whether there has been any negotiation and, if so, what have the parties been talking about? Usually, the judge says that the ton of evidence party has been most reasonable, and the judge will give what the ton people have offered on a plea, with an admonition that if the defendant loses at trial, he will get a lot more.

This is followed by the request, more like an order, for defense counsel to talk to his client. "Talk" means time to stop the stonewalling. Defense counsel comes back with an adjusted suggestion, and it is then back and forth, and in the meantime, half the day is gone. I hated these things. You knew that by standing up for your client, you were annoying the judge, and your client would ultimately suffer. So it was refreshing to have this judge dispense with that kind of formality. Prospective jurors were brought in, and the jury was selected.

The case begins, and after opening statements, the evidence starts. As usual, I'm nervous as a cat, but after the jury is placed in the box, I most often can settle down and do my thing. The first witness is the lady who tells her bit. She puts out the garbage, and then this big guy comes along and pulls a gun on her. She mentions her dog in passing. My turn to cross, and what I want to establish is that her dog is a monster, something like the Hound of the Baskervilles. "Isn't it true that your dog is a seven-foot-high German shepherd?" I ask.

She answers with this: "Partly."

This was an important part of the case, and I was completely thrown by her response. I have to pause and explain that when the Ten Commandments of trial practice came down from Mount Whatever, it was etched in stone that thou shalt not ask a question as to which thou knowest not the answer. In my view, the etcher never tried a case. My worry is that if the question is not asked, then the jury will think you are hiding something and that the other part is nothing more than a lapdog, and you know it. I therefore plowed ahead with the next question. And the other doggie part? Thankfully, came the answer: "Doberman."

So we're looking good. Now we have to deal with the police officer. The cop comes in and relates what he did and is very clear about it. Memory is sharp. No doubt about what happened. What the prosecutor did not ask him about is that when he showed up and made his investigation, he initially wasn't going to arrest the defendant. Gun owners are extraordinarily sensitive about their gun permits, and so the defendant, when confronted by the police, asked if this episode could possibly affect his gun license—his permit to carry. The officer, who was prepared to make a report and let the defendant go, said that that might be a possibility, upon which my client asked for the officer's badge number.

Now asking a cop for his badge number is the same as asking about his love life or maybe asking for his social security number. The policeman was happy to pony up his badge number, and the defendant could get a good look at it, but that would have to be at the police station. So my unfortunate client was arrested. On cross-examination, I tried to elicit details about that part of the incident. I was dealing with an experienced police officer who knew the drill. Any question asked by the defense that might possibly help the defendant elicits a form of total onset amnesia and necessitates the answer that he simply can't recall. Never mind the complete clarity when questioned by the DA. Police officers have an antenna that immediately spots these types of questions, and lo and behold, they aren't able to recall anything, including what street the police station is on. Since on cross you can lead, a question such as "Isn't it true that the defendant asked for your badge number?" is permissible. The more the officer answers that he can't recall to a series of questions, the clearer it becomes to the jury what the answers are. So Mr. Amnesia left the stand, and I next had an opportunity to question his partner.

The partner was new to the police department and had not yet learned how to forget. There is a story I heard one time from a veteran policeman about a typical rookie cop. A body is on the ground with a man standing over it holding a bloody knife. The rookie runs up and says to the knife holder, "You better get out of here before you get in trouble," sort of the way the police are supposed to react in light of recent events. This officer came in to testify. He had been sequestered as a result of a motion I brought. He had no inkling of his partner's forgetfulness. He tried to be as unhelpful as his partner but slipped up when he seemed to remember some details of the badge number request. That's all that was needed. The case was submitted, and the defendant was acquitted. Mr. Baba was profuse in his thanks and left, secure in the knowledge that his gun permit was safe.

It is surprising how many lawyers would have leaned on the defendant and had him accept the continuance without in the lower court or folded up the case in the superior court with no trial. It is these little cases that never make the news and have no importance to anyone but the defendant that are the lifeblood of the system. This charge, should it have had a different result or even if he had taken the lower court offer, may have resulted in the loss of his gun permit and thus his livelihood. And what does this case show? Forget the "killer" cross-exam rules and go with your gut, and this: cops are difficult witnesses. Accept that as a fact. They make an arrest and are convinced of the defendant's guilt and are not there to help you, the defense, present your case, or even to be fair. It is part of the business.

Another case presented a different problem. My client was charged with receiving stolen goods and, unlike the previous defendant, had a record—not an upstanding citizen. The difficulty was that the case was being handled by a brand-new assistant DA who I would describe as a looker, who was wearing a low-cut dress. Please don't be upset at my lack of PC-ness. Since she was new, she had an experienced DA at her elbow, whispering sweet (legal) nothings to her as she tried to prosecute the case. It was also clear that, in addition to providing her with legal pointers, he was also hitting on her, in the parlance. The hitting would probably go a little better if her newness won the case, and so he was working hard to achieve that and possibly other objectives. The case went on with the two of them at the prosecutors' table, ganging up on me and my unfortunate client.

Finally, the closing arguments came, and of course, the defense goes first. While I was arguing, the two of them were at their counsel table in a tête-à-tête about, I'm guessing, what she would be saying in her closing to follow shortly after mine. You could hear them whispering as I was attempting to argue my case. Finally, I stopped and stared at them. It took them many seconds to realize that I had ceased speaking. The jury got the idea of the prosecution's lack of politesse.

But that wasn't all. In her closing argument, she was demonstrating something, I forget what. As she made her demonstration, she bent low, practically into the jury box, so it was likely the jury got a good look. I thought this was grossly unfair, but what could I do? That dress is now on the Prosecutors' Wall of Shame in a nearby village. I thought that all was lost, but there wasn't enough silliness already baked into this trial. There was more to come, and I feel certain it rescued our case. There was the luncheon recess, and afterward, the judge came back to charge the jury.

There is a part of the charge that has to do with circumstantial evidence. The usual is that the mail is not there and later in the day the mail is there, so circumstantially, one can infer that the mailman has been to the mailbox. Duh. Occasionally, there is a departure from this charge. I know one judge who charged that if you came back to your car and your radio antenna was bent (remember those?), you could conclude that your car had been vandalized.

I didn't win that case. Here, the judge, apparently tired of mailmen, decided to try something else. It went like this: "If I was sitting in the middle of the Sahara Desert and a camel rode in from the west with a bottle of gin, and a camel from the east with a bottle of vermouth, and a camel from the north with some ice, and from the south with a glass and some olives, you would be warranted in concluding that I had ordered a dry martini in the middle of the Sahara Desert." Inferences having been explained, an inference that may have been drawn might have been one about activities during the lunch hour.

This apparently overcame the haberdashery ploy since the bemused jury acquitted my defendant in short order. Any lesson here? Maybe expect the unexpected and be ready to capitalize. And the nuttiness I mentioned at the beginning? This was certainly Exhibit A. It would be hard to say that my mere presence resulted in these unusual happenings, but these kinds of things seemed to follow me around despite my best efforts at good behavior.

At this point, I was trying a lot of cases. I've told you about three difficult ones that I didn't win and two where I had success. Here's another case that I recall caused a great deal of anxiety. I had a client charged with two counts of assault and battery by means of a dangerous weapon. This was way back when discovery was minimal. I knew little about the case except that the victims had both been stabbed. I didn't know the extent of the injuries, so I asked my client. He told me the wounds were minor. I was suspicious, so I asked him if the victims had gone to the hospital. He said they had. Still suspicious, I asked if they had been placed on the danger list.

"Naw, just the critical list," was the answer.

Thus reassured, I made ready for trial. His story was that he was attacked by these two huge guys. He defended himself as best he could. He was just a little guy but strong. The big guys had the knife, and during the struggle, the knife somehow got twisted back against them, and they got cut. With this lock of a story, we answered, "Ready for trial."

I had long since avoided the bloody noses, but that didn't mean that I didn't become nearly hysterical when I had to try a bad case—let's be honest, a good case also. What amped up the anxiety in this case was the judge. There had been a report of a case involving our judge where the defendant had been offered a sentence on a plea of not less than three years nor more than five years and turned it down. The defendant had lost the trial and been sentenced to not less than thirty nor more than thirty-five years. That case was appealed, and the appellate decision was that this was not a problem, all perfectly legal and certainly not cruel and unusual punishment as forbidden by the US Constitution.

Memory doesn't allow for whether there were negotiations in this case, but I knew we were dealing with a judge who wasn't afraid to hand out the time. Each of these two charges carried only a maximum of ten years, but still, plenty of firepower, and the sentences could be imposed consecutively.

We were on trial, and after the prosecution rested, the defendant testified. This was long ago, and I don't remember much about the evidence. He was a good witness and was a local boy from Dorchester, a sort of most favored nation in the Boston area. The victims were from out of town and not terribly likable. Still, the issue seemed very much in the balance. Closings were made, and I did what I usually do, which is to try and give a summation that does not amount to a concession. Indelible in my memory is the jury returning after a wait and, with my heart in my throat, seeing the judge at the bench slowly looking through my client's probation file. As the jury announced its verdicts of not guilty, I watched as the judge slowly, and it seemed reluctantly, closed the probation folder. *Whew*, was all I could think.

I had come a long way since those initial days of jury inexperience. I had tried a lot of cases and, in that latest year, tried at least a dozen and won more than my share. It was an exciting time, and I thought I had accomplished a lot and knew a lot. I became involved in a new strategy (things were always changing) where the office set up what they called vertical defense teams. Previously, cases appealed from the district courts to the superior court had been assigned new attorneys from the superior court staff. The idea was it made more sense and made for more effective representation to have the same attorney throughout.

I had assigned myself to a drug case in one of the district courts. It was a case that arose out of one of those undercover drug sweeps in one of the neighboring towns. My client was charged with two counts of distribution of a controlled substance. I knew how carefully these operations were run. The undercover would contact the seller, make the deal, and then report to the supervisor. The drugs would be handed over, and the means of identification would be established. The operation would run until enough of the targets had been involved. Warrants would be sought, and arrests would be made.

My client was free on bail and came to my office for an interview. He denied selling to anyone. He said that yes, he had been a user and past dealer, but that during the time of this operation, he had been with his girlfriend, staying off the streets in an attempt, so far successful, to kick his habit. I thought I was ever-so-smart and barely concealed my disbelief. These drug sweeps were airtight, right?

Later on, we went to court for a preliminary hearing. My client's case was called first, which was unusual because the usual was alphabetical, and he wasn't at the top. A police official took the stand and moved to dismiss my client's cases. "A mistake had been made," he said, "and the wrong person had been arrested."

I passed my client as he was on his way out. "SEE!"

Big lesson learned: never, never disrespect the client's story. The risk is, as here, that the client is actually telling the truth. No harm was done, and ultimately, if I had to, I would have worked with the client's story. It is not up to me to distinguish the truth of the charge. That is what is known as prejudice in the truest sense and, in the vernacular, as selling out. Emphatically, you run with the client, even if that seal looks an awful lot like that bird, and burgundy is a subspecies of the color red, and picked hickeys don't require a tourniquet. I did that, and look what happened. If the defense doesn't succeed and you have presented it in your most persuasive manner and the jury doesn't accept the defendant's story, it's on the defendant, not on you.

# 12

## End of an Era

**So by now, you should** have the picture, which is that it is a real challenge to operate as a public defender. If a challenge is valued, then this is the career for anybody as I was already sure it was for me. True, the government has all the cards, the judiciary is against you, and the appellate courts are government rubber stamps. This only makes it more of a challenge and ratchets up the glory of the public defender job. If that isn't enough, frequently, your client is also against you and submits complaints to the public defender organization or to this: the Board of Bar Overseers, code name BOBO.

BOBO is the organization that is engaged in keeping the lawyers on the straight and narrow. It's where complaints about a lawyer's behavior end up and where they are treated with varying levels of severity. It is a little hard to say that BOBO actually encourages complaints against lawyers, but that's what it sometimes feels like. Early on, I felt it was necessary to prepare to counter any action BOBO might contemplate, so I founded an organization—Board of Bar Overseer Overseers, code name BOBOO. I felt BOBOO was necessary because it was clear to me that, insofar as the criminal business was concerned, BOBO didn't have the faintest idea and was in need of some oversight. I was the only member since solicitations for membership were laughed at or ignored.

The charter of BOBOO was to forcefully meet any suggestion of wrongdoing by myself, the founding and only member of BOBOO. For years, nothing happened, and I was seriously thinking that BOBOO would have to be disbanded. But sure enough, after a long period of inactivity, a BOBO person telephoned. Some former client had written in to BOBO that I had done something egregious, like fail to provide him with limousine service to and from the courthouse. A very nice and well-spoken BOBO person wanted to know what I had to say about this. There was a short conversation, and I was thankful for the existence of BOBOO because after a moment or two, the caller very kindly reminded me "that I didn't need to shout."

Even though your client could be an enemy, that need not always be true. Over time, I was able to develop a sort of bedside manner that I used so that, despite being paid by the government and my client knowing nothing about me and preferring F. Lee Bailey, I could develop a fair amount of trust. Eliminating the use of the word *bozo* when speaking with or about your client is a very good first step. If you can gain some confidence from your client, then it is you against the government, and your client has been eliminated as an adversary. This is helpful because the other side presents enough challenges in and of itself.

The government controls everything or almost everything. But the one thing the government does not control is the jury. Not only does the government not control the jury, but it can be made to actually fear the jury. But that fear can only be instilled if one can try cases and can implant in the mind of the prosecution that one has a chance of winning. One must also, most importantly, be able to try the cases that look hopeless because some defendants just do not want to plead out and, better yet, every now and then, one of these cases will win and infuriate the opposition. The projected bank robber case was, to all intents and purposes, a loser, and yet look what happened.

My job is not to fear the jury but to embrace it, love it, cajole it, and feel comfortable in its presence. If I cannot try cases, my clients have no chance. This is easily said, and most lawyers, including myself, feel anxious at the thought of trying cases. What do you think went through my mind when I had to try Mr. Burgundy Jacket or Mr. It's Not a Bird, It's a Seal. Even worse, Mr. Hickey. Help! But I was able to do it, and these clients got their comeuppance without having to plead and were able to take their shot at the glory of an acquittal. It is very important for some to be able to go to prison having lost at trial rather than pleading out. They can always maintain innocence and say that all the witnesses lied or, even better, that the lawyer sold them out. Very understandable.

Now let's say you are a public defender, and you have a bow and arrows while the prosecution has bazookas. You are trying to dispose of a bad case, and the government is being unreasonable. You are going to go to trial and hope for the best. There is one important thing you need to do before you get a jury and start off on your journey, and that is to take anything you learned or even thought about learning at law school and put it in the dumper. I took the trial practice class at HLS, and this was mostly worthless for what I later did. When cases are tried, you are not a lawyer; you are an actor in a stage play in which something very important to your client is taking place. You do not need to be trained as an actor, but you need to be acutely aware of what is going on in your little scenario and to take advantage whenever the opportunity presents itself, and rarely will there not be an opportunity.

Expect the unexpected and be ready to capitalize. For sure, some Looney Tunes event is bound to occur in any trial, and it is up to you, the defense counsel, to take advantage. It goes without saying that it is easier to spot these happenings if you are just a little looney yourself, and on that score, I am certainly of the first rank as by now I have most certainly demonstrated.

I can't leave this period of time in my career without mentioning this episode. I also offer it in support of my theory that generally, some oddity seemed to occur in any court proceeding in which I was involved. I was driving on my way to a movie one evening when I was stopped by a member of the MDC police. The MDC police are long gone, but they then patrolled the Metropolitan District Commission territory, which consisted of parklands mainly in the Boston area. This occurred on the James R. Storrow Drive adjacent to the Harvard Stadium. I was driving behind another car which had just passed me when a police cruiser raced by and pulled over the car in front. I slowed down, and the cop jumped out and signaled me to pull over also, which I did. Now he had two cars for the price of one, a superior effort on his part. After a long wait, I was cited for going 50 in a 35-mile-per-hour posted zone. My movie plans were curtailed, and I made other plans with my chagrined passenger.

So what to do about this? First of all, nobody has gone 35 on that stretch of road since it was built unless they wanted to get run over or receive the bird flip from cars speeding by them. Second, this was just part of an annoying "crackdown" on speeders which was nothing more than a thinly veiled program of raising revenue. Third, bad impact on insurance rate and fourth, a minor criminal record.

In those medieval days, speeding was a criminal offense and would appear on court records. Since speeding was a crime, one could even appeal to the superior court and demand a jury trial. But a first step would have to be to serve notice to the local court that you were contesting the matter, which is what I did. I sent in the ticket, checking the box for a hearing. Shortly, I received a summons, and I went to court on the appointed date. I sat in the hallway and waited and waited until finally, the case was called, and I was before a court clerk who could dispose of the matter by denying the government's application for a complaint. After being informed archly that the true charge was "overspeeding" since when one drives, one is speeding, and overspeeding is, of course, driving over the speed limit, the clerk heard me out. He wouldn't refuse to issue the complaint as I requested. He had his pat story ready that he himself had once been stopped and was going only 26 in a 25-mile-an-hour zone and still had to pay.

Finally, an accommodation was reached that the police would recommend filing the complaint without a finding of guilty on payment of court costs. This had to be done in front of a judge, just as if it was a major felony case, so I went into the courtroom and waited for the judge to appear, which he did after a while. It was later in the morning, and the courtroom was empty. This was not a particularly important matter, but, of course, "self for lawyer has fool for client" resonated here.

The judge I knew something about. He was among the rarest of rare birds—a triple eagle. A triple eagle is a diplomate of the three BCs: Boston College High, Boston College, and Boston College Law

School, and is treated in Massachusetts with the same veneration as is the Quetzal bird in Guatemala. But I knew more than that about this judge, and that was he had apparently not done well in judge school, and the reason I surmised this was because he didn't like to send people to jail, an absolute necessity for high judge school marks.

I had never had cases before him but had been in juvenile court where he ordinarily sat, and I had seen his reluctance to send kids to the reformatory. This was neither here nor there as far as my appearance on a speeding ticket was concerned, I thought. My case was called, and I stood, identified myself, and was profuse in my apology that I had been going too fast. I was admitting to the offense and noted that the prosecution and myself had an agreed disposition. The police officer started to speak but was interrupted by the judge who said this: "Not guilty."

The policeman continued, "But, but, but we have—"

The judge said, "That's okay. It's not guilty" and darted off the bench.

By this point, I was nearly a hundred yards down the street fronting the courthouse and also driving very, very slowly.

So I had saved myself a criminal record and an increased insurance charge and, who knows, a BOBO intervention. In later years, I had occasion to return to this same court, and by then, this judge had since retired and been appropriately venerated by a portrait hung in that very same courtroom. It was off to the side and smallish and hung in a darkish space. Nevertheless, as I passed by on the way out of the courtroom, I couldn't help pausing and lighting a mental candle to this remarkable man who had saved this fool's ass.

This event, plus some of the others I have recalled and mentioned in the preceding pages, convinced me that I was surrounded by some sort of magnetic field that guaranteed wherever I went, something weird would take place. For instance, there was no reason whatsoever for the judge to find me not guilty of the speeding ticket. It was just that these strange things seemed to happen in most of the cases I handled. I recall a case I had in a district court fairly early in my practice. I was representing a man who was charged with indecent assault on two young boys and had a couple of cases against him. It certainly looked like my client would go to jail. We had talked it over, and he was resigned to the fact he might have to spend some time behind bars. Not a lot of time but enough to make life uncomfortable for him.

There was a conference with the judge. I walked into the lobby, and the judge says, "I suppose you're looking for a suspended sentence," something I hadn't even considered as a possibility, but in the nick of time, I heartily agreed. And that's what the defendant got, a suspended sentence. I recall walking with the defendant after the dispositional hearing, and we couldn't help marveling at the turn of events. It was like that *Star Wars* guy saying to the judge, "You don't need to give my client time."

But this was the sort of thing that seemed to follow me around. I became used to the idea that something strange was about to happen every time I stepped into a courtroom. It wasn't necessarily a good thing, but more often than not, my client benefited. And, of course, there was the stupidest argument ever made. This just didn't happen to other lawyers. And there was the martini judge. I used to ask other lawyers about their experiences in their practices, and it seemed as if it was all fairly prosaic. Nobody had a case where there was an Arnold Palmer or a Rob Roy in the middle of any desert you could name. A lot of this stemmed from my personality and from the fact that since I was clearly only approximating a lawyer, the recipients of my representational efforts were dealing with the unexpected, and thus bizarre results were often produced.

This was a remarkable period of time. My career had advanced from the total neophyte to the point where I knew a thing or two. In those six or seven years where I was doing jury cases, I tried many cases and many difficult cases. But I was, after almost ten years, burnt out. I found myself working on a difficult case and, much as I could usually muster up enthusiasm for any case and any client, I just found that for once, I couldn't. Other things were also swirling around—personal things—and I made an abrupt decision to quit the Defenders.

The chief counsel, who viewed me generally with suspicion if not overt hostility, saw a chance to send me to a galaxy far, far away and so tried to interest me in heading up an office that was being created to handle appointed cases in the western part of the state, the far western part. I wasn't interested. I also had this nagging feeling that if I didn't make a move, I would wind up being a lifetime public defender, and I didn't want that. So I was gone, and I was out of the legal business, and for how long, I didn't know nor even if I would ever be back.

And so closed out an initial run at law practice. I had been at it for almost ten years. I had taken on every responsibility I could and tried a lot of cases. I had obtained the jury experience I had coveted when I started with the Defenders. I began as someone with no experience and much anxiety about my future. Now, leaving the Defenders, I felt accomplished and was filled with a belief in my abilities that I had not had when I began. I had been fortunate to have worked with many able and dedicated attorneys who taught me a lot and who helped me when I was about to fall off a cliff. I had received good evaluations in the main from my supervisors, although I was often graded as weak on finesse.

There was still a little of this from court personnel: "Oh no. Not this guy" when I stuck my nose in a courtroom. I was learning to trust that "activist" in me that was soaking up the experience, and certainly, as time went on, I would learn to be more genteel in my approach. And what a marvelous experience it was. And that's how I learned—by doing—and I did a lot of doing during those nearly ten years. But I was truly exhausted, and I needed to rest and recharge and think about what was next. So off I went to what I didn't know.

# 13

## Another Chapter and a New Leaf

**And so began a period** of time outside the practice of law, the details of which are unimportant. I was living near the Boston Waterfront, which had undergone a renaissance and was now the hot spot. My marriage had ended, and I had three small children I saw on weekends. I knew, however, that something in my life was out of joint, so about a year after leaving the Defenders, I made an adjustment that adversely impacted the bottom line of many distillers, local barrooms, and dram shops. Just how many, I don't care to think about.

I am not a proselytizer, but at the Defenders, drinking, sometimes heavy drinking, was a way of life. Particularly with some of but not all of the senior attorneys, it was a ritual. I found myself joining in since there were often case discussions and small talk and attitudes from which I learned. Many is the night when I thought I was about to be on my way home, I would hear "Just one more!" which usually meant a lot more. So I quit drinking—as it turned out, for good. Within a short period of making that very substantial lifestyle change, I was back at it and had opened an office in downtown Boston.

Initially, I had been in touch with several criminal defense attorneys, asking if they could take me on. I was told by a few that, in view of all my experience, they would be unable to sufficiently compensate me, while others said they weren't currently hiring. If I was so experienced, then my own practice seemed to be the way to go. So I opened my own office. It was centrally located but in a building with no lawyers. I had been absent from the courts for about a year and a half and had no clients. The problem was how to reestablish myself.

I went to a used office furniture place and bought the basics—a desk, a bookcase, a couple of chairs, a table. That's all I needed. The office was spare, but I liked it. For the first time, I was the one picking my own stuff rather than government-issued. I was finally on my own and not part of some organization with someone looking over my shoulder. But I needed to find a way to get started. I sent out announcements about the opening of my office to people I knew. This generated exactly zero in the way of business.

It's trite, but it's worth saying here: where there's a will, there's a way. The Roxbury Court had an informal system for doling out court appointments. Business in the Roxbury Court was so brisk that the public defender's office couldn't handle all of it. There was a sign-up book in the clerk's office. You put your name in the book before the start of court, and the judge would go down the list and assign lawyers from the list as needed. This was ideal for me, and I received my first cases using this system. I remember my first day there, literally shaking with nervousness upon receiving my first few assignments—I had been away for that long.

The difficulty with this procedure was payment. The hourly rate was $25 for out-of-court time and $35 for in-court time. Most of the assignments involved very little, so my bills tended to be small.

The bills had to be signed off on by the judge who disposed of the case, and many just let the bills sit for months before approving them. Then the treasury likewise took its time processing them, and payment was not received until long after the services were rendered. To fill this payments void, I was able to build up a small private practice representing people I had met through my work in the Roxbury Court. It was a hard time, and I was making next to nothing. But I soldiered on.

I developed a routine around the court-appointed cases, which went as follows: I would do the appointed case and file my bill with the court. If the case was not finally disposed of and it was appealed to the superior court, I would tell my client that I would be willing to handle the appeal, but I would ask to be paid. I would tell my client, now my former client, the alternative would be a new court-appointed attorney in the appealed-to court in the event he or she decided not to retain me. This got me very little in the way of work, but occasionally, I was hired. Just because I was sober of body didn't mean I was sober of mind as this next case clearly shows. Quite the opposite.

I was assigned in the Roxbury Court to represent a man charged with driving under the influence. There was a bench trial, and the defendant was found guilty and received a committed sentence of six months, which, naturally, he didn't want to do. So an appeal was entered. I offered to represent him on the appeal for a few hundred or maybe just a hundred, thinking the case could easily be disposed of with a suspended sentence in the appealed-to court. I was really scrambling to find money wherever I could. By this time, the juries of six had just started up in some of the courts, so the case went to the jury of six session of the Boston Municipal Court since the Roxbury Court had yet to have its own jury session.

Prior to appearing in that court, I obtained the defendant's record and saw that this DUI charge was what? His sixth? What am I, out of my mind? The sentence in the lower court was a gift. No matter, he didn't drive drunk, he said, and so the case had to be tried, and my mantra that I could try anything was going to be put to the test.

The trial date arrives, and the defendant comes to court dressed in a sparkling white suit, white shoes, and, I think, a white hat. "Dude" is written all over him, to be kind, but also accurate. He is also ossified. The first witness for the government is the unfortunate woman who was at the stoplight when my defendant whales into the back of her car, apparently unaware that there is stopped traffic in front of him. The police are called and give the usual litany of how the eyes are red and glassy, there's a strong smell of alcohol, the defendant can only stand by holding on to whatever is handy, etc. The government rests, and my client takes the stand and with great lucidity testifies that he was not drunk and that it did not happen that way.

Just the opposite, she rear-ended him, he says, and he produces a picture of his taillight with what looks like a pinhole in it. This is all being done with as much aplomb as I can muster. There is a recess and, gulp, I'm going to have to argue this thing. Which I can do. I've argued a lot of this type of case. We return to court, and the judge calls us up to the bench and in a confiding voice says, "You know, I haven't heard any evidence about public way," a necessity in drunk driving cases.

Quickly, I replied, "Your Honor, neither have I, and I have a motion." One never knows how fast one can write until needed.

A required finding motion was filed and allowed, and a not guilty verdict directed for my client, who wobbled his way out of the courthouse. I'm not sure I ever was paid the whole fee or was even thanked. And the public way that the Commonwealth forgot to give evidence about? Washington Street, certainly the most public of ways in the City of Boston, if not the entire Commonwealth. Looks like the karma was still lingering even after my few years away.

I was scratching around to find business wherever I could. It was definitely a hard time, and I had to rely almost exclusively on the appointments I was getting in Roxbury. There was very little work, and what work I was getting from the court I wasn't being paid for due to the delays in having the bills approved. People that I had represented would occasionally drop by but just to shoot the breeze. I was thus gratified to learn that the security guard in our building had been arrested. I managed to have myself retained as his counsel. My retainer was a fraction of what I had asked for, but given the shortage of business, it was enough for me to file my appearance with a promise of the balance in the near future.

The total fee was ridiculously low to start with. I never knew what to charge people, and since I wanted to be sure to be retained, I always charged too little. My client had a personality one would not expect for our building, which had some pretensions. It was near the Avenue Lafayette (ooh la la) and had been recently rehabbed. My client's idea of a hello was a glare, and smiles were forbidden—always.

The details of the case are sketchy in my memory. It was a barroom altercation. The victim was a police officer doing a detail at that particular establishment. The charge was assault by means of a dangerous weapon, a pool cue. The odd part about this case was that the police report was filled with misspellings, which raised the question in my mind of the policeman's sobriety. Even the simplest words were misspelled. The case eventually went to trial in the six-person session. It was just a two-person case. My client testified, as did the arresting officer. I cross-examined the police officer about his spelling acumen, and he had an unusual answer to each question: "I didn't go to Harvard." (Had he gone to Yale? I didn't ask.)

I hate to admit that in my closing argument, I was not the nice man that I usually am and argued that the part of his testimony where he said he didn't go to Harvard was the only part of his testimony that could be believed. This argument I am ashamed of, but it shows you what lengths I will go to on behalf of my clients. The defendant was acquitted, and I am even more ashamed to admit that, despite this herculean effort, the defendant showed his gratitude by stiffing me for the balance of my fee in spite of repeated requests. I saw him every day upon entering the building and was shown the usual grimace but no money. I chalked this all up to experience in the private counsel wars. A lesson I was slow to learn was to be paid in advance or don't take the case.

Eventually, I reached the point where I would not file my appearance unless I had "Mr. Green," as the pros call it. Once I file my appearance, I am stuck. I would never have had the nerve to go before a judge and ask to be let out of a case because I wasn't paid. "Too bad for you," would be the response.

I would go to my office every day and sit with little to do because of the lack of business. The building was on the upswing, and soon Mr. Surly Security was replaced by someone who could muster an occasional smile. My rent was ultimately raised to an uncomfortable level, and the management began to get edgy on account of the clients who dropped by my office and didn't conform to the building dress code. Unfortunately, the management office was on the same floor as my office and contiguous.

I had one client who occasionally came in unannounced early in the morning. I knew he was showing up when there was a metallic clink down the hallway. He had just finished his nip and disposed of it in the ash receptacle by the elevator. I enjoyed his repartee, and he would sometimes slip me a few dollars for the case I had represented him on months before and never paid the whole fee. But he was noisy, and the management was not amused by the same things that amused him and produced his raucous laughter, which could be heard throughout the corridors. And so time for some new digs.

My new office was a few blocks away and even more remote than the old. It was off the elevator and then to the right, down a long hallway, and then to the right again and down another long hallway to the last door on the right. I was next to a podiatrist's office, and the walls were thin. I learned a few things about feet for the few years I was there. But it was my space, and I quickly developed a fondness for it. Sparsely furnished, I tried to give it a little panache by purchasing a replica of the old-style candlestick phone. I had an ancient typewriter that had margins I could never get straight. Along with the phone and a glass-front bookcase, it had the look of something from 1890s Dodge City—a place where sometimes I felt like I was a resident. I had an answering service because I thought a human voice was more appealing than a machine. I would check in daily and receive the usual advice that I had "no calls." Depressing.

There were little bits and odds and ends of things to be done, so I was at least a little busy. I represented a man involved in some sort of check scam where he was part of a ring. Thousands of dollars had been stolen from some local banks as a result of a check kiting scheme. I was taking some risks that I probably should not have been taking. My client requested that I give him a ride to court one day, which meant going to a section of town I was unfamiliar with. The pickup and return were accomplished without incident.

Later, I learned that a few weeks after, someone unhappy with the fact my client had decided to plead guilty, and possibly cooperate with the prosecution, broke into his apartment and shot him in the back several times. My client fled by jumping off a second-story balcony and somehow managed to survive. This happened about the same hour I had picked him up a few weeks previously. Pretty scary.

There were other clients as well who demanded the type of attention that I ordinarily would not have given. It was all in the pursuit of a dollar to keep things going. But it was only a matter of time before another of those unusual cases would come my way and reemphasize that most important facet of the criminal justice system—the jury.

# 14

## A Very Serious Case

**I continued my efforts to** get business by putting myself on the list at the Roxbury Court. On one of those occasions, I was assigned a case that I paid little attention to. The charges were serious, but the case would be going to the superior court, and I figured I would not be involved after the district court probable cause hearing was held. The case, as expected, was bound over to await grand jury action, and I imagined I would be out. I did my usual, which was to offer my services, but for a fee.

To my surprise, the defendant agreed to retain me, and a fee was agreed upon. He didn't have the fee upfront, but since I was always in need of money, I, as usual, undertook to take the case on his promise to pay. My memory is not terribly good on this, but I believe the charges were attempted murder, attempted robbery, attempted rape, and assault and battery. "Serious" is an understatement to describe these charges. The fact that I had stopped drinking had its effect. I was no longer the jocular, happy-go-lucky warrior in which every legal matter I participated in produced an arguably unprofessional courtroom whirlwind, and I had become a much more sober and matter-of-fact person.

This did not mean that underneath it all, I wasn't still a little unbalanced, maybe even more than before, but one had to scratch the surface a little harder to find that out. My out-of-court professionalism had occasionally risen to a high level as exemplified by the manner in which I accepted payment from my client. I embarked upon a procedure whereby I left a small envelope taped to the exterior of my office door. The defendant's girlfriend would drop by after hours on her payday and leave a few dollars for me as part payment of the retainer and slip the envelope under the door. I was sure that the State Street guys were doing the same and that some humongous corporate client was slipping six-figure checks under the office door while the staff was out for lunch or maybe out to lunch.

The defendant had been in custody on another charge when the case began, and I had to go to the Suffolk County House of Correction to interview him. The county prison was still on Deer Island in Boston Harbor—a remote location—and a demanding drive was thus necessitated to make a client visit. (For those not in the know, Deer Island was no longer an island but connected to the mainland by a narrow causeway.)

I remember sitting on the steps of the main prison building while interviewing my client and admiring what had to have been the most gorgeous view of the Boston skyline. Progress, however, resulted in the replacement of the prison with a sewage treatment facility. Now Boston has good water, and the lovely view is gone since the treatment facility, regrettably, is off limits to the public.

Eventually, the defendant was out of prison. He had posted bail on this new charge, and we made ready for trial. Finally, we are in a trial session in the superior court, and we have a jury. I had done my best to be prepared, but I was not ready for the spectacle of the testimony of the victim. She could hardly speak. Her voice was slurred, and one arm hung uselessly at her side. She claimed that her speech and physical impairment came as a result of a beating administered by the defendant. The testimony was absorbing and moving. There were, however, two problems with the government's case, one of which I knew about and one which came up during the trial. The first was that the witness had a record. She had half a dozen convictions for prostitution—sex for a fee, as it is now called.

I was able, as is proper, to impeach her credibility by having those records introduced into evidence. In those days, the entire record went in, including the defaults, the probation violations, and the punishment, although record-keeping was not as extensive then as it is nowadays. In its zeal to advance the interests of the government, the high court has now ruled that the entire record may not be admitted. All that can be established is that the witness was convicted of such and such. No penalty, no defaults, no probation violations can be mentioned. The juicy details, which made the record so impeaching, are now banned per order of our legal higher-ups. Regrettably, a weapon taken out of the hands of the defense.

The other problem for the prosecution was that out of nowhere, the witness maintained she had been beaten by a baseball bat. Nothing in the pretrial discovery made mention of a bat, and it was clear the government was surprised by this testimony. The police detective, who was seated at the prosecutor's table while this testimony took place, tried to cover for her. When his turn came to be a witness, he testified that he remembered her talking about a stick when he had initially interviewed her. Yet as I was able to point out on cross-examination, a stick was a dangerous weapon, and no effort had been made either in the district court or in the superior court to seek charges involving a weapon. Even though the victim's record of convictions and the inconsistencies in the prosecution's case were damaging, the outcome remained very much in the balance.

The closings were finished, and the jury went out. A long wait. I knew the clerk from my many forays into the trial sessions, and he let me know where he stood: "I don't know what your client is thinking, but he is going to be doing a lot of time."

A while later, the jury came back and found the defendant not guilty on all the charges. There was no gasp, no cries of disbelief. It was just one of those serious cases in the lives of people who come before the bar of justice that receive little attention. The jury was thanked and discharged. My client was taken downstairs and held pending a check for warrants. A bailiff showed his displeasure with the verdict by growling, "You'll be back" at the defendant as he was placed in the elevator.

After a wait, my client was released, and he collected a check for his bail money from the clerk's office. We then went to a local bank where he cashed it, the proceeds of which were to be the balance of my fee, and which he graciously and gratefully paid. When I look back on this case, I wonder how I had the nerve to have tried it. These were very serious charges, and the defendant would have received a heavy sentence should he have been convicted. When we had left the courthouse, such was our elation that it seemed as if our feet never touched the ground on the way to the bank—like walking on air. I had done the job for my client, and he was most thankful. It was a great feeling, a real accomplishment. Little can compare with the exhilaration we both felt. And his girlfriend of envelope fame? Overjoyed. And as far as I know, this client never did come back.

So that was that, and I moved on to other matters that had been neglected while I prepared for and tried that case. Or at least I thought that was that. A few days later, I picked up the morning newspaper and happened to notice an article from a noted columnist in the local news section. And there it was, rearing its head again—the bane of the system—the stupid jurors. The columnist lambasted the jury for its decision in that case and went so far as to reveal what he thought were "facts" about my client's background in an attempt to shame the jury for its decision. It was a story written by someone who didn't attend the trial and only got news about the trial second-hand from the disappointed detective who had tried to cover for the baseball bat testimony.

The column, written by the cop-friendly columnist, is another expression of the system's paranoia about the jury. Shoving people into prisons would be such an easy job if only we could get rid of the "stupids" that make these terrible decisions. Thank you, Mr. and Mrs. Juror, for the work you did in that case. My client I ran into numerous times later on, and he was doing well. Years later, for some unknown reason, I went to check the docket on that case—I was having a hard time remembering the charges. I wasn't able to look up the case because my client had, sometime previously, gone to court and had the entire record sealed, as was his right. Good for him.

I had learned at some point that this case was the last trial for the assistant DA before he moved on to something else. He was an extraordinarily effective prosecutor, even though he didn't win that one. He went on to author a widely used treatise and served with distinction as an appellate court judge. Rarely, I would see him on my way between the courts and my office. We would nod hello. I feel sure that the memory of this case, though not uppermost, is something he can't help thinking of when he sees me. It is, of course, difficult to know what's on any person's mind, but a guess would be that this man is not thinking that but for my efforts, an innocent man might have been convicted. Somehow, this thought pleases me.

So the 'stupid' jurors had struck again, and I had been a part of it. The government went off licking its wounds, but it would be back and would redouble its efforts to get any defendant. Also, the ill wind that had quieted somewhat was now blowing again with renewed intensity. I had to say, however, that the columnist's screed blasting the jury did not target me. Perhaps I was too inconsequential to be noticed despite my efforts in that case. I was still flying under the radar while the war zone went on somewhere above me. I returned to my isolated office and went back to the slim pickings of my practice and tried to remain viable. Not for long did the vagaries of my existence leave me be, and I soon was involved in another of those strange cases.

# 15

## Ghost of Elvis Past

**I have no recollection of** how this came to be my case. I had taken on a number of private cases from a certain family, which was good for what little business I had, since most of its members were in trouble at one time or another. This was because there was no getting around the fact that they were all troublemakers. The charge against my client, a woman and a member of that family, was arson. She had burnt up her grandmother's apartment—totally burned it up. The apartment was destroyed, if not the entire building. There was little question she did it, but her mental state was very much at issue.

In a nutshell, it appeared she became furious at her grandmother because she, her grandmother, was dating Elvis Presley's ghost and interfering with her own attempts to have the ghost date her, and she retaliated by torching the apartment. It was complicated, but something like that, and Presley's ghost was at the center of it. An interview with the defendant left no doubt that she was—how does one say it with delicacy?—daffy.

I considered just trying the case and maybe having her testify, which would certainly show her unbalanced mental state, but yielded instead to the standard approach, which is to have a psychiatrist examine her and be ready to testify with an "expert" opinion. I am always nervous with this type of case because I'm afraid that the psych might come back and say the client is fine but the lawyer? I asked around and obtained the name of a psychiatrist who had testified in mental illness cases previously and was reputed to be a defense guy. The mental health business is a little vague, in my opinion, because of the range of conclusions that are often produced over just one person.

As it turned out, I had screwed up, per usual, because this psychiatrist came back with a report that supported the government. In effect, it concluded that my client should be held responsible. Not to worry. This was the usual odd turn that seemed to occur in virtually every case I was involved with. So it was back to the drawing board. Another psychiatrist was found. I held my breath while I waited for the results of his examination. This time, the right conclusion was reached, and he would testify that mental illness had compelled her to act and she should not be held criminally liable.

The case went to trial, and the dueling psychiatrists testified. My first shrink had now become the government's leading witness since I had been required to let it know about that first report I had received. The star of the show was my client, who sat at the counsel table and looked the part. Glassy-eyed, no interest in the proceedings, and incommunicado with counsel. The judge also was sympathetic and helped with his rulings and his charge. The result was as it should have been—not guilty by reason of insanity.

My client, eventually, after a number of hearings in which she was represented by other counsel, was committed to a mental institution. I was interviewed by a newspaper reporter after the trial because the case had gathered some interest. What had raised the reporter's curiosity was that it turned out there was a secure mental hospital for men but not for women. It seemed that the fact that women mental patients were not regarded by the state as having the capacity to be as violent as men was a violation of women's something, although the issue only had currency for about half a day. The presence of press made me nervous because I was worried a reporter might discover a not-so-well-guarded secret that I had little idea what I was doing, especially in this type of case. But the verdict was correct, so whether I did or didn't mattered not at all.

I wasn't quite through with this client. Her grandmother decided to hire me to see if I could secure her granddaughter's release from the mental hospital, a tall order. She gave me my ultra-small retainer with a promise for more. I went to several hearings and argued for her release, but she was just too mentally ill for me to succeed. The grandmother had developed a fondness for me, along with those other members of her extended family. She would call me occasionally and say she had more of my fee. One day she calls me, and she wants to pay me more of what she owes. Always in need of some cash, I rush up to her place on Huntington Avenue.

I arrive at her apartment, and the lights are low and some mood music is playing. I realize that the grandmother is putting a move on me, and I'm going to have a hard time doing a fend job and still get the money. I finally made good my escape by asking, "What would the Elvis ghost think of all this?" As I said, one needs to be resourceful in the criminal business.

# 16

# Jury Trial Success

**Back to the usual routine,** which was periods of quiet with little to do, followed by short periods of frenzied activity. A case came my way, court-appointed again, from my contacts with the Roxbury Court. There had been a celebration of sorts at the Harriet Tubman House, a local community center, for the members of some school organization—a graduation or prom or some sort of festivity. Everyone was dressed up for the event. The locals were not included and decided they wanted to attend. The partygoers resisted, and soon there was mayhem. In the subsequent melee, shots were fired, and in another part of the fracas, one of the partygoers was stabbed in the groin by one of the interlopers. The injuries were serious.

I was representing the alleged stabber, who was charged with assault and battery by means of a dangerous weapon. There were two codefendants who were the shooters. The case finally, after the usual backing and filling, went to trial in the Suffolk Superior Court. We had for a judge a man from the western part of the state, whom I got along with instantly—a rare occurrence. A jury was empaneled, but not before we were brought to the bench and asked our opinions as to the length of the trial. This was important because the jury needs to be told the approximate length so that the prospective jurors can ready their stories as to why they should be excused from service. It is usual that most called for jury duty want to avoid service and offer a variety of reasons.

Some judges are lenient and let jurors walk away, and others will accept almost no excuses. Curiously, those who eventually do serve mostly think that the experience was worthwhile. Two days was the consensus. Two weeks later, the case went to the jury.

The reason this case took so long was that one cocounsel had a not very good case, and he was trying his best to help his client. The issue was identification, and so there were endless questions as to how far away the identifying witnesses were from his client. Could it have been two feet? Could it have been two feet, two inches? Could it have been three feet? This went on endlessly until the case stumbled to a conclusion. I did my usual for my client, and he ended up with an acquittal, which made us both happy.

One of the exasperating things about jury trials is the wait for the jury. Normally, the jury only returns just after your client has gone to the canteen for chips, a sandwich, and a soda, usually the fifty-ounce size, and that's what happened here. Upon his return, my client didn't want to lose his feed, so he brought it into the courtroom. In the excitement, he spilled his drink, which he had placed under the counsel table, kicking it over when we all stood for the jury's entrance. Fortunately, he was able to help with the cleanup since he was cleared and brought along the usual handful of fifty napkins.

It was not known at the time, but the "how far away" attorney was on his way to becoming famous. I was headed in the opposite direction because, rather than ask all those questions, I was making my cross-examinations as short as possible. Something like "No questions, Your Honor." I must have been doing something right because the two codefendants were convicted, and Mr. Famous-to-Be's client received a sentence of ten to twelve years.

Historically, lawyers don't stand out in the long-term scheme of fame. Like, who do we know who still is famous after, say, a hundred years who was a lawyer? Saint Augustine? Was he a lawyer in addition to being a saint? Some famous people were also lawyers, like presidents, but that is not what they were known for—lawyering. Still, the temptation always is there. High-profile cases get you known, and enough of them might send you to the top of your profession. My worry always was that in these types of cases, a certain perspective is lost. Must talk to the press. Need to perform for the cameras. What about the client? This is why, at all costs, I always tried to avoid cases that had exposure to the public eye. Also, if one has a limited knowledge of what one is doing, it's best not to let the rest of the world know.

Like many of these cases, or at least the ones I handled, there seemed to be something extra that came along afterward. I suppose I had worried when I first started about how I was striking the jurors. A lawyer I shared space with claimed one time that I was the least image-conscious attorney he had ever known—no, make that person. This meant I got comments like maybe I should stand a little closer to my razor and suggestions that I try to leave the mustard on my sandwich and maybe discontinue using an eggbeater to comb my hair or shining my shoes with sandpaper. Later on, a temporary inattention to dental hygiene resulted in my giving a new meaning to the phrase "talking out of the side of one's mouth." Still, I thought I was doing a decent job in my courtroom presentations.

In all cases, there is a juror who is selected to be the foreperson who guides the deliberations. In this particular case, a woman was selected as foreperson who evidently was surprised and not pleased with this eventuality. She was the one who had to announce and did announce the various verdicts. By chance, I bumped into her months later on an elevator in the building where I then had my office. Any reservations I had about my rapport with the jury evaporated when Madame Foreperson very sweetly asked me if I was busy while her boyfriend was out of town. I resort to the attorney–client privilege here, and I'm not saying anything more. But whatever your questions are, all the answers are, "I can't recall." Obviously, whatever was following me had just drawn a little nearer.

This case also was a lesson in working with cocounsel. I say "working with," even though in reality you are "working against." If you can establish that you are a little better at some things than cocounsel, it may work in your favor. For instance, the fact that my cross-examination of certain witnesses consumed all of forty-five seconds and cocounsel's cross took an hour and forty-five minutes and accomplished less helped put the jury on my side. He was a time-waster as opposed to my succinctness. When the jury starts to squirm, it's time to sit down. Most jurors have other lives, and wherever you are going with your questions, they will get the point rather quickly.

# 17

# Another Era Ends

**I had run into the** man who had been the stenographer in the stupid jury case. He had passed the bar and become a lawyer. He was now sharing my office space and some of the expenses. I had practiced for another ten years, and my feet were dragging. I was now living a distance from the office, and my commute had to be by car for lack of public transportation. This could be anywhere from an hour to two and a half, and on rare occasions even longer. Disputes with my office mate about how to split the phone bill and other issues were not helping. And the same as before, a case came along that I just was having trouble mounting enthusiasm for.

I was going to the office less and less, and finally, I decided to take another period away from the legal fray, and just like ten years ago, I had no idea what lay ahead and whether I would ever practice again. I had remarried, and my wife had a good job in tech—good meaning well-paying—and I had started up a little business that, even though it made no money, was something that I enjoyed, especially since it didn't have the pressures attendant with law practice.

I did, however, have one remaining case that needed to be tried. It was in an adjoining county where I had had mixed success. The charge was distribution of a controlled substance. The police had received a tip and had set up a surveillance in a high-rise building. My client was allegedly out in the parking lot dealing narcotics. In time, the police discovered his identity, obtained a warrant, and arrested him. Not a particularly good case, but we were going to go to trial. We went to the courthouse for the arraignment. This was managed quickly, and a date for a preliminary hearing was set. At that next court date, and as we were waiting for the case to be called, my client nudged me and let me know he got the blood test. I hadn't the faintest idea what he was talking about, so I mumbled something like "Good for you."

Then it dawned on me. At his arraignment, he had been advised of his right to take a drug test to see if he was a drug-dependent person. My client's inattention produced the blood rather than drug test. I was touched. Here was a defendant who would do whatever he could to try and help himself, including not knowing what people were talking about.

Soon the date for the trial arrived, and we went forward with a jury. I don't remember much about the case, except that we had an alibi witness, a rapper whose name I have not been able to forget—Beamo Blast. The alibi didn't work, and my client was convicted. I had already concluded that our judge was not fond of me, to make an understatement. It was just one of those things that happens, and there is little that can be done about it. I just hoped that she didn't take her dislike out on my client, for whom I had developed a liking. He was an earnest type who had come from somewhere in the

Caribbean. He had little of a record and had made the mistake of trying to make a little extra money.

My hopes that he would receive a light punishment vanished when he was hit with a sentence of not less than nine years nor more than fifteen years in the state's prison. The fifteen years was the statutory maximum. To my way of thinking, the case was only worth a year or eighteen months in the house of correction. The judge knew that parole was possible at one-third the minimum, so she cynically, I thought, gave the nine years to ensure that he did at least three years.

There is a sentence review board that, at that time, met twice a year to review sentences to the state's prison. At my suggestion, the defendant filed for a review. The review board is a panel of three superior court judges who pass on sentences imposed by other judges in the superior court. As one might expect, the superior court bench is fairly tight, and as a consequence, not many of these sentences are reduced. So that every sentence isn't appealed, there is a warning that sentences are capable of being raised as well as lowered, and occasionally, one is raised to keep the board from being overwhelmed with appeals. I attended my client's hearing and spoke for him. The sentence in his case was so out of line that I thought we had a good chance.

After the hearing, we were notified that the sentence had been lowered to six to ten years. This was gratifying, but still, in my opinion, a far too heavy sentence. Ultimately, I learned he was transferred to the county prison, where he did his time, which is where he should have served his sentence in the first place. An early parole would mean he would "only" have to serve two years. I received many cheery letters from him thanking me for my efforts and letting me know how he was doing. A nice man. I wished him well. This result was an unfortunate down note from my final trial before another stint away from law practice.

Over this second go-round, I had many, many clients. There was one person who was not a client, although she had plenty of contact with the criminal courts. She had just shown up at my hard-to-find office one day. I have no idea how she got my name or office address. She came by often because, it seemed, I was one of the few people who would listen to her. The day she showed up, she presented the same as she did each time I saw her—shaved head, jack boots, and military fatigues. Her life, it appeared, was one long struggle for women's rights, and she was continuously at war to achieve those rights. She would tell me about her battles with the authorities at the courts in Middlesex County, where she was a fixture until she was barred from the premises. She would wander through the courthouse denouncing anti-feminism wherever she found it, which was nearly everywhere.

When the authorities tried to shut her up, she would yell, "This is America! I have a right to speak!" Several arrests for disorderly conduct and disturbing a public assembly were putting a crimp on her activities.

For some unknown reason, I gave her my home telephone number, and I received many middle-of-the-night phone calls because this is America, and she needed to speak. There was something engaging about her, and I was always happy to listen to her diatribe whenever she stopped by or called.

One day, she came by unannounced. She was pushing a wheeled contraption onto which she had loaded a filing cabinet. It was a two-drawer letter-size cabinet, and it weighed a ton. Unlike file cabinets today, which fold up when you so much as touch them, this one was built to last. Sheepishly, she asked me if I would keep it for her and, of course, since this is America, I said I would. She didn't leave me with any particular instructions—just keep it. I did that, and I never saw her again.

A few years later, I received a phone call from her, and she said she was calling from the British Isles and, of course, it was also the middle of the night. She was just saying hello, and that was all, and that was the last I ever heard from her. But the file cabinet has gone with me to many different office locations, and it has continued to stay with me throughout my retirement. Hard to say what this means, but it has become a treasure that ties me to my past and also to all the, let's call them, unusual people I have had the pleasure of dealing with over the many years of my career.

So off to something else. Where it might lead, I had no idea.

# 18

## Dead Man Walking

**I had now left my** office in other hands and essentially retired. It had been a very busy twenty years: ten at the Defenders Committee and now ten years in private practice. It was something that I could look back on with pride. I settled into a new life miles away from the hub of the universe in a much smaller and quieter urban area where I had been living for the past three years. I could afford to run my little business the way I wanted to.

The fact that in reality it was little more than a hobby and made me no money didn't matter at this point. I had dreams of this placid lifestyle continuing well into the future. I was also hopeful that the general weirdness that seemed to follow me like some great miasma and which seemed to enter into everything I did had largely dissipated, if not disappeared completely. What I did not know is that the on-again, off-again strangeness which was part of my existence had mutated and reenergized itself and was about to resurface in a new form of nuttiness beyond comprehension—and it happened this way.

My wife and I were returning from something, a short vacation, a family visit perhaps, and we stopped in the vestibule of our building to pick up the mail. We must have been gone for a while because there was a pile of mail to be looked through. We searched and threw out the junk and kept the stuff we knew we needed to open—bills, notifications, personal stuff. There was one letter that was a curiosity. The return address was the office of the Dean of Harvard Law School, and it was on expensive-looking stationery. It was also addressed to my wife. What would the Dean of HLS be writing to my wife for? I knew right away what it was, and I couldn't contain myself. I knew something had been missing the few months I had quit my practice and was overjoyed that the craziness had returned in all its savagery. My wife opened the letter, and this is what it was about. The law school had received news of my recent demise and was writing my wife to express its condolences.

It is rare that one gets a chance to see what an organization thinks of you before the actual event, and I was oh so glad to have that opportunity. For whatever high regard I had for HLS, it went a few notches higher upon reading this letter. After an expression of sympathy, the letter stated, "We were saddened to learn of the death of John F. Wood Jr."

A few bars from the pop song "Oh Yeah!" might be appropriate here. I'll bet the flags all flew at half-staff and classes were suspended for the day. You could hear students whispering to each other in the hallways, "Did you hear that John F. Wood, the younger of that name, passed away?" I'm wondering who the "we" referred to. But it got better: "We will remember him as a valued alumnus."

That's it. Nothing more. I was not remembered for anything else. It's hard not to conclude that this wasn't code for "And he never contributed a nickel." Couldn't they have done a little better than that? After all, I had early in my career briefly mentored a Harvard Law professor who had some interest in the operation of the public defenders' office and also addressed Harvard's voluntary defenders on the subject of investigation in criminal cases. I had also participated as a judge several times in the Ames competition, Harvard's moot court and, even more, had labored tirelessly in the trenches of the criminal courts for more than twenty years. I mean, I had actually practiced. Even though I didn't make the law review, I'm still entitled to speak in Latin—*sic transit gloria*, as it is said.

It took us a while to compose ourselves, and of course, we knew what had happened. My father, the senior of that name, also a Harvard Law grad, had died the year before, and the records office had just gotten around to screwing things up. My wife suggested I should call and straighten this out. But I saw a great opportunity here and, as a consequence, I did nothing. The result? None of those dun letters telling me how much the law school needed a contribution and reminding me of those wonderful days when I was there as a happy student contemplating all the money I would soon be making. I became a dead "valued alumnus" walking and found that the very thought of this put an extra spring in my step. My wife still received the occasional letter, the widow's letter it's called, that went something like, "I'll bet your unfortunately recently deceased husband told you all about those happy days at HLS and wouldn't you like to respond with a donation?"

We had to think about that. So, yes, I was back on track. The lifelong lunacy that surrounded most of what I did had now resurfaced in all its incomprehension.

# 19

## Return of the Native

**Life continued on its merry** way for a few years, and everything was on an even keel, more or less. But, as ever happens, the world changes and circumstances necessitate that one adapt. A big change was that the tech industry began to downsize, and my wife lost her job. I had expected that I was pretty much out of the legal world, but I did read the Boston papers and kept in touch that way with what was happening in the courts. I didn't feel any strong desire to return. We were happy where we were, and I knew that going back to Boston would involve a hefty commute. Eventually, I got the spousal sit-down, which was, essentially, that I needed to give up this faux business that wasn't generating any income and get back into the real world.

What I was most familiar with, of course, was practicing as a public defender, and I set about finding out how I could get back. I was in touch with an attorney friend who was still involved, and he gave me the lay of the land and a person to contact.

The entire public defense apparatus had drastically changed in the three years or so that I had been away. What had been the Massachusetts Defenders Committee was now the Committee for

Public Counsel Services or CPCS. It did not have the resources to handle all the court-appointed business, and as a consequence, county associations had been founded to handle the overflow. There was a vast difference between the county associations and the Committee. The Committee was comprised of salaried employees, whereas the members of the county associations, known as bar advocates, were paid by the hour and had to engage in a cumbersome billing process. CPCS had secretaries, investigators, health insurance, pensions, office supplies, office space, telephones, research, a library. You name it, they had it.

The bar advocates had none of these. What they did have was a certain independence, which to me was worth giving up all the things that CPCS did have. Ostensibly, the advocates were under the supervision of the Committee, but the supervision was loose, and the advocates had a certain amount of freedom to operate as they wanted to. This was important because, as time went on, it became clear that what had once been an organization of talented, experienced, and dedicated lawyers now operated largely as a hidebound, nitpicking royal pain in the ass.

I telephoned the director of the bar advocate organization for Suffolk County, known as the Boston Bar Advocates. I asked about job openings, and she informed me there were no openings and wouldn't likely be any for another six months. I asked if I could at least meet with her, and she was agreeable, so an appointment was made. The following day, we had a nice chat at her office, and I showed her my résumé, which, of course, showed all my previous experience. She finished reading it and then asked me when I could start. Was the next day good? It was, and I was in the superior court the following day, taking cases.

It wasn't long before I realized how much had changed and also how I had lost a few miles off my fastball after the long layoff. Paperwork was different, there were now juries in all the district courts, and money was pervasive. There were fees the defendants had to pay for nearly everything. It took me about an eighth of a second to develop a hatred of these fees, which were a killer for the clients who had no money. They were indigent, after all. There was the hated $150 legal counsel fee and a victim witness fee that varied in size depending on the court. These fees were imposed on every person who received appointed counsel. I turned blue in the face explaining to clients that I didn't get the counsel fee and double blue asking the courts to waive it and the victim witness fee. "They are nonwaivable, Counselor," was the smiled response. A little venom has resulted in this digression.

Soon after my return, I was in touch with one of the few lawyers I had remained in contact with. He had some office space available, and shortly, I had an address, a telephone, and business cards. The focal point of this new office was the letter from HLS to my wife mourning my recent demise. I had it expensively framed and matted and now hung it near my office door. As I left, I would glance at it, and it never failed to put me in a good frame of mind as good as could be in the public defender business. I savored my continued existence long after my expiration, and the sky seemed just a little bluer, and the sun shone a little brighter on my way to court each morning as I went out to enjoy life beyond the grave.

This new office was in a suite of other lawyers. These were regular guys who had small practices. Some were specialists in some areas, and others handled pretty much whatever walked in the door. This suite was located not in the prime lawyer area but close enough to the courts to make it convenient. Parking was also available, although not so convenient but at a workable price. There was a certain decorum to this office, not fancy, but the lawyers were expected to project a certain professional image. The fact that I had a desk that was, on close inspection, nothing more than a folding banquet table did not fit this image, and I took a lot of heat for this, including suggestions that I keep my office door closed. This table, however, I had mated with the "This is America" file cabinet, whose owner had not yet shown up. The two together met the exact dimensions of a desk, and the folding table had a gorgeous imitation mahogany—or was it rosewood?—finish which made it quite elegant. Unfortunately, the metal folding legs could not be concealed, which resulted, of course, in the razzing.

I continually pointed out that should we have to move, which was something that appeared to be imminent since our building was scheduled for rehab, I would be the first one out the door carrying my desk in one hand. The filing cabinet was a different matter. It weighed, as I have mentioned, a ton.

As soon as I was settled in my office, I received my court assignments from the bar advocate gurus. In view of my long experience in the Boston courts, I was assigned to the Boston Municipal Court and the Suffolk Superior Court. This was in line with the general practice, which was for each advocate to be assigned to two courts. I was pleased with these assignments because it would mean the most challenging cases. I, of course, needed to get up to speed on the many changes that had taken place while I was away.

In my first appearance in the municipal court, I had to fill out a form called a notice of assignment of counsel, the NAC. This form was a necessity in order to be paid. It had something like five or six carbons attached. The last one was canary—or was it goldenrod?—because nobody makes forms that are yellow anymore. At the bottom was a line that said "authorized signature." So, what the hell, I signed it. I'm an authority. The form, after being submitted, came back with my name crossed off and the judge's signature under it, followed by a knowing smile from the court. I didn't know, but as usual, I learned by doing, often the wrong thing.

These forms were separated into their respective parts, and one was given to you, the appointed attorney. It was the last one and the least legible. The originals would be collected by the clerk's office and then sent to the CPCS payments unit, which would enter them into its computer. Good. Great. Very efficient. But some of the courts were short on staff, and the collection process would take a while, or some of the forms would go missing. And after the collection, some courts would hold onto the forms for weeks and would not send them along until enough were collected to fit into a small truck. Payment delayed. And suppose your form was lost or mislaid? You needed to furnish CPCS with a copy in order to get paid. Your copy was the last copy. Do you think the judges followed what was printed on the form, the part that said press down hard? Forms with no legible signature went into the CPCS reject pile, so the chase would be on to find one with a signature visible to an electron microscope.

CPCS received their nice shiny paychecks twice monthly while the advocates struggled with the constant payment mess-ups. My dander is still up about this even after years of retirement.

# 20

## Back for Real

**Gradually, I was acclimating myself** to being back in harness and used to all the changes. My general impression was that the system was now far more punitive than it had ever been. More crimes with higher sentences in addition to the dreaded fees. Probation as a weapon had also increased in use with the addition of many more restrictions on behavior. Otherwise, it was much the same. The government had all the power. No dismissals without its assent. They controlled the list and were backed up by heavy penalties for small infractions. The size of the criminal code had grown. The crime of assault and battery by means of a dangerous weapon now had numerous subsections to protect the elderly, the young, the blind, the poorly dressed, and people walking their dogs.

The DUI statute, which used to be about a page and a half in the code, had now increased to over twenty pages. There were so many subsections that they had run out of letters of the alphabet. It was clear that the lawyers had been at work since I had been away. But there was still this—the jury. And if I could try cases, maybe I could keep this dangerous adversary at bay. As I went along disposing of cases and engineering pleas, I knew that the day when I would actually have to go to trial would eventually come along. Would I have a good case—a so-called triable case? Would it be something I could handle? Would I be successful? Time would tell. Would a few bars of "Que Sera, Sera" be appropriate here?

The way the system works in the BMC is that cases eventually reach the trial assignment list if some sort of resolution has not been previously worked out. That list is called, and if the case answers ready, the case may be sent to a trial session where a judge is supposedly waiting to try it. The system is basically the same in the district and superior courts, with some variety in details. There was a game that went on in the municipal court because, of course, judges differ in their approach and some are regarded as more desirable than others to try cases. The state of readiness of defense counsel often depended on which judges were in the trial sessions on any given day.

In order to keep everything on the level, the judges assigned to the trial sessions, usually two, were supposed to be kept a secret. It was discovered that the names of the trial judges for the day were posted early in the morning on a board in the judges' lobby. An enterprising attorney would be dispatched to the lobby and, on a pretext of some sort, would take a peek at the board and thus find out who those judges were. Where appropriate, the lawyers could now prepare their continuance motions.

A lot of cases are sent to these trial sessions. This does not mean these cases are going to be tried. As a practical matter, it just means these cases, after a few months of backing and filling, will now merit a discussion as to a possible resolution, particularly if the witnesses are there and ready to go. The presence of witnesses often has a distressing effect on the defendants and encourages a settlement. After my return, I had many cases that went out to the trial session, and none of them had as yet resulted in a trial. I was still looking for that nice easy case with which to get my feet wet after my few years' layoff.

Shortly after my return to practice, one of those cases that was sent out to a session for trial went to one of those judges where a lot of lawyers were making use of the famous quote "ready until reached." I wasn't worried because this case looked like a natural for a plea, even though the defendant had one of the longest records I had ever seen. It was mostly minor offenses, but a lot of time had been served in the house of correction. The defendant, in addition to the new charge, was on a suspended sentence of eighteen months to that same house of correction. The new offense, assault and battery on a police officer, appeared to be a strong government case and constituted the violation of probation on the old case. I must have suggested that perhaps he consider wrapping up the new case with the old, possibly by way of concurrent sentences. It seemed logical. I didn't say he had to do it; it was just a suggestion.

I was immediately and abruptly told I was being fired. I was selling him out and a lot of other things as well. There was no reason for any of this, just a part of the business from time to time. I now realized I had a wild man for a client, and if I were to remain on the case, it would be an adventure, to say the least.

I cannot be fired from a case without the permission of the judge, so I brought the fact of my client's displeasure to the attention of the court, and that meant a hearing would be necessary. The normal course at these hearings is that the defendant expresses his grievances about the attorney, and almost always, the attorney is allowed to withdraw. Formally, the attorney files what's called a notice of withdrawal of appearance, and new counsel is appointed. The reason the withdrawal is almost always allowed is because the courts would rather not force defendants to work with lawyers they are having difficulty with. There is a limit, of course, but the first time the court usually goes along. I was more than willing to step aside and did not oppose the defendant's motion to discharge me.

If I withdrew, the case would go back to the assignment session, and new counsel would be appointed, and I would thankfully be rid of this client and the difficulties representation of him would present. The case would have to be continued in order to give the new lawyer a chance to prepare, and there would be more delay, which could conceivably benefit the defendant, as he well knew.

It is now beginning to dawn on me what is going on here. The judge, aware of this client's long record, is out to flatten him and doesn't want the case to get away from him. Knowing that allowing me to withdraw will mean that he will likely not be the judge on the case, he unbelievably denies the joint motion for my withdrawal. The judge was a former DA that I had cases with, and he knows me and doesn't listen to this sell-out nonsense and tells the defendant that I am the best bar advocate ever and the case is mine, and furthermore, we are going to go to trial right now, and now means *now*.

So that's it. I am stuck with Mr. Difficult, and a jury is about to be empaneled. Further, my dream of a nice easy winnable case has gone south. The judge knows the facts of the case and, talented as he has represented I am, believes nobody can win it and he'll be able to wrap up the defendant with, in his opinion, a well-deserved lengthy sentence. In addition to the suspended sentence of eighteen months, there is a maximum sentence of two and one-half years on the new charge, which could be ordered served from and after the probation violation for a total of four years—a substantial piece of time for a not very significant case.

Here's the background story. The defendant had recently been released from the house of correction. He had been out just a matter of days and had just started his probation. The original sentence was a two and one-half year split sentence, a year to serve the balance suspended, which is now the eighteen months hanging over him. The defendant, after that year in the joint, thinks he will feel better if he smokes a little crack, and for sure he will, so he's got a piece and a pipe and is preparing to light up in a downtown back alley. And this is what happens next. The Boston Police have a bicycle patrol working, and it is specifically designed to patrol those places where the crackheads are hiding and where the patrol cars can't go, namely those back alleys.

Two cops on this bike patrol spot the defendant, who drops the drugs and the pipe while excusing himself in haste. There is a chase. The defendant is cornered and, allegedly, turns and shoves cop number one off his bike. In the process, the cop damages a fingernail, and his uniform is ripped, and his pride is injured. My amiable client is arrested and charged with assault and battery on a police officer.

The trial commences, and I'm thinking maybe I ought to go back to being deceased. The policeman is a good witness. My client is not going to testify. I cross-examine the cop at length, the case is argued, and after a while, a small miracle occurs, and the jury is hung. I'm thinking now I've still got it, baby, and better the case will now go back to the assignment session, and I'll be rid of this man who unfortunately now is beginning to warm up to me. He's actually speaking to me. The jury is excused, thank you very much, and we're done, and I'm thinking I can tiptoe out of this case. But no tiptoe or soft shoe or anything. The judge is out to drop my client down a well somewhere, and to that end, we are going to try this case again, like right away. I can't remember whether it was the next day or a few days later, but it was soon.

Now we are back in court, and we empanel another jury. This time the partner shows up, so now we are being doubled up on. He saw the whole thing in even more detail than the victim officer. I cross-examine both with as much ingenuity as I can muster. Essentially, the defense is that the police later went back to find the crack evidence, couldn't, and so in the absence of a drug charge, the assault and battery charge was manufactured. I might also have suggested that the cop flunked bike school and didn't know how to ride and therefore wasn't pushed off his bike but fell off. Also, I dimly recollect asking questions about this bike school, which it turned out was somewhere near a resort community in the west, and the whole thing was paid for by the taxpayers. The jury retired, and this time they got it right or wrong, depending on which side you're on, and the defendant was acquitted. So yay!

My first case since my return from the boonies, and it is a winner. The basis of the probation violation is the new case, and my client has just been acquitted of that, which will mean no probation surrender, and I will be done. First, the judge has to give thanks to the jury. The word *hollow* comes to mind when the stoked-up judge states his appreciation for the jury's (dis)service. Worse, as the jury files out, my client does this. He had a loud voice, and this courtroom had good acoustics. He looks at me and with a laugh booms out, "You—are dangerous," a remark unfortunately heard by the judge. But, I don't care because it's all over. I have a satisfied client. Again, the defendant will have to be put back on probation because the violation was the new arrest, and he has just been found not guilty of that.

But that didn't happen. It is important to remember that judges are not necessarily Abe Lincolns up on the bench. It is sometimes more like this: malice toward all and charity for nobody. The judge gets hold of a probation officer and instead of dropping the surrender, a new violation is dreamed up. Apparently, the defendant failed to report within twenty-four hours of his release. This is the thinnest of grounds for a probation surrender. Nobody ever does that, and nobody ever gets violated for that. I protest. I need time to prepare. Nevertheless, I get ready to do what I can for my client. My motion to continue is denied, and we are going to have the hearing *now*, even though the jury has barely left the courtroom.

But it turns out the probation officer who witnessed the defendant sign the contract and can verify the defendant's signature is unavailable. I move to dismiss. Not at all. Denied. I can't have time to get ready, but the government? That's different. Take all the time they want. The next day, I file a three-page motion asking the judge to recuse himself. He won't. There is a brief hearing in which I raise every possible objection I can think of. It doesn't work, and the defendant is sentenced to the remaining eighteen months on his probation.

We're not going to take this lying down, so we appeal. I'm upset, and I have received permission to handle the appeal, even though I haven't the faintest idea how to write a brief and have no familiarity with the appellate process. While we're waiting for the case to be docketed in the appellate court, a case is handed down from the Supreme Judicial Court which has something to say about probation surrenders, and it is not helpful for us. Here's the story in that case.

A man is on probation on a charge of operating under the influence. While on that probation, he is arrested on another driving under the influence. He goes to trial on the new case and wins. He is found not guilty. The only grounds for the probation violation is that new arrest on which he has just been acquitted. Everything else is in order. Reporting, paying fees, whatever else is required. The hearing judge on the probation surrender doesn't dismiss it but finds him in violation and sentences him on the suspended sentence anyway. The case is appealed. And here's the ruling, and this is why one goes to law school.

The standard for the jury is beyond a reasonable doubt, but the standard for a probation surrender is the preponderance of the evidence, a lower standard. This means that the judge can find to a preponderance that the case constituted a violation, even though there wasn't enough evidence to convince a jury to the higher standard of beyond a reasonable doubt. The cons would have a word to describe this decision, and it is not complimentary: that word would be *slick*. That way, the government wins, and the defendant stays in jail. This is why I was always at the bottom of the pack at HLS, and the opinion was written by a Harvard guy. There is just something that strikes me as wrong about this.

The defendant wins his case but loses and goes to jail? Why not say that the court in those circumstances will not allow the judge to go behind the jury verdict and make what amounts to a different decision? Why not say that the judgment of the jury is binding and it cannot be used as a probation surrender? Why not? "Mr. Wood, you are not thinking like a lawyer!" That's for sure.

Now let's say that you have a client that has fallen victim to the preponderance rule, and you appeal. Your argument is that the evidence doesn't even meet the preponderance standard. You are guaranteed to be backstopped with this—the "plainly wrong" doctrine. The appellate court will not touch the lower court ruling unless it can be shown to be plainly wrong. Good luck with that. That decision essentially undercut the appeal we had in our case.

It was months before the case was docketed in the appeals court, and the defendant, with his sentences aggregated, would be released soon, so ultimately, the appeal was dropped. So the battle was won but the war was lost. At least the defendant did not have to do an extra two and a half years that the judge would certainly have given him if he had been found guilty. So there was that. A pretty good beginning. Nice to get the first one out of the way and have it be a victory. Que sera? It was also reaffirming to realize that the lunacy associated with all my courtroom endeavors was back, refreshed and in full flower, and ready to be tapped, I hoped for the benefit of my clients.

This was not quite the end of it. Many years later, I bumped into this client in one of the sessions in the municipal court. He was there for who knows what. I asked him if he remembered me, and he did. His record was on the counsel table, and it was considerably longer, but I could still lift it. We stepped outside for a moment. His eyesight was poor, and he had some difficulty walking. He had led a rough life. If he was up against it and he needed something, he just took it, which naturally led to some opposition and frequent stays at government expense. In a few moments, I found the entry showing the only not guilty on his extensive record and showed it to him. We whooped it up for a few minutes, so much so that a bailiff poked his head out of an adjacent courtroom to see if everything was all right. It was a nice moment, and it made me feel, just for a few minutes, dangerous all over again.

So I was back in harness for real. I had actually been back for a few months, but it had taken a while to get that first trial. It was a real shot in the arm to have it be a winner, and I felt as if I had shaken off the rust accumulated during my short layoff. I could feel the beginnings of a new energy coming into focus, and it was a good feeling. The few years I had been away had been good years. My life had stabilized, and the cyclone that usually surrounded my personal life had disappeared over the horizon. The tornado that was an on-again, off-again part of my professional life was, however, about to resume. The previous case was but an inkling of what the future held, although I didn't know it at the time. My general view was to let me make the subsistence money that was being paid to the public defenders and let me keep a low profile.

The result in this case made me more aware than ever of the importance of the jury as a means of neutralizing the evil forces of incarceration. This was a first-class example of how the system operates and of what I have said about the judges, which is it is their job to help the government win. Probation is an integral part of sticking people in jail as can be seen from the decision which allows judges to operate with a free hand in probation surrender hearings. I saved my client some time but couldn't keep him out from under the probation violation. So what, you say? He deserved the time? I don't want you on my jury.

# 21

## Probation Surrendering

**So probation and its attendant** preponderance of the evidence sank my client. Probation had become endemic in the criminal business. Virtually every case disposition had probation attached to it. Formerly, it was parole that followed the cons after they got out from behind the walls. Truth in sentencing killed that because parole had become virtually nonexistent. No more two-thirds and one-third parole eligibility on the minimum sentences after the truth in sentencing law, which was passed shortly before I returned to practice. Whatever the sentence was, it was essentially the time that was served.

Probation was now the means of keeping offenders on the straight and narrow after their sentences were up or of keeping offenders in line as an alternative to time in prison, at least in theory. This meant more probation officers and many, many more probation surrenders. The secret true purpose of probation is to make life miserable for anyone who is on it. Reporting, home visits, program requirements, and now the hated fees. The probation situation is so bad that many facing time refuse to accept it as part of a plea bargain. Naturally, the opposition thinks that this means the defendant has no interest in behaving once out of prison, so more time is asked for as part of plea negotiations. Many are happy to do increased bids so they are completely free once they've done their time.

Probation means a lot of things and the worst is the money. Years ago, the legislature decided that it wasn't enough to simply behave while on probation, but there was a need to really rub noses in it, so they invented the PSF—probation supervision fee—which was, at the time of my retirement, $65 per month. Probationers were paying their overlords to be nasty to them, something that was received with a great amount of enthusiasm. In addition, there was a victim witness fee on all cases, a counsel fee, and a DNA fee if the case was a felony. If it was a drug case, there was also a drug analysis fee, which was automatically included as a part of probation. Yes, a fee was collected so that a defendant had to pay for the privilege of the government proving its case.

Probationers were stacked up against it as soon as they were released from prison. Fortunately, jobs were waiting for them that didn't require background checks and interviews, and that was in the drug trade. Did I mention that one condition of probation was to "seek" employment? Nobody ever understood what "seek" meant. In addition to the fees, the government had figured out something else helpful to those stepping out of prison and "seeking" employment, and that was to suspend drivers' licenses. This stupidity was good for the prison business because an early violation of probation was often operating a motor vehicle after suspension of license, and if one never had a license, there was the suspension of the right to operate a motor vehicle. And suppose the time had passed for either of these suspensions and one went to get back the license or right to drive and be legal. Fees—hundreds of dollars. Screw it. Just drive and try not to get caught was a frequent approach.

A facet of probation often was for one convicted of stealing money to pay the money back. As a result, probationers were saddled with amounts they could never hope to pay, and their lives were completely ruined. Defendants would see that they could avoid going to prison and would accept probation with all its murderous terms, only to live to regret it.

I was in the habit of advising defendants who accepted probation to carry a little notebook around with them. Anything that had to do with probation, I would recommend they keep a record. After all, the probation department was keeping a file on them. Why not keep one on the probation operatives? Yet I don't know anyone who ever did. Probation surrender hearings involved probation officers referring to their notes about missed home visits, missed reporting dates, nonpayment of fees, and job-seeking insufficiencies, along with other failures. It would be nice if the probationers had a few notes of their own to contradict what the POs were saying.

Here are some examples of probation cases I handled. These may seem to be extreme examples, but they are not too far from the norm. I was in court one day and was assigned a client on a probation surrender. I am assigned many of these cases on my so-called duty days. The defendant was released, and a date set for a surrender hearing. The fact that bail is not requested usually means that the violation is not considered serious, and there is an expectation that the defendant will likely be allowed to remain on probation and not go to jail. Before that can happen, a hearing in front of a judge is required.

I knew that this case was a failure to pay restitution. A digression—the pros always remind me it is really reparation. Restitution is giving back the thing that was taken; reparation is making the aggrieved party whole, something that was required in this case. I made an appointment for the defendant so I could prepare for his surrender hearing. He arrives at my office at the appointed time, and he presents as a shy, self-effacing man. He sits, and I ask him about his matter—how much of the restitution (reparation) has he paid?

"Over a thousand dollars," he answers.

I congratulate him and think that this will be an easy hearing. Most defendants who owe money have paid next to nothing. He is paying and just needs a little more time. So I ask him how much he owes, and he says, "One hundred and seventy-two thousand dollars."

And I say, "What?"

And he says, "ONE HUNDRED AND SEVENTY-TWO THOUSAND DOLLARS."

I ask him if he can write a check. Okay, it's a joke, although we don't laugh. I ask him how he is managing to pay. He has a part-time job and is paying, what, maybe a hundred a month? I make a calculation, and he will need more than his current lifetime to pay up, but only if he can continue at the current rate. Not only does he have this order, but he was required to serve a six-year sentence before he started to pay. So there were six years when he could have been paying, and to boot, this order is being enforced by another six-year suspended sentence. (A video clip of the disposition in this case has been added to the contemplated late-night television series *Judges Gone Wild.*)

I leap out of my chair and start screaming, "Do the time. Do the time. That way, the order is extinguished, and you are free."

No. No. He is going to pay, he says, and it is clear that the insanity that is part of the criminal courts has now enveloped him, and he has become one of the truly lost.

I don't recall what happened to the case. Probably, the court put a further court date at which time he will have paid a little more, and he will then be surrendered again. This will continue until he either dies or the court takes pity and tires of squeezing him. I can't help recalling that the judge who imposed this order and sat on this unfortunate man's trial—I was not his trial counsel—was a former public defender. Mark this: former public defenders and defense counsel who become judges are the worst when it comes to sentencing.

Former PDs and defense counsel think they have the inside track on how evil the defendant population is and are thus way ahead of former DAs in handing out the time. This client had a business, a travel business, which he claimed failed, and that was the cause of the loss of his customers' money. It was stealing, claimed the government. He went to trial, lost, and got whacked. I couldn't remember if this former PD judge was one I had supervised in my earlier days, and if so, he was one of those who sought a different line of work as a result of one of my unsubtle evaluations.

Another probation case I was assigned to was similar: a huge payback after a theft. The stolen money was used to go to the casinos and was ultimately lost there. There were two defendants, and they had both worked for a large corporation, which was the victim in the case. The amount in question was a mere $55,000, and since there were two, they were jointly ordered to pay back the money (in legal terms, they were jointly and severally liable). They had seen the door instead of a prison sentence and thus reluctantly accepted the probation order rather than do time.

Unfortunately for my client, she had started to pay and had paid a small amount when her codefendant promptly died, and now it was all on her. She came to my office and begged me to help. She was working three jobs and had no life whatsoever. Before we went to court, I did a little research and found out that her aggrieved employer, who was getting the payback, earned billions the previous year and paid no income taxes. Further, the company was now, as a result of her conviction, not obligated to pay the substantial pension she had earned during the many years she had worked for it.

We went to court, and I'm jumping up and down like a possessed person and waving my printouts of the corporate balance sheet of the poor aggrieved former employer who needs the extra $55,000 tax-free to shore up its multi-billion-dollar bottom line. The judge shuts me up, but she is good, and she remits the order and terminates the probation. Outside the courtroom, I have a client who has been transformed. She is awash in tears and can't stop with the hugs. I am so happy for her and glad I had brought along extra hankies. A special moment and altogether a very nice day.

One of the things about probation is the probation officers themselves. It is a good job if your role in life is to find things wrong with other people's behavior. You get to make home visits and show up unexpectedly. You get to criticize everything about the probationers. You can bet that their job-seeking has not lived up to the probation department's manual of job-seeking standards. The probationers have to report. The probationer never shows up at the right time, and better yet, the officer can make sure he or she is out of the office so the visit is never recorded. Probationers are required to give an address where they can be located. Many have just finished a sentence and understandably want to spend time with a girlfriend or whomever. They prefer not to furnish the probation department with the satellite address and so give their mother's address. The probation officer visits and is told by the mother she hasn't seen him in weeks. Dimed out by the family and placed in violation.

As crushing as probation terms were for most defendants, there are a very few who look at probation a little differently. I was retained to represent a man who had been charged with a DWI. He had been with friends on a warm afternoon, and they had some wine. On his way to pick up his wife after she finished work, the drink hit him the wrong way, and he was observed driving intermittently on both sides of a two-way street. He was stopped by the police, arrested, and charged with the DWI.

He was dressed in his "wife-beater" shirt with his head where his arm should have been and so photographed in the booking procedure. That booking photo was gleefully displayed by the police at the top of the arrest report, with an arrow drawn to it from the narrative underneath, in case anyone missed it. My client is just a sweet, hardworking family guy who is terribly upset and sheepish about the whole incident. We go to court, and I get him the most lenient disposition I can.

The case will be dismissed at the end of a year, and there is no finding of guilt. Of course, he has to pay thousands in fees mandated by our money-oriented legislature, which constantly has its hand out. There is the head injury fund, the broken kneecap fund, and the hangnail fund, which all get a piece of my client. There are programs that cost and other innumerable fees, and of course, the probation supervision fee, which every probationer must pay for the privilege of getting yelled at.

So here's what happened with this man: he loved being on probation. He reported. He paid his fees. He went to all his classes. Everything was up to and beyond snuff. Now the fun of being a probation officer is, as I have noted, to be able to yell at people and criticize their very existence. This man's probation officer would come back from lunch, and there would be my smiley client who had arrived early and was now waiting at her office with all his paperwork in order and his probation fee attached to the properly watermarked and government-approved paper. His hair was neat, his clothes pressed, and his shoes shined. The probation officer would show up with a scowl at the ready, but there was nothing to scowl about since my client presented in all his neatness and happiness. This put his probation officer in an even worse mood than she had worked up during her lunch hour, getting ready to meet with the day's failures. Soon, the officer had enough, and she did finally get to yell at him. And this is what that was: "Don't bother reporting anymore!"

Probation has different effects on different people. Some seem to be able to grudgingly accommodate themselves to it, and others just can't or, rarely, like the previous client, actually bask in the idea. There is always the risk that not living up to the terms of probation means being sent to prison, and it is this thought that keeps many in line. If the end of a probation surrender hearing, as sometimes happens, is the imposition of a sentence, most probationers can face it with some equanimity.

A client I had in a local district court back in the dark days when I first started out had a different reaction. This client had a surrender hearing scheduled and had a six-month house of correction sentence hanging. I met him at the courthouse and then went to talk to his probation officer. This officer was something like the assistant chief and very well respected. He had been a star pass catcher for the Boston Patriots before they became the New England Patriots. He was beloved as befitted his past, and his word was good, or so I thought. Mr. Catcher said he wasn't recommending time for my client and would ask that he be reinstated to probation as the violations were minor. I informed my client I thought there should be no problem, and we went before the judge.

It all went smoothly until the judge unaccountably revoked the order of suspension and sent my client to jail. Before my client knew what had happened, he was whisked off to the courthouse lockup. We had apparently forgotten that the judge is the one with the robes and has the final say. This was early in my career, but already these strange things were happening—and it was about to get stranger.

The lockup was directly under the main courtroom. As the session attempted to continue, the noise from muffled swears and hammering on the cell door wafted up into the courtroom, and it was becoming difficult to continue. Finally, the judge yelled at the bailiff to "bring him up." The police prosecutor knew the judge to have a temper and tried to restrain him. It didn't work. I was reminded of the "Holiday" poem, which I now paraphrase: "From down in the dungeon, there arose such a clatter; the judge sprang from his bench to see what was the matter."

But what was brought up was definitely not the jolly old elf of poesy but rather my very steamed client. He is put in the prisoner's dock, and the judge warns him he is going to give him more time if he doesn't go downstairs and shut up. Remember, this is before the days of transcription, and my bloody but unbowed defendant utters these immortal words: "Go ahead, you bald-headed motherfucker!" This wasn't the "give me liberty or give me death" thing, but it wasn't bad.

It took a while, but calm was restored, and yes, the judge was bald-headed. And yes, the defendant was punished with an additional six months, which he had most happily earned. And so off he went to jail with a smile on his face. Visions of sugarplums? Undoubtedly.

# 22

## Stand by Me

**As bizarre as some probation** matters can be, there is nothing as wacky as this: the standby counsel. In the court appointment business, the appointed lawyer does the work, files motions, arranges the court dates, handles the trial, and argues the case. In standby counsel situations, the lawyer does nothing except stand by while the client represents himself. As standby, you are available to be consulted if the defendant has a question. The best part is that you are getting paid while all this is going on.

Standby cases are almost always going to be trials and since usually the defendant you are standing by for has no idea what he or she is doing, they are slow trials. Since you are paid on an hourly basis, you are going to get paid a bundle—or what constitutes a public defender bundle—for doing absolutely nothing except from time to time needing to answer some silly defendant's question. You are also out of circulation for days at a time and can avoid the heavy lifting you may have to do on other cases. One of your cases is called for trial in the assignment session, and the call goes out, "Where is defense counsel?"

The session is notified you're on trial, standby, and that case you would prefer to avoid has to be continued. For these reasons, standby cases are coveted by the public defender bar or at least they should be. You sit in a chair in a courtroom and view the action and work hard to stay awake. I regret to say that despite all my efforts, I only had a few of these in my career. The slightest bit of unhappiness with my efforts always elicited a suggestion from me that the client could represent himself (go *pro se* in legal Latin speak), and I would be delighted to be standby.

One of these was a client who was charged with driving under the influence. It was his third offense, and in an early conversation with him, it was obvious he knew a lot about driving under cases—a lot more than I did. As the case progressed and I became dumber and dumber about this type of offense, the defendant was happy to take over the running with me as standby. Good news, and now I would not have to worry about a case that I could possibly lose.

Eventually, the case comes up for trial, and the judge tries to talk the defendant out of handling his own defense. The judge thinks that the defendant will stumble all over himself and the case will take a few weeks to try. The judge doesn't know how wrong he is. A jury is assembled, and the defendant goes to work. He is whirling and twirling and spinning like a top. He is masterful and he has the jury eating out of his hand. I had counseled with him, so I knew he would do well, but even I am impressed, and the judge is amazed. Any efforts by the judge to steer the case in the government's direction are batted away like so many flying insects.

The case is argued, and shortly, the defendant is acquitted and carried out of court on the shoulders of the assembled to cries of "Bravo" and "Well done." Of course, the rules are that the jury did not know of the two prior DWI convictions lest this prejudice their view of the defendant's dance. Everyone is happy with the result, and I congratulate him on his victory.

Now here is the thing that entranced me throughout this trial, which despite fears to the contrary, only took maybe a day. The defendant came to court with his legal paperwork in a canvas briefcase-type bag. It is usual for an attorney who is on trial to take out the paperwork and place it on the counsel table and then put his briefcase off to the side somewhere—on a table or a chair over against a side wall. This defendant did not do that but instead placed his bag gently under the counsel table where it rested comfortably next to his feet. I noted that at intervals, maybe every ten or fifteen minutes, he would reach into the bag and remove a plastic bottle with a label on it that read "Smart Water." He would then refresh himself not by taking big gulps or several swallows but instead with little sips. *Nips* would probably not be a good word to use in description.

Perhaps it was my imagination, but as the case progressed, this defendant appeared to get smarter and smarter and the whirling and twirling even more pronounced. I just couldn't help wondering, as I watched this show of legal acumen, what might be discovered if the contents of that bottle were subjected to a chem test. I guess we'll never know.

This next case, in my opinion, belongs in the Standby Counsel Hall of Fame. The defendant was charged with possession of a handgun, possession of ammunition, and assault and battery on a police officer. I was assigned standby counsel from the beginning. The defendant was in custody, so I had to see him at the jail, a stone's throw from my office. The defendant and I got along well. This was chiefly because I was accommodating of his various requests on account of I knew I was going to get paid a bunch for doing next to nothing. The defendant wanted to see me? I was there. He wanted some paperwork? I had it for him. Some research? I printed out the cases. Some photographs? I had an investigator get as many photos as he wanted. There was nothing of any complexity involved.

Eventually, the case is sent out to a trial session in the Suffolk Superior Court. We have a "Let's move it along" type judge who sentences with a heavy hand. My client comes into the courtroom, and the first thing he does is to spread out his photographs on the counsel table, which is maybe eight-by-four feet. Virtually the entire table is now covered with four-by-six-inch photos. We go through the preliminaries, and a jury is finally empaneled. The government puts in its case, which is as follows:

The police drive up and see a crowd of people gathered in the middle of the street. As they get closer, they see the defendant break from the crowd and run off down a side street. He appears to be carrying something. He runs by some bushes and appears to toss whatever he is carrying behind the bushes. The police, who are now in hot pursuit, find a gun behind those bushes in the area of the toss. The police attempt to arrest the defendant, who has gone down an alley. In an effort to escape apprehension, the defendant conks a police officer over the head with a brick.

The gun is tested and found capable of firing, as is required under the statute, and it is loaded. The police witnesses take little time in testifying in what they think is an open and shut case. The defendant is this little guy who has this impish smile on his face throughout. His cross-examination of the witnesses follows this same procedure. Before asking a question, the defendant would pick up a photo, look at it, put it back down, then pick up another and put that back down. He would do this until he found the photo he wanted among the seventy-five or so he had on the table, or he would decide he didn't want to use a photo and go on to ask a question. This was taking a lot of time, of course, and Mr. Hurry Up on the bench was going batty with the slow pace. Obviously, the judge felt he couldn't bark at the defendant to get a move on for fear the jury would sympathize with him.

But here is where the defendant did something extraordinarily clever. He asked a question that no lawyer would ever ask. On cross-examination, he asks one of the officers, "What made you think I was the one with the gun?"

I cringed, and the judge licked his chops. The answer took a minute or two but was basically, "As our police car approached, we saw you look in our direction, run by the bushes carrying something, make a throwing motion, and then when we tried to arrest you, you assaulted my partner in an attempt to make good your escape, and later we found the gun where you had made the throwing motion." What this answer did was to make it clear that the police did not actually see the defendant throw the gun into the bush. As good as that was, this was where the defendant sealed his case.

The government called a ballistics expert to testify that the weapon was capable of firing. In order to qualify under the statute, the weapon must be able to discharge a projectile. Normally, in these gun cases, the ballistician is asked if the weapon was examined for fingerprints. The answer usually is yes, and also, usually, no fingerprints are found. That is because the gun oil on weapons is not susceptible to holding fingerprints, the witness always adds. The follow-up question is, "Do you ever find fingerprints on weapons?"

And the expert usually says, "In only about 5 percent." This line of questioning is to show that the absence of a fingerprint doesn't mean that the defendant didn't hold the weapon. In this case, the surprise answer from this particular ballistician was that prints are found in about 20 percent of the cases.

The defendant, on cross-examination, does his photo routine and hops from one foot to the other and, with that impish little smile, asks the witness this: "Is that 20 percent of 100 percent?"

You could almost hear the jury say, "Oh, how cute!" But only if it was loud enough to be heard above the judge's grinding his teeth.

The case took about five days to try. In the end, the defendant is cleared of the weapon and ammunition charges, but he is unable to get around the assault and battery on the policeman charge. The judge now exhales and whacks the defendant with the maximum on the assault and battery, two and a half years in the county prison. While everyone does their best to keep a straight face, the judge is careful to say that that sentence is required because of the defendant's bad past, and he was not at all influenced by the acquittal on the gun charge. Or the fact that his mother, watching from the back of the courtroom, cheered loudly and turned a somersault when the acquittals on the weapon and ammunition charges were announced.

The defendant had waited almost two years for his trial, which time would be credited to his sentence, so he would be out soon. I gladly filed my bill for "working at nothing all day" as the song goes—and best of all, the assignment notice was in the computer, and the bill was processed for immediate payment.

# 23

## Fun in the Appeals Court

**I have mentioned the appellate** courts in connection with the appeal on the probation case. These constitute the Valhalla of the entire system and are best approached on one's knees, continually salaaming to whomever one needs to deal with. The courts are in the "old" courthouse, recently opulently and expensively rehabbed as befits the courts' station, and ensconced in impressive marble columns so that one can appreciate the great majesty of the law. These courts maintain they are open to all for redress of legal wrongs, such as in the rare case where the defendant wins and the decision can be reversed in favor of the prosecution. And I swear by the defense lawyers' mantra that the case better be won at trial because the appeal is normally a guaranteed win for the government. This next episode of legal hopscotch involved a bunch of unnecessary ring around the rosy that resulted in my taking most of the day to accomplish something that should have taken a few minutes.

I had tried a case that I didn't win at trial, something not terribly unusual. Actually, the principal charge was a not guilty, but the client was convicted on a lesser charge and received a sentence to the house of correction. I thought there were some good appellate issues, so I filed for an appeal, claimed an appeal as it were, and then prepared a motion for stay of execution of sentence. The idea behind this type of motion is to allow the defendant to remain at liberty and on bail while the appeal is being heard. This is real tilting at windmills. These motions are vigorously opposed by the government, and you have to show that the appeal is a sure winner in order to get relief.

When I say I prepared a motion for stay, I mean that I engaged someone else to prepare the motion because legal writing is beyond me, I can now confess, or I should say that I can do it, but I'm of the opinion others can do it better.

So my whiz kid legal writer guy cobbles together a motion for a stay, and it is a beaut. Thirty-five pages of cites of cases and legal reasoning that cannot be denied. We first carry this weighty thing up to the trial court, where we file it because to start the process, it has to be heard by the trial judge. This hearing lasted about a minute, and the motion was not unexpectedly denied in short order. Trial judges are not in the habit of ruling after a defendant's conviction that some or one of their rulings was a mistake and allow the motion. Now we can go to the appeals court and ask for the stay, but we need to hurry because we are at the last day that we can file or else we are time-barred, as is the expression.

We know there is a filing fee in the appeals court of $150. That's a tough amount for poor people to pay so someone can stamp a docket number on it and log it into a docket book. This is the kind of job a lot of people would want—$150 for a few minutes' work. But there is a way around it, and it is called *forma pauperis* or something like that; maybe it's the *formam pauperam*. That's because Latin is still spoken in the higher echelons. The lawyer's dictionary has the correct spelling. It means that you are alleging that your client is a pauper and can't afford the fee. That *formam* has to have an affidavit of indigency in order for the filing fee to be waived. We put together an affidavit and attached a copy of my appointment, the trial court's finding that the defendant was indigent, and a copy of the docket sheet that showed my client was in prison.

I signed the affidavit stating the information was true to the best of my information and belief and on the basis of that requested that the fee be waived. Our shoes were shined, and we were looking neat and appropriately dressed. We pushed our way through the stacks of brochures describing how user-friendly the court is. We were respectful and approached the clerk's office, bowing and genuflecting appropriately.

Almost anything I became involved with in the courts seemed to take an odd turn, and this was no different. The clerk, this very nice person, looked over our submission and made a face. This meant there was going to be trouble. She pointed out the affidavit of indigency was not signed by the defendant but instead by me. We called attention to the documents we had attached in support of the *formam* affidavit. He had been found indigent, was represented by appointed counsel, and was in prison. She countered, "Well, how do I know he didn't hit the lottery?"

So we were going to go off into never-never land doing what should be something simple. I had been dealing with clerk's offices for thirty years or so and knew that kindness and solicitude were the best ways to operate, so I put aside some rash thoughts that instinctively came to mind. After a little bit of back and forth where we tried to suggest we didn't know there was a lottery agent in the prison, we retired to lick our wounds and consider our next move in this chess match. To get an affidavit from the defendant would require drafting a new one and then going to the prison and having the defendant sign it. This would additionally involve getting the car out of the not-so-close garage, driving to the prison, which meant a trip on the Southeast "Distressway," finding a parking spot at the prison, an always iffy adventure since only two spots were reserved for lawyers, and then hoping that the defendant was available or that the count was not on during which no visits were allowed. The count consumed at least an hour in which it literally was "One, two, three, etc." All of this would be time-consuming.

Resourcefulness kicked in. I knew that my client had a woman friend who had access to a bank account that she used to send him money for his canteen, so I thought, we'll just pay the fee. I knew my client well and was sure he would approve. I called and reached the friend. She's on board. We pick her and the money up, drive back to the garage, and walk her, the cash, and her heart condition up the hill to the courthouse. We're thinking we're good here and we can finally get this thing filed. We are now well past the lunch hour and hoping this can be done before dinner time. We approach, hats in hand, thinking we can't be denied, produce the money, and start peeling off the $150. I present the money, and the opposition, the same person, who is now sticking to us like flypaper, says, "We don't accept cash" with an expression of utter triumph.

But we are nothing but resourceful, and I'm thinking we can easily get around this latest blockade, so I tell the stakeholder, "Give me the cash and I'll write a check." This is said within earshot of Madame Clerk.

I know that at first I don't hear this, but I think the clerk said, "Are you with a firm?"

When it finally enters my consciousness that she is actually asking me this, I answer that I am not, and so what? Well, incredibly, they only accept checks from "firms," which means essentially the gang of twenty-two or who knows, maybe only a select number of the gang of twenty-two. I tell her proudly that I am a sole practitioner and am informed just as proudly that checks from sole practitioners, particularly sole practitioners who have a large criminal defendant client base, are treated with rank suspicion and not acceptable. Threatening is a criminal offense, and if I am not careful and follow a certain impulse, I could find myself going to a place where it will be easy to get my client's signature on the *formam*. But calm and resourcefulness win out. I know there is a post office nearby, and I run off and purchase a money order, and the thing is done, and the sun has nearly set. We leave with our many thank-yous echoing off the marble walls. It didn't take long, but in a few days, we were notified of the usual: motion for stay of execution of sentence *denied*.

This is just another episode in the public defender business, where you as the defender are treated as a second-class legal citizen. It used to be that when spotted by a functionary in any criminal court clerk's office, you were treated as if you didn't exist. I must say the situation has improved because nowadays, after a wait, clerical staff will mostly ask if you can be helped. I remember in my early days when I was in the court of the Cadillac judge that the rule was never to wait on any public defender if it could be avoided. I would go to the clerk's office and be ignored. I usually wanted to see the court papers, something most attorneys didn't do. It would take many long minutes before I could be offered any assistance, and I would always bring along some reading material to occupy the waiting. As I say, that has changed, thankfully.

# 24

# Self-Improvement

**The criminal justice system is** always looking for ways to improve itself. One of these self-improvement inventions was a program whereby lawyers were asked to engage in a process of judicial evaluation. Lawyers would receive an email claiming that they had appeared before certain judges, and they would be asked to participate in a confidential evaluation—heavy emphasis placed on the word *confidential*.

It was promoted as an important piece in improving the quality of the judiciary. I wasn't about to put myself on record as to my opinions on various judges, no matter how confidential, and these requests I forwarded with alacrity into the delete box. I had a lot to do and, particularly as a public defender, I was busy for some of the reasons I have already outlined, such as getting paid, preparing cases, and dealing with clients and an unfriendly judiciary. The speed with which I disposed of this request was accompanied by the following thought: how are we, the defense bar, expected to give an unbiased "evaluation" of judges who deny our motions, give us a hard time at trial, and sentence our clients to lengthy prison terms while telling us how they are sending messages to the public? And furthermore, why is it the obligation of the lawyers to get involved in this?

There is the assumption that lawyers and judges exist in some kind of clubby atmosphere where what happens in the courtroom is forgotten. Let them call in retired judges or judges from other jurisdictions to do this job and leave us lawyers alone. Let them police themselves. And how are the judges going to take criticism? It is emphasized that these evaluations will be held in strictest confidence and no one will have any idea who is saying what. The emails stop short of saying it's open season on the judges, and there is no suggestion that this is a time to anonymously settle some scores. Anyway, I ignore these emails and go about my business.

Here is a feature of this which I find bizarre. If one does not respond to this request, there is a succession of emails advising you that you only have a short time left to do your evaluations—like you are missing out on the opportunity of a lifetime. Your participation will be a cathartic event, and through your evaluations, the sins of the judiciary will be washed clean and the legal world will be a safer and saner place. It is emphasized how important this is for the health of the judiciary and you are, again, given a multiplicity of assurances that none of the judges will ever know even if you write a stinko evaluation. You have to wonder if some secret judicial cadre is holding it against you if you don't cooperate.

It's only however many more days you are warned until the window will close and you will no longer have an opportunity to trash, or maybe butter up your favorite judges is the tenor of this succession of reminders. At the risk of being labeled an outlier, I pay no attention to these requests.

Reality and common sense are two items in short supply in the judicial world and particularly in the criminal courts, but sometimes either or both manage to protrude into the ongoing daffiness. And it did at long last do just that, and this is how it happened. I was involved in a case that was being conferenced at the bench. There are three of us—two lawyers and the DA—and we are waiting for something, maybe the stenographer has to retrieve her backup tape—something. There is dead air while we are waiting, and there is thus plenty of time for something unusual to happen, and, for sure, it does.

The judge is standing at the side of her bench, beaming kindly in our direction when, out of the blue and apropos of nothing, the judge mentions that she just got her evaluations. So that's okay, and nothing off-kilter has happened yet, but there is a gentle stirring of a breeze off in the distance. We are holding our collective breaths that this is the end of this, but no, she follows this up with a statement that she got one bad one. Okay, we are heading onto thin ice, but sanity still prevails until she adds this: she thinks she knows who it is. *What?* There is a pause, but suspiciously left hanging was the unsaid comment, "And I'm going to get that sucker if it's the last thing I ever do," to lift a line.

The three of us are now looking at each other. We can assume that the judge doesn't think it was one of us or she wouldn't have mentioned this. So is this what happens? You do the evaluation and say you don't know how this judge got past the judicial nominating committee, even though you do know, and the judge is going to suspect it's you and have it out for you? Or have it out for members of the bar in general? Suppose the judge is wrong and thinks it's you and it isn't? Are the judges going to be able to respond to criticism and think maybe they should do things a little differently? Or is criticism going to merely reinforce some behavior that is, let's say, not judicial?

In addition, I wouldn't want to be in a position to have made negative comments or positive comments and then appear in front of a judge and have the judge do something that would make me wish I had never said what I said. Judging, I would imagine, is a hard job. Who am I as a lawyer to be put in the position of critiquing a man or woman who is saddled with the obligations of being a judge? So I never responded to these evaluation requests. But I have wondered occasionally if the fact that a judge has been unusually harsh either to me or one of my clients where that might have come from. And so the eleventh hour has passed, and the window has closed, and I have not responded with my evaluations.

What do you think follows on the heels of that? An email that wants to know *why* I didn't participate in the judicial evaluation process. Are they keeping score somewhere? Begging your pardon, but that went into the delete box even faster than the initial requests, if that's at all possible.

# 25

## Eyes Open and Mouth Shut

**I have postulated that there** were these weird happenings that seemed to follow me, a sort of living force, a sort of psychic magnetic field that complicated everything that I did. And yet it is clear that a lot of these things were my own fault and that I should take responsibility for them. Still, I am not so sure; I like the magnetic field idea. This occurrence can only be described as awkward, at best, and it was entirely my fault.

I had a brief hearing in a session in the superior court that had gone well. It put me in a good mood, and jauntily I left the courtroom. There were a number of people in the corridor, and as I left, I caught the eye of a woman passing by and, for no reason that I can think of, I winked in her direction. Generally, I had a happy life as a public defender and so went about my business, often winking and smiling and skipping as befitted a "valued" Harvard Law alumnus. This wink didn't mean anything, just one of those happy-go-lucky things that I occasionally did. There was no particular response that I can recall. To the best of my knowledge, I had never seen this person before.

I had a hearing scheduled in an adjacent courtroom, so I hung around for a while until that session started. That session began and lo and behold, I see this person again, and that's because she's mounting the podium where the judge sits and sitting where the judge sits, and the reason she is doing this is because what? She is the judge! It now dawns on me I had managed to wink at the judge who I am now going to be asking to allow a very important motion in a pending case.

My first reaction was that I had been had because judges don't ordinarily wander around in the corridor with the hoi polloi but are escorted up a back elevator by court officers who then sneak them into their lobbies through a side door, presumably to avoid being accosted by a dissatisfied litigant or attorney. If I had had the slightest inclination that she was a judge, I would have been my usual reverential self. She looked at me with a bemused expression, which was hard to do because at this point I was only a foot tall, but she did grant my motion. Maybe the wink helped. I had many cases with this excellent judge. You have to wonder.

This next gaffe was all on me. After 9-11, courthouse security was very tight. The superior court had moved to the old federal courthouse building in Post Office Square. The strict security mandated by the federals, who had the oversight of the building, resulted in long lines waiting to be cleared for admission. This included the lawyers who were in some ways treated as if they were responsible for 9-11. Usually, these lines were inside the courthouse, but occasionally they backed out onto the street, always a pleasure in the frequent inclement weather. It was so bad that the lines sometimes doubled back on each other like those lines for the security check at the airport.

One afternoon, I'm in one of these lines, and the doubled back line is there, although fortunately, this part of the line is inside the building. A lawyer I know is standing facing me in the doubled-back portion of the line, and he has a plastic bag looped over his arm. I say jokingly to him, "I really admire your handbag"—something like that. What I didn't see was the female judge moving outside the line just behind him. She hears my comment and thinks it is directed toward her. She falls all over herself, thanking me for my appreciation of what apparently was her favorite accessory.

What do you say here? "I didn't mean your handbag. I mean, it's just as nice as this plastic bag I was complimenting." You can't say that. You can't say, "I didn't mean your bag, but now that I think of it, I love it." I just smiled and let it ride. I had a lot of cases in front of this judge and always thought I did pretty well. I'm sure it was my legal abilities, and the handbag episode had nothing to do with it.

I can't help recounting this story about that judge. This happened before the purse incident. The judge was new and getting her first taste of sitting on the bench. She was presiding in a session in the municipal court when an arrest comes in, and I am assigned to represent the defendant. The charge is fugitive from justice from some other state. Normally, in fugitive cases, the bails are in the neighborhood of eight quadrillion because the court wants to be sure that the defendant is held for that other state. The question of bail comes up for a hearing. It turns out that the defendant has not yet gone through the booking process at the local police station. Unbelievably, the judge tells the defendant, who is wanted for something like an axe murder, "Now I want you to go down to the police station and get your picture and fingerprints taken, and then come right back, and we'll decide on bail."

This is one of the few times that I felt like asking to approach the bench and say, "Are you nuts?" But I didn't. The defendant was released to be photographed and fingerprinted, and sure enough, the defendant did not reappear. It's been twenty years, and they are probably still looking for him. The bad side of this was that for the next few months, every defendant who appeared before this judge got smoked on bail. She learned in a hurry.

In another "how could I possibly," I had a case in the superior court that was standing for trial. It was a bad case. Three kids, supposedly involved in a gang initiation, had shot this unfortunate man in the back as he was walking home in the wee hours of the morning. The only thing that might have saved him was that he was heavily intoxicated at the time of the shooting. My client was not the shooter. The shooter was a codefendant, and a third kid got away. We were before a judge that had a reputation for being heavy-handed on disposition. There is some sort of break in the action during a pretrial conference, and the three lawyers, me plus cocounsel and the DA, are at the sidebar. We are waiting for something—the stenographer, I don't remember.

There is some small talk, and the judge mentions that he is concerned about the weather report for the weekend at "the heights." It is the week before Thanksgiving and the end of the football season when all the big rivalries are played. The heights is Chestnut Hill, where Boston College, a wannabe national power, plays its football, and this is an obvious reference to the field conditions for that big game. Some big end-of-season rival was on tap, like Penn State or maybe "The Cross," as is locally called Holy Cross. Before I can even think about wiring my mouth shut, I say that I'm more worried about the weather in New Haven. This, of course, without saying more and as everyone knew, referenced the Harvard-Yale game.

There is a sudden silence—the silence that you hear when time is needed to reflect on whether what was said was actually said. I'm thinking I'm insane. I have a bad case, and I'm telling the world's biggest BC booster that his school is a nothing compared to the Ivies? And he's the judge, and I'm not, and I've just told him I'm Chevy Chase and he isn't? I better win this case.

The case goes to trial. The charges are assault with intent to murder, assault and battery by means of a dangerous weapon, possession of a firearm, and possession of ammunition. I do a good job for my client, and he is convicted only of the possession of the handgun. The shooter is convicted of all the charges. It was clearly a compromise verdict as far as my client was concerned. Since it was the week before Thanksgiving, many jurors had travel arrangements and were in a hurry to reach a verdict and continue with holiday plans. Given more time to deliberate, I felt as if my client might have been cleared of all the charges. I don't remember who won the BC game, but in the important game, it was Harvard, naturally.

The maximum penalty on the handgun charge is five years. It is traditional to sentence to state prison in terms of years with a maximum and a minimum term. Four to five would be the ordinary maximum sentence. Instead, my client received a maximum of five years and a minimum of four years, eleven months. I wondered what happened to the extra thirty days, so I guess my client caught a break; and for sure, BC is the head of the football universe. The codefendant received multiple sentences all to run from and after, amounting to something like thirty-seven to forty. Yikes. And his counsel didn't give two shits about Harvard-Yale.

But I was not quite through with doing some quick thinking that got me into disfavor. This involved Mr. BC Booster again. I had a client who was accused of perjury, and the perjury had been committed in a murder (capital) case. This was one of the most difficult clients I had the pleasure of representing, and yet despite all my efforts, he wouldn't discharge me or go *pro se* with me as standby. I had by then adopted a policy that I would never move to withdraw. If there was to be one of these attorney-client breakups, then the client would have to be the one who initiated it. The case is in the later stages of the pretrial folderol, and it has now been sent to a session for some sort of preliminary foolishness. The defendant is pondering whether he is going to go to trial and is now before this judge. Thank goodness it isn't football season or I may have put my foot in it again.

The judge has my client on his feet and is warning him of the seriousness of the charge and asks my client if he realizes he could get life imprisonment if convicted. This was part of a hearing to make sure the defendant knew what he was possibly facing if he went to trial. I worry a little that the client, who had indicated he wanted a trial, is going to waffle because of the possible heavy hit. And I know this—the judge is wrong, and that's because I do those things that I should do, which is to read up on the penalties for the various crimes. Perjury in a capital case can result in a life sentence, but where the perjury in a capital case is committed before the grand jury, as was the case here, rather than at trial, the maximum is twenty years.

I haven't yet learned my lesson that sometimes it pays to be dumb, but if not that, then maybe a little diplomacy should be used. Instead, I stand up and tell the judge he is wrong and explain it. At least I had enough sense to not use the word *wrong*. The unsaid part might have been something like, "How about getting with the program, Judge, and bone up on the law?"

Now this judge, like most judges, thinks he does know the law and, in fact, is reputed, as are many judges, to be a good "law" judge. All judges pride themselves on that, so he's not going to let this Ivy League guy who doesn't know squat about football tell him what the law is. He charges off the bench so fast that the bailiff can only declare the court in recess well after the judge has disappeared into his lobby. He obviously thinks he's right and I am wrong and has gone to his lobby to look up the statute.

We wait awhile, and then the judge comes back out, and nothing is said because, of course, the judge has now acquainted himself as to his error. I was, however, cheered by this: the case went to a different judge for trial. I remembered the four years, eleven months in that other case and was glad we avoided the possibility of nineteen years, eleven months on this one, with a comment such as "I'm glad you reminded me of the twenty-year maximum, Counselor."

The case eventually did go to trial, and the defendant was found guilty. His sentence—two years in the house of correction. Just like all the cases I get involved in, that case had its unusual aspects, which I will not go into except to say what else is new? The defendant was asked if he wanted to appeal. No way. He was happy that the sentence wasn't a lot more, so maybe the judge's warnings had an effect.

# 26

# I Get Blamed

**Those were just silly little** things where I got myself into minor scrapes due to my own poor behavior. Now I was about to get myself into an imbroglio, and I hadn't really done much to accomplish that. I had practiced for a while and been back on the current tour of duty for a number of years. I had so far steered clear of serious trouble and actually done quite well. I had tried many cases and met with considerable success. BOBO had been eerily quiet, and none of my supervisors had me on the carpet. Furthermore, the clientele seemed to be appreciating my efforts. I had not bothered to alter my unorthodox approach, but since I frequently tried cases where I was working for a solo defendant, I had not rubbed shoulders with a "real" lawyer who might have been able to spot my already noted unusual behavior. That was about to change.

A case came up which seemed somewhat routine. However, there was a codefendant who was represented by an attorney on the staff of the feared Committee for Public Counsel Services. I had had little to do with CPCS or its lawyers but knew enough to keep my guard up. Several calls to that lawyer to discuss the case went unanswered.

I thought it might be a good idea if counsel conferred to work on strategy. The lack of response was not unexpected since the prevailing CPCS attitude was that bar advocates were the panhandlers of the legal business and weren't worth bothering with. I did what I was supposed to do in preparation for a trial, including some investigation.

I was my client's second lawyer, the first having been discharged due to my client's dissatisfaction with her efforts. The charges against both defendants were a number of counts of assault and battery and assault and battery by means of a dangerous weapon. Eventually, we are in court, and the case has answered ready for trial. What I was not prepared for was the setup, and this was an omen as to what was to follow. CPCS had apparently been contacted by the British Broadcasting Corporation, the BBC, which was planning to do a program or maybe a series of programs on American justice. CPCS, ever on the lookout for advancement, had sought out a case which they apparently thought to be a sure winner.

The idea was to try the case, of course win, and be glorified on a worldwide TV series. I had not been told about this in advance, so I show up in court with my client and see all the cameras and lights, and now at this last moment, I learn what the setup is. This is going to be a three-ring circus, and my job is to look stupid and let the CPCS lawyer win. Looking stupid is one of those things I do easily, but appearances are deceiving, and it is something that I am not, although Mr. CPCS, who has no idea who I am, assumes that I am just that. I confer with my client, and we both agree we want none of this TV stuff and object. We weren't consulted and therefore feel we shouldn't be part of this. So we complain, and the judge agrees, and the camera people are told not to film us. They, the BBC, will only film the CPCS part of the case.

It is clear that Mr. CPCS thinks he has a winner for the codefendant, although the reason for that thinking has not been explained to me. There is an added factor which is part of the abnormality that permeates everything I do in the criminal courts, and that is our judge is the previously mentioned winked at. This is known only to me and perhaps the judge, who I am hoping has forgotten about the entire episode. What this adds to the mix, I can only guess.

The case is about a stomping that the victim received at the hands of a number of people, the two defendants being the only ones charged. The weapons are shod feet. I watch as members of CPCS scramble to get the best seats in camera range so they can appear on television and be seen by millions.

We start with the preliminaries, and I am watching what is going on. The very first thing is the clothing. I'm fine with how my client appears. He looks natural and relaxed in what he is wearing. Not good for CPCS. A team is dispatched to local stores to buy shirts, ties, and jackets so the defendants look like they stepped out of a catalog. In my opinion, this is a bad idea. We looked like we were trying to sell something to the jury. If they are innocent, the clothes are not the things that are going to win it for us. I go along with this reluctantly. At least, I think, all the price tags were removed, but the defendants looked unnatural, and it was a giveaway that my client, at least, was in custody. The CPCS group had added a second seater whom they wanted to get BBC airtime, so there were five of us at these two enormous tables set side by side across the room.

Meanwhile, the prosecutor was up in front of the clerk's bench at a small table. It looked as if the prosecutor was being overmatched, and the sympathy was going to be with him. It didn't help that our defendants were these two very big guys.

We start the trial, and the issue is identification. It is clear that the codefendant has a different approach, even though the general theory is the same. I had done some investigation and looked at the photo books that the victim had viewed to aid in making his identification. I noted that the photo books had categories of people divided up according to height, weight, hairstyle, etc., and that my client appeared in several of these categories. So I thought there was at least an argument that there was suggestion in the ID process. CPCS had not done any of this. The victim testified first, and what is clear about him is that he is an excellent witness.

The DA in this case is also doing a good job. He is not overplaying his hand but putting forth what he has, which is credible testimony. The victim now has to be cross-examined. I forget who went first, but my rule of thumb is to be very careful with good witnesses. If I am not careful, my questioning can result in hurting my client's case. Not the same with cocounsel. His questions were based on the idea that cross-examination could be a "killer cross"—lots of tricky questions and insinuations.

Cocounsel wanted to home in on the witness's ability to observe, recollect, and relate, so as part of this series of questions, he asks him this: "Do you know how many trees there are on your street?"

To which the witness responds with some venom, "No, do you know how many trees there are on your street?"

I won't say that was the end of the case but close. The detective who conducted the investigation testified, and I tried to introduce the photo book. This is opposed by Mr. CPCS, who feels that it in some way damages his case. The judge won't let the photos in, apparently on the theory that the photo book has changed from the time the victim viewed it. I am now a social outcast. My cocounsel decides

I should argue first, and he will argue second and clean up the mess that I have made. The closings are done. The Commonwealth does a good job. I watch my cocounsel's closing argument and note that he has what in the business is called a "tell," which is body language that communicates when he is blowing smoke, which is often.

The jury is charged and retires to deliberate. The cameras have been rolling for the whole case and now await the coronation. Within twenty minutes of retiring, the jury sends in a question. They wonder if they can see the photo books. The judge sends back the message that the books aren't in evidence, and they have to decide the case based on what they have. At least it showed that my approach was of interest to the jury. At the end of the first day, there is a partial verdict. The jury has decided on one of the codefendants. This is sealed, awaiting the verdict on the other.

The next day, both are convicted on some, but not all, of the charges, but on at least one each of the principal charges. Of course, this was not the plan. And the defeat was certainly not the fault of Mr. CPCS. In the spirit of camaraderie, I am told that I am being investigated by the CPCS high command for grand malfeasance. I was worried enough that I hired a lawyer. Nothing much happened. Wounds were licked, and a lengthy affidavit cataloguing my mistakes was filed. Motions for new trials were filed on behalf of the CPCS client and also my client. CPCS had now taken over my client's case and was also representing him.

This affidavit shot itself in the foot because one of the things complained about was that I had not sought to retain an expert on eyewitness identification. Mr. Affidavit needed to check his own eyesight because he failed to note that my predecessor counsel had prepared a motion for funds to hire such an expert, and it was noted in the docket that motion had been filed, heard, and denied. I was able to ask if I had to raise that and other issues multiple times. Nothing ever came of this. It was just a nuisance. I had to spend hours and hours answering the thing when I could have been preparing my cases.

There was a silver lining to all of this, however. The Boston Bar Advocate contract was expiring, and CPCS was looking for a new organization to take the bar advocate load. I was contacted by an attorney who wanted me to be part of a group that was preparing a bid. I had known her for years and knew her to be an accomplished criminal defense attorney, and I was flattered that she asked. I advised her that in view of the recent flap with CPCS, I thought it better if I not be a part of her group and possibly prejudice her application.

Reluctantly, she agreed, and so I was now free to do what I most wanted to do, which was represent my clients and avoid involvement in administrative matters. I was relieved because I had had enough of those duties when I was earlier with the Massachusetts Defenders. As it was, there was plenty to do in maintaining an office and being sure that my clients received my best efforts. And also to see that I got paid, and that was not always the easiest thing to accomplish.

# 27

## Adventures in Payment

**I've already mentioned the forms** that had to be filled out and the low-tech way in which these initiated the billing process. Screw-ups were endemic, and time had to be spent fixing them. Payments were handled by the computer people at CPCS, and calls about unpaid bills were largely ignored. It took a lot of persistence, but it was usually possible, with a lot of effort, to have errors rectified.

I learned a little about how the system worked and was able to avoid most snafus. In the early days of computerized billing, bills could not be rendered until the case was closed, and this might mean months before a bill could be submitted for payment. Since lawyers weren't getting paid until the case was over, there was the feeling, if anyone cared, that lawyers might be hustling their clients into a disposition faster than was in the clients' best interests in order to expedite payment. Eventually, this was changed, and payment could be had at the end of each month, even if the case was still ongoing.

Billing was laborious and required entry into the computer in time increments of whatever it was—ten minutes—something like that. The case had to be on file in the CPCS computer system for one to be paid, and the only way this could happen was if the notice of assignment of counsel, the NAC, had been transported to the CPCS computer center at its downtown headquarters and the information loaded into the computer. No NAC on file, and the "not on file" notice showed up. One could still enter the data, but one wouldn't be paid until the NAC was entered into the system at the CPCS end by their computer nerds.

I quickly learned who at the clerk's office was responsible for sending the counsel assignment forms over to CPCS and made sure I was on his good side. Other lawyers should give me thanks for my work in assuring that the forms reached CPCS posthaste. Even after the forms had purportedly gone to CPCS, the "not on file" problem might persist. A solution often was to check the court case folder, as, mistakenly, the form that was supposed to go out to CPCS may have been misplaced into the case file. A pleasant "Would you kindly…" worked wonders.

A lot of money was spent on the state's obligation to provide lawyers for indigent defendants. Despite a lot of talk about how this was a worthwhile objective, there were many who thought the whole idea was bogus. No love was lost, of course, in providing funds for lawyers to represent criminals as opposed to giving tax breaks to large corporations being wooed to relocate to the Commonwealth, and various efforts were launched to cut back. One was to tighten up on the standards for what constituted indigency.

The way in which it was determined that a defendant was indigent was to have a probation officer fill out a mandated form, a questionnaire about finances. One would be back in the tank, trying to interview a client who was having a hard day and trouble remembering his own name, only to be elbowed aside by a probation officer who wanted to know if the prospective client owned property or stocks and bonds and maybe had an estate plan. If it turned out that the arrestee was making more than seventy-five cents an hour, then he or she did not qualify for a "free" lawyer. This money-saving ploy was eventually abandoned because then there were too many defendants who didn't have lawyers, and in trying to represent themselves, the system threatened to slow to a crawl. Other plans were launched to cut back on the funding, particularly if the economy had soured and there was a looming budget deficit. The ambition to stamp out the alleged cheating by the lowly bar advocates finally gained traction in the creation of an Audit and Oversight Committee, a wing of the dreaded CPCS.

The CPCS people were paid salaries, so their budget was manageable. The bar advocates were paid by the hour, and so a shooting war began with the oversight committee over whether the various hourly billings were justified. Extra pressure was applied every year because no matter how much was allocated for the Commonwealth's constitutional "free lawyer" obligation, there always was an overrun, and the legislature would be asked for a supplemental appropriation. This was always because not enough money was approved in the first place. In an attempt to control these rogue bar advocates, daily and yearly time limits were imposed and tracked by the Committee. Little notices would show up on the computer warning that limits were approaching or had been surpassed, and pay was being docked—backed out of the system, in the lingo. Bad as this was, there was something even worse: the so-called spot audit.

Here is an example of how that worked. You would submit a bill for a case you had poured your life's blood into. It would be a trial and therefore would have the most billable hours. You would also have grossly underbilled because in the sound and fury of the trial, you would have lost track of how many hours were actually involved. It would also be that sizable bill that needed to be paid immediately in order to meet the pending office rent payment. You would hit the submit button, and up would pop a sign that the bill was being subjected to a spot audit and you needed to justify your hours, which would mean a huge delay in payment.

I was in the habit of keeping my billing records on small scraps of paper. I would send these in, and a month later, I would receive a note that my paper scraps were mostly illegible. I would make them more legible, and then I would get a note that they weren't detailed enough. Stupidly, I fired off that I wasn't writing essays on the six minutes it took me to engineer continuances on some of my cases, and further, I was wondering how the audit people thought there was any time left over after the billing machinations to actually represent clients. This was met, as one can imagine, with scorn.

My reward was having all my bills for the previous five years looked over. Gleefully, they were able to sniff out a few hundred dollars that they took away from me, wrongly, of course. I considered a lawsuit to recover the money and thought I would have a good chance as a small claims action would be heard in the municipal court where I dreamt I would be treated like a favorite son. Fortunately, I quickly realized this was the thinking of a crazy man, even beyond my usual parameters, and let well enough alone.

Later, when billing issues came up, I took a more cautious approach and met with better accommodation. As a result of the savagery with which bills were scrutinized, means of various complexity were devised by some in order to meet the criticism that hours billed were not sufficiently explained. I saw lawyers in court who had specially devised forms with adhesive-backed peel-off strips that they could stick in their files and record their times as they were actually occurring. It would go like this: "Counselor, your case has been called."

"Give me a minute, Judge, I'm busy."

# 28

# The Ongoing Craziness

**In the meantime, the usual** wackiness continued. Every day, it seemed, presented some new event that was out of kilter with the somber ongoing mood of adjudicating the unfortunate defendants guilty and sending them to jail. These moments provided some levity and some relief from the terrors perpetrated by the system. Here are a few of them.

I was often in a particular courtroom—the first session—in the superior court. In this courtroom, as in many others, there was no place to hang coats. The lawyers' enclosure had a rail behind it, followed by rows of seats for the spectators and those waiting for their cases to be called. Many attorneys, myself included, draped their coats over the rail such that the top half of the coats hung into the gallery. On one occasion, after whatever I was doing in court had concluded, I collected my coat and put it on. I noticed that something was missing—the top button. I examined and noted that where the top button should be, there was nothing. There was no tear in the coat, no loose threads, just a small hole where the button should have been attached. I was sure the button had been there when I placed the coat over the rail in the morning.

Someone, I concluded, had spent his morning picking the thread that held the button and then removed both the thread and the button. Who would do something like that? Did someone need a button? Should I take this personally? I was baffled. Subsequent to that, my coat went someplace else, even if I had to put it on the floor.

Another time, I was involved in a trial in one of the district courts. The details of the case have long since been lost to memory. We had reached the point where the closing arguments had been given and had arrived at one of the most important parts of any trial—the charge to the jury. Everyone puts on their best clothes and most serious faces and prepares to pay little attention to what is certainly the most boring part of the trial. By this point, most of the jurors have already made up their minds which side they favor, and they are able to tune out this part of the proceeding. Some judges of lengthy experience can give the charge pretty much extemporaneously, but others, not so sure of themselves, adhere to reading the charge from a book which contains the charge verbiage. The judge in this case was of the latter, a reader of the charge.

The seriousness of this part of the proceedings is reflected by the fact that the court is closed off so that there can be no interruption of the ongoing ennui. The clerk was at his bench directly in front of the judge. To pass away the time, the clerk was playing with a rubber band, snapping it back and forth between his fingers. We were in one of those modern circular courtrooms which had a well of some size in the middle, situated in front of the counsel tables. At some point, midway through the charge, a snap misfires, and the band goes flying into the ozone—like Longfellow's arrow shot in the air—but unlike

Longfellow's, which landed "we know not where," we knew where this one was going to land. And it did, smack in the middle of the well.

The clerk slouches down and turns, expecting some sort of reprimand. But he was saved because, even though everyone else saw this unexpected happening, the judge had his head down and was deep into reading from his charge book. He hadn't noticed. The incongruity of this resulted in the courtroom exploding in silent laughter, silent enough so that the judge never noticed. The entire courtroom, except the judge, was having a hard time keeping it together. I don't remember what happened to the case, but everyone had, for a time, completely lost it.

I can't help remembering this, which speaks to how on their toes some members of the so-called criminal element are. The situation in the district courts was that the defendants were brought in for every court date, no matter how inconsequential, and from wherever they were held. Case on the list for motions? The defendant was to be brought in. Pretrial conference? The defendant had to be there. Nothing going to happen? The defendant was transported anyway. Prisoners held in the jail or the house of correction would be in court without fail by around eight in the morning.

I would arrive at court at eight-thirty or eight-forty-five, and I would be advised by one of the bailiffs that my client was in the lockup waiting to speak with me. For years, this went on like clockwork. Snowstorms, monsoons, heatwaves, traffic tie-ups—nothing defeated prisoner transportation. Then, one day, transportation didn't show up. Nine o'clock came along, and no prisoners. The court was at a standstill. Judges who hop on the bench at nine precisely so they can start issuing default warrants against late arrivals were losing their tempers.

Finally, around ten o'clock, the sheriff's vans arrived, and the prisoners were brought upstairs, and the courts could begin their daily business of handing out the day's misery. So what had happened? Apparently, on the way out of the parking lot, the van with the prisoners held at the county lockup had just lightly bumped another vehicle, nothing but the most minor of fender benders, and so lightly that it was a fender bender where no fender was bent. It was nothing more than a little jolt. But what was heard from the prisoners in the back of the transportation van was, "Oh my neck, oh my back, oh my knee." They had to be taken back to the facility and checked out by the medical staff, else there would have been a deluge of lawsuits. Just because those guys were in jail didn't mean they were stupid. Quite the contrary, always looking for a slight advantage.

I'm in the municipal court, and it's a slow day. People are sitting on benches trying to stay awake. Some are in the back, sitting as close to girlfriends as propriety permits or maybe even closer. Defendants are waiting for cases to be called. All cases are called by the clerk in a loud voice, which is good for those who are hearing impaired. Several cases have been called and moved along, and the clerk now picks up a file and calls out the name of the next defendant: "Prince Charles." There is a slight buzz in the courtroom as various reveries are interrupted with the thought of, *No!* With this, a lanky young man comes to the front and stands in the box where the defendants stand. This was definitely not *that* Prince Charles. I insisted on being assigned this case. I did my paperwork to perfect my appointment and obtained contact information as my new client had been released on his own recognizance. He was charged with tagging, an offense wherein those attempts to beautify the city were unappreciated by the city fathers. A while later, I called the phone number I had been given, and this very pleasant woman answered. I asked to speak to Prince Charles, and she answers with this: "Which one?"

I was used to unusual requests from clients, and this one occurred back in the dark ages, a few years after I had begun with the Defenders. I was in one of the district courts and had been assigned to represent a man who was in custody on some long-forgotten charge. I went into the lockup to speak with him about his upcoming hearing. In those early days, the lawyers were allowed into the holding areas to speak with clients, a policy which has now changed. He was an unkempt man with a serious mien who spoke in a low voice as if the two of us were involved in some grand conspiracy. While speaking with him, he asked me if I would do something for him, and I, always glad to assist, offered to be of help.

At this point, he pulled out of his court papers a moth-eaten sealed stamped envelope and asked me if I would be kind enough to mail it for him. Not a problem, I assured him. I noted joyfully that the letter was addressed to one Alexei Kosygin, with the address being the Russian Embassy in Washington, DC. I knew that Kosygin was, at that time, the Chairman of the Russian Supreme Soviet, and I was naturally perplexed as to why my client would be sending a letter to him. But, of course, I complied and dropped the letter into the nearest mailbox, duty-bound to follow my client's wishes. Whether this had any impact on world affairs or the fall of the Berlin Wall will, of course, never be known.

This is just a small sampling of episodes that contributed to the general loopiness that surrounded the operation of the Massachusetts criminal courts, usually on a daily basis. Exposure to this kind of activity took some getting used to. For my part, I adapted rather quickly and, as I have already described, was in short order able to contribute my own brand to the ongoing silliness.

# 29

## The Juries Work Wonders

**In among the ongoing frivolity,** there were cases to be tried, and I was trying a lot of them. These are all cases which demonstrate the power of the jury to do things for clients, even though the evidence against them is strong. This is not to point out that I am some kind of trial genius, but to show that just doing my job, which was to present my clients' cases as best I could, would, on many occasions, produce results. I had learned that my client's version of the case was my brief and that I was duty-bound to present it on his or her behalf.

It continued to amaze me that what often appeared to be utter nonsense, when presented in my thoughtful and sincere way, resulted in an acquittal. I was, of course, bolstered by my highly developed skill, which was that I could try anything, and in many cases, that meant trying nothing. In addition to presenting many non-defenses as ironclad reasons to acquit, I was also perfecting techniques which I hoped would one day earn me a position in the top echelon of public defenders. I hadn't achieved that yet, but I was drawing ever so much closer.

Here is an example. This was not a case that would make the front page, but in terms of its importance to the client, it was right up there with famous cases. My client was charged with larceny. He was caught leaving an MBTA commuter train carrying the trainman's bag, which contained the receipts from collected tickets. The train had pulled into the station, and while the conductor was busy, my client had allegedly stolen his bag and was making his getaway along the station platform. He was arrested along with his girlfriend, who was with him. They both were charged with larceny. My client claimed he had seen the bag and picked it up and was planning to bring it back to the trainman in order to protect it from thieves like himself.

To make sure that there was no interruption in this plan, he had apparently covered the bag with a folded newspaper. All attempts to end the case short of trial were unsuccessful. He wasn't going to plead guilty. The trial began, along with his girlfriend as his codefendant. We had the same judge as in the "dangerous" case, all set to lower the hammer. My client testified to his story, and after both parties rested, the case was submitted for the jury's consideration. I proceeded to give what I thought was one of my lamer summations and then sat and waited for my client's blood to be spilled.

Shortly, the jury comes back, and the verdict is not guilty, to the disbelief of the judge and the prosecutor, although my client, living in his own special world, was sure this would be the result. I had long since learned that unexpected results in cases I handled were the norm, but even I was surprised by this one. We are happy with the acquittal, but there is a certain amount of puzzlement. Could the story that our hero had protected property from mischief, rather than mischief being in the making, have been bought by the jury?

This can only be speculation, but this circumstance might have contributed to the result.

At the close of the government's case, the judge had ordered, on motion of the codefendant's lawyer, a judgment of acquittal against the codefendant, a woman, and made something of a display of this. This left my client to take all the weight. An examination of the venire provided a possible answer, I suspect. In a by-chance rarity, the entire six-person panel was male. My guess? Possibly they thought she was just as involved as he was, and if she was going to be let go, then he was too. Another fine example of the jury at work. My delight was that in some way, I contributed to this happy, for my client, result. This was the type of case I would gladly try, even though no one else would go near it. No matter that, in my mind's eye, I was the recipient of the Mason scowl that this was not what was meant by defending the unjustly accused.

Now, if that case was bad in the sense that I had no business winning it, it does not compare with this one. I don't know whether this was a sweeter win than others, but maybe this case should be followed by a slight feeling of guilt. But only slight. This case involved a cashier at a parking lot—a big parking lot run by the transit authority, the T. The defendant was charged with larceny. This lot had several exits, and one was on the top floor away from the main office and therefore not under surveillance by the garage management. This top floor exit was the one manned by my client. Allegedly, he had a scheme whereby he would disable the car counter at his gate for some of the cars, collect those garage fees, then discard the tickets pertaining to those cars and keep the proceeds. He would report a reduced car number on his worksheet and turn in a ticket count that matched the altered car number.

I interviewed the defendant, and he was adamant that the garage counter system was foolproof and he couldn't possibly have defeated it, and he was innocent. My investigator located an expert in garage technology. We explained what my client had said, and asked him to investigate. We went to the garage and showed him the gate. "Couldn't possibly be defeated, could it?"

"Sure it can," he says and shows us that, despite the defendant's claim, there was a switch on the gate's housing, which when thrown, deactivated the gate's counter. So sayonara to Mr. Expert. Unfortunately for my client, there was a master counter in the garage headquarters that could not be gamed, and it was this that led to the investigation. After one of his days on duty at the upper level, my client's car was searched, and excess tickets were found hidden under a seat, as well as additional cash on his person which gibed with those tickets. Adding to the case against the defendant was that one of the managers had hidden himself in a parked car near the gate and videotaped my client coming out of the booth and doing something in the area of the cutout switch. Still, in the face of all this, the defendant maintained he was innocent, and I took careful note of his complicated story. It must have made a big impact because I don't remember it.

Now we are in the trial session, and we have a judge who is a hitter, in the vernacular. We empanel a jury, and this is where if there is any explanation of how this case came out, it is here. We had run out of challenges, and there was still one empty seat to be filled. A practicing lawyer is called to fill the last seat. Generally speaking, I have an aversion to lawyers on my juries and challenge them. I have no particular reason for it; it's just something I do. But since we were out of challenges and the government had no objection, this person was seated. The case then proceeded to trial.

The defendant testified. No memory survives as to what that was about. The case is argued; the jury is charged, retires, and after a wait, returns. The judge is sharpening her axe, but too bad for her because the verdict is not guilty. So how could this have happened? It is no more than speculation, but I somehow have a hunch the lawyer did it for us. Lawyers like loopholes, and my bet is he found one for us. There's also this: the T is not a terribly popular organization, and this may have helped. So another stunning victory and a happy client. Whatever I was doing, and I don't know what that was, was working. I was trying cases nobody else would think of trying—and winning.

In another case, the defendant was charged with multiple larcenies that occurred at a local hospital. He had been a floor worker, a member of the cleaning staff in this hospital, and there had been thefts from patients' belongings. Two of the cases had been dismissed because, in one, the victim was from another country to which she had returned, and the second could not be located. That left this one case as to which the defendant denied his guilt, and so the case would have to be tried. My client was a likable man that I got along well with. No settlement could be reached, and so a jury is empaneled, and the case starts.

A victim testifies that she is missing some property and puts my client near her room. A second witness claims he saw my client with his hand in the victim's property bag and there is some follow-up that since my client was a floor sweeper, there was no reason to be going into the patient's property. This case looked strong for the government. After charging the jury, the judge left the bench. Seconds after he left, there was a knock on the jury's door. They had a verdict.

The judge, upon leaving the bench in that courthouse, walked down a corridor and boarded an elevator which took him to his chambers on the sixteenth floor. The courtroom is on the second floor. As he stepped off the elevator on sixteen, he was met by a bailiff who informed him the jury already had a verdict and he needed to return to the courtroom. The verdict was announced and it was not guilty. I am sure that this case represents the all-time record for fastest acquittal, something of which I am most proud. My disgruntled prosecutor, the lead prosecutor for the municipal court, threw up his hands in disgust and swore he wouldn't try any more cases against me. And he didn't. He quit and became a defense lawyer—and not a bad one at that.

My client, of course, was relieved and happy with the result. It is usual to never see clients again after the fact, although occasionally it happens, as it did in this case. About a month later, I'm walking down Congress Street, a main thoroughfare near the courthouse, and I hear a gleeful, "Mr. Wood, Mr. Wood."

I turn and spot this former client. He is driving one of those vans with the sliding door and he is leaning out and waving. He was laughing so hard I was afraid he might jump the curb and take out a few parking meters. A happy client. A not guilty verdict is something shared and not forgotten.

And there is no forgetting this one—a case involving a failure to register with the sex board. An entire apparatus had grown up to protect the citizens of the Commonwealth from the sex predators roaming the streets and threatening the well-being of the citizenry. The chief, but not the only means of keeping track of these myriad offenders, was the imposition of an obligation to register with the local police department. Tabs could be kept on them lest they even thought about becoming sexually offensive. This disgusting apparatus made life unlivable for anyone caught up in the machinations of the process. This type of case, failure to register as a sex offender, became endemic and threatened to displace the drug cases as the most popular means of incarcerating defendants. Lengthy house of correction sentences were possible, and multiple offenses called for even stiffer penalties. The defendant either did or did not register with the sex board, so these cases were simple cases and usually were pleas. There were numerous ways one could be guilty of the crime of "failure to register." In addition to just the registration itself, one might be guilty by giving false information, failing to give notice of a change of address, or failing to verify registration information.

In this case, the defendant was charged with just the initial failure to register. At his trial, he was found not guilty, and I have no idea how I managed to win that one. I recall that the defendant was nervous and so certain he was going to be found guilty that, when the verdict was delivered, he had to ask me what had happened after the actual event. I was pleased to give him the result. I remember distinctly some of the testimony from that case. The defendant had been released from prison after serving a sentence for something involving a mega sexual offense. He had been sentenced to the state prison with a period of probation to follow. Upon his release, he had reported to his probation officer as required. The probation officer advised him of his obligation to register with the sex board as a convicted sex offender. In addition to just advising him of this, the officer provided a registration form, read it to him, filled it out, and had him sign it.

Even better, the probation officer put it in an envelope addressed to the sex board, put a stamp on it, and told my client he needed to mail it. There was a post office on the first floor of the building housing the probation office, and the PO secretly shadowed my client to make sure he actually mailed it. He did mail it, and that fact was observed and testified to by the officer. Regrettably, the receptacle into which my client tossed the envelope was labeled "Trash" rather than "US Mail."

I should note that the defense in the case was not that my client did not know how to read, although it could have been. For my own part, my client's cavalier attitude toward the sex board registration rigmarole earned him a high place on my personal list of favorite clients, I am ashamed to confess.

# 30

## Those Impossible Cases

**But what about some of** these other cases where there could be no optimism? Cases that can be described as "dead and buried" or from the government's point of view as "shooting fish in a barrel." These would be the open-and-shut drug cases where the undercover officers make buys from the unsuspecting dealers. No amount of fancy footwork could possibly help the unfortunate defendants, one might guess. These drug cases gave the government a good chance to fill up the prisons and keep the prison personnel employed, as well as the police drug details. In the big cities, and to a lesser extent in the towns, these drug cases took a familiar form. Trained undercover operatives would be dispatched to buy from putative drug dealers. The deals would be made, and the unfortunate drug dealer, thinking he or she had just made some money, would find himself or herself arrested, either on the spot or later as part of a wider drug sweep. The latter was usually the operation in the towns, and the on-the-spot arrest would be in the cities where, in cop speak, it would be called a "buy-bust operation."

The drugs purchased by the UCs (undercovers) would be analyzed and held as evidence. These cases always involved the same format: I came, I saw, I bought, and I arrested. Essentially, there was no defense to these cases, except that as it turned out, there was, and for enterprising lawyers, there were opportunities.

Here is a case that shows how the jury can work favorably in one of those open-and-shut cases. My client was charged with distribution of a Class B controlled substance—crack cocaine. He had a codefendant, a woman who was charged as a second offender and was facing a five-year mandatory minimum. The amount of drugs was infinitesimally small. She had a few kids, a family, and not wanting to face this draconian penalty, had skipped town. As if she could be blamed. My client did not have a prior drug offense so was not facing a mandatory sentence.

The story was that he and the woman were standing in a doorway on a side street in the South End of Boston when they were approached by a man who wanted to buy a forty. This meant drugs of a certain size. As everyone knows, this stuff is not packaged and labeled like food in the supermarket. The woman says sure and hands over a piece to the man who is an undercover cop. He looks it over and says, "This is not a forty. It's too small."

The woman then supposedly asks my client if he has any, and he produces some, hands it to the woman, who then hands it to the UC, who is now satisfied that he has a forty. He pays over $40 and takes off. The signal is given to the waiting "buy-bust" squad, and both are arrested and charged. The $40 are made up of two previously marked twenty-dollar bills, each one of which is found on either defendant.

My client tells me that never happened. He was there, but the deal was exclusively with the woman. He never gave her anything. The reason he had one of the marked bills was because she owed him $20, and she paid off the debt after the transaction was done. Not a great story, but it had some ingenuity to it, and it certainly could have been true. And since the codefendant woman is on the lam, she is not there to contradict it or possibly support it. So the case is going to trial.

Now there are a number of things in this case that are a help. The first is that when the UC approached the woman seller, she asked, "Are you a cop?" to which he answered he wasn't, which, of course, he was. In these types of cases, the government brings in a pseudo-expert on drug dealing who explains how drugs are packaged and sold. They qualify the expert by asking how many drug transactions the putative expert has been involved in, and it's always in the hundreds, all of them in downtown Boston. The jury gets the idea that there are drug dealers behind every lamppost. The purpose of this testimony is not to acquaint the jury with the obvious manner in which drugs are sold but to give a false impression of the size of the problem. And this is all sanctioned by the appellate courts as part of their opinion that the general public is brainless and needs the testimony.

I usually attempt to exclude this testimony, but this time I don't because I want to be sure I'm able to cross-examine the expert. And I do. And yes, lying is part of a cop's job when it comes to waging war against the drug trade, but not otherwise, of course. And I have him explain about the UCs and how they go to acting school, how they dress, how they throw alcohol on themselves, and all the things they do in order to convince would-be sellers that they are not cops but real, honest-to-goodness druggies. I'm thinking that maybe I'm scoring some points here. The balance of the government's case is put in.

Now it is the defendant's turn, and he is agreeable to testify, and he does, and I thought rather well. I also know my client, and I know that he has an electric smile that will light up a room. I want him to smile at some point in his testimony. He has told me that after he received the twenty from his codefendant, he went to the corner sandwich shop to buy a sandwich he favored, called a "steak bomb." I also knew he smiled every time he mentioned the bomb. Finally, he does mention it as part of his testimony and produces his signature smile, and it does light up the room, and, I'm hoping, also the jury. At length, his testimony is concluded, and the case is submitted.

The jury went out and stayed out for an inordinate amount of time. To shorten the story, ultimately, a mistrial was declared—a hung jury. The jury refused to convict, one suspects, because of the unsavory tactics of the government and maybe the smile of my client. On the date for the retrial, the government, unsure of its prospects, offers the defendant a plea deal, time served, as he has a few jail credits from when he was first arrested. The defendant walked out of the court a free man. A nice outcome. This shows that these open-and-shut cases are not that at all. The jury did at least refuse to convict the defendant, even if it did not deliver a not-guilty verdict.

If that case was an example of how juries looked askance at these types of cases, it has to take a back seat to this one. This client was charged with distribution of a controlled substance, crack cocaine. I have mentioned that these cases are ordinarily of the "shooting fish in a barrel" variety, and this case was of the smallest barrel type. According to the testimony, an undercover police officer bought drugs from the defendant. The defendant removed the drugs from his mouth, where he was keeping his inventory in tiny plastic bags. As in the previous case, the government produced an expert who testifies to the ins and outs of the drug trade. That expert had been to DEA school, FBI school, and local cop drug school and participated in hundreds of arrests.

The object of this testimony was again to try to paint a picture of how bad the drug epidemic is. Civilized society and the world, in general, are being ruined. Downtown Boston was awash with this furtive drug trade, and this was, shamefully, interfering with important local businesses such as the pickpocket and prostitution trades.

Despite attempts to have testimony of this type excluded, appellate courts have uniformly decided that this "expert" testimony is to be allowed on the theory that the jurors, deemed incapable of understanding on their own, would never be able to grasp that drug dealers hid the drugs in their mouths so they could be swallowed if an arrest was imminent. This opened up opportunities. As in the previous case, I was able to cross-examine these experts on the expertise with which they prepared themselves to pose as druggies so as to facilitate the deal. In addition to the usual, they knew that drug dealers generally favored Newport cigarettes, and so that was what they carried to put their buys into. This sneaky behavior did not amount to "legal" entrapment, but it was unsavory, and I suspected the jurors would not like it.

Whatever I argued in this case escapes my memory, although this must have been part of one of my finer "I could try anything" performances. The jury retired to deliberate. A while later, the parties were summoned to the courtroom as we were told the jury had a question. Upon entering the courtroom, we saw the judge over by the entrance to his lobby. He was holding the paper on which the jury question had been written, and he was laughing. We were shown the jury question, and it was this: Had the plastic bag, which allegedly was taken from the defendant's mouth, been tested for the defendant's DNA?

It is often possible to get a read on the jury's deliberations from their questions. This jury was having a problem with the credibility of the police. The question was answered in the negative, and the jury resumed its deliberations. The result eventually was a mistrial, a hung jury. On strong evidence, the jury refused to convict. The evidence of the machinations of the UC to convince my client to make the sale were part of the evidence. I reemphasize, trying cases, especially the "unwinnable" ones, is of the essence if one expects to be able to fully represent one's client.

A nice part of the result was that the DA on the case was making his swan song before going on to bigger and better things. Was I sorry to have squashed his expectation that his final case would be a resounding victory? Of course not. The result was a boon for the defendant, who later was able to plead his case out on favorable terms. Even better was the recollection that this was the second "swan song" case that I had ruined, something which I am embarrassed to say pleases me even more.

# 31

## You Can't Win Them All

**Among the parade of wins** on unwinnable cases, there were those that more nearly represented the norm—cases of such difficulty that there could be no expectation of a win. I was certainly losing my share of these, despite my many winning efforts. This case was one of those hard-to-win cases, but I am particularly fond of it for reasons I don't fully comprehend.

This was an armed robbery case. The defendant was alleged to have relieved the victim of her gold earrings at gunpoint just outside a T station. The police showed up after the event and checked out various T stops and located the defendant, who matched the description given by the victim. A search produced a handgun and the earrings. He was arrested and charged. He claimed he wasn't the perpetrator and had an alibi. He was home with his brother and was helping him out of his apartment at the time the robbery took place. The brother needed the help because he was a paraplegic as a result of having been a victim of a shooting. The case went to trial, and it went like this: the victim testified that those were her earrings and that was the gun that was shoved into her face, and that's the so-and-so who did it, and she would never forget him. Some not-so-nice testimony was that her attacker had not been so gentle in removing the earrings but instead had ripped them off. At the conclusion of this ultra-believable testimony, the prosecutor announced with a smirk, "Your witness, Counselor," and the judge, with a benign smile, as I remain glued to my chair wondering what I am going to ask, said, "Mr. Wood?"

*Yes, Your Honor, I still remember my name.* Cross-examination starts off with something like, "It was a dark and stormy night, wasn't it?" as a prelude to suggesting an identification of the assailant would have been difficult. This is before the government's rebuttal, in which it establishes that mercury arc lamps had previously been installed, making the area as brightly lit as the surface of the sun.

After my lame cross-examination and the government resting its case, it is the defendant's turn to present a case. I put the brother on the stand. He does okay and is clearly sympathetic. The jury is also sympathetic and convicts the defendant of unarmed robbery instead of armed robbery. So this was another case where the defendant wanted his trial, and I made sure he had one. These are important cases. Respect the wish to go to trial and be able to try the thing. No matter how bad the evidence, sometimes good things will happen. No acquittal here, but a conviction on a less severe charge and a reasonable sentence.

No matter how important it is to be able to try cases, and especially important to try the bad cases, there are some lawyers who just won't. This brings into play an important skill, which is how to get fired. The easiest way is to make it clear to the client that you are not going to try the case. That will certainly result in your getting fired. And that's what happened to the court-appointed lawyer in this case. The case was particularly bad on its face because it was a sexual assault on an underage female, a type of offense not particularly popular with even the most forgiving of jurors. These cases usually present as he-said, she-said contests and are thus triable since there is a chance that the defense side will be believed.

Unfortunately for this client, the aunt of the underage arose at night to use the facilities and observed the incident, so the case became a lot harder—a he-said, they-said type of case. In addition, after the police had obtained a warrant for the arrest of the defendant and went to his house looking for him, they couldn't find him until they noticed some movement in the pile of laundry in the bathtub. This was where my client had been hiding in order to avoid being arrested. So consciousness of guilt was added to the mix.

The attorney originally assigned took one look at the case and decided it was time to jump ship. There are many ways to engineer a dismissal, but there is one surefire way, and that is to tell the client that he or she has no chance. Every con knows there is always a chance, and even some clients just want the trial no matter what—they are constitutionally unable to plead to any charge. What the assigned lawyer did was to write a well-drafted letter of a page and a half on heavy, lawyer-type stationery, summing up the "damning" evidence in the best legalese, informing the client that there was no chance to win the case and the only thing left to do is to plead. Not said but understood is that the lawyer is not going to make the effort to try the case. She was fired almost before the letter was read in its entirety, and ultimately, I was appointed. My new client made it clear he wanted his case tried, and I made it clear I was going to do just that.

I prepared the case for trial. There was one hiccup. On the day the trial was to start: I was so agitated I had a minor auto accident on the way to the courthouse. After the resultant delay of a day or so, the case began. The evidence against the defendant was strong. The "they against he" testified, and the police glowingly told of my client hiding under his laundry. Since none of my cases ever have anything like legal symmetry, there is always something unusual, always. In these sexual assault cases, the victim has to testify about where the male has placed his member and thus has to describe the male appendage so as to fulfill the physicality of the sexual assault. In many of these cases, as here, the victim is youngish and resorts to some unusual descriptive language.

Words like *pee-pee* or *wee-wee* are those frequently employed. In what must have been a first in the annals of recorded legal history, the male appendage was described in this case as a "giraffe." What the jury made of this, I'm not totally sure. What you, the reader, make of this is up to you. I did my best for my client, but my best didn't take very long, and it only took a little more than a day to try the case.

My client seemed happy with my efforts, so that was a good thing. What was not expected was that the jury was out for the end of the first day of deliberations and then the entire next day. Finally, on the morning of the third day, the jury announced it was deadlocked. Well, you can't win them all, and the judge, an experienced jurist, pulled a fast one. But there was nothing I could do about it. She sent the jury back to deliberate one more time but, by the tone of her voice, made it clear to them that they would likely sit up in the jury room until hell froze over if they couldn't reach a conclusion. She suspected that there was a holdout or two. Soon the defendant was convicted, and he and his "giraffe" received a state's prison sentence—although something he could manage. I don't remember any particular moves I made in this case, but still, keeping the jury out for this length of time shows that I must have done something to impress, and the defendant didn't have to plead. Another well-served client had his trial and came close, at least, to a hung jury and possibly a better outcome.

Sometime later, on one of the many days I was in the Suffolk Superior Court, I stepped onto a crowded elevator, and the judge from this case was a passenger. Elevators and sidebars are where much of the loopiness in this courthouse seems to occur. The judge kindly asked me if I was still doing public defense, and I answered that I was. She seemed gratified and told me admiringly that what I was doing was "God's work." So that's her opinion, anyway. Laudatory though it may be, I'm sure there are many who would disagree; and I might be one of them.

# 32

# Day Care Adventure

**A woman came to my** office and presented me with a rarity—a representation where I was actually going to be paid—a private retainer. I hadn't any idea where she got my name. I questioned her about it, but she never revealed her source. Referrals come from unexpected places, and here is one that I cherish.

I had a prospective client come to see me about a matter. He had my business card, and I was curious as to where he got it. He told me he had found it on the floor of the jail down on Nashua Street, where it had apparently been tossed by another well-served client. Good to know that satisfied clients were passing my name along. As to this new paying client, I charged her my usual rock-bottom fee and was engaged.

The charges against this client were assault and battery by means of a dangerous weapon and assault and battery. The story was that she was running a child care center and that she had struck one of her charges, a two-year-old, with a bat. The case was pending in a local district court. An interview with the defendant shed a little light on the case, and at this point, I don't want to spoil the story except to say this was going to be a difficult case, not a "fun" case, if there is such a thing. We went to court, and I was prepared for whatever, which is usually what occurs in any criminal matter in any criminal court. The case was called, and per usual, the judge wanted to know if the case could be disposed of without a trial, in other words, with the judge avoiding *work*, which is, of course, understandable.

Another factor in this case was that it was clear the defendant was actually guilty, but since the crime wasn't terribly serious and the defendant had no previous record, it seemed that a suggestion from the judge to impose a light disposition would be acceptable. Furthermore, the government had said it was not going to pursue the assault and battery dangerous weapon charge, and that matter was dismissed at the very beginning. This left only the charge of assault and battery. I was brought up to the bench with the prosecutor. The judge heard us out and offered to continue the case without the entry of a finding of guilt, the case to be dismissed after a number of months. I communicated this to the defendant.

She surprised me by saying she would have none of it. The sticking point was she would have to admit the offense, which she would not do. I had to be careful how I advised her because, after a trial, she could be found guilty, and she'd have a record of conviction and, although it seemed unlikely, possibly go to jail.

It is important to note the facts of the case—the "true" facts as the redundancy has it. Not only had my client committed the offense, but she had sent a note home with the victim, a two-year-old, stating that she had done it. In other words, she had freely and voluntarily admitted to the assault. More than that, it almost seemed that she was proud that she had done it. She had also admitted the assault in several separate interviews she had with investigating authorities who were considering whether she should continue to be licensed to run a day care. This obviously made this case the kind of case I was familiar with—the case with no defense—and I was puzzled as to how I might conjure up some magic to assist my client.

The court went about some other business. The case was called again. We weren't going to plead out, even though it was suicidal not to. A jury of six was selected. The judge brought me up again. "Can't we get rid of this case?" I knew the judge from his former incarnation as a prosecutor. I'd had cases with him and knew him as somebody you could work with, as opposed to some of the others who were impossible. The judge sweetened his original offer. He would waive all the court fees and allow my client to not report to a probation officer during the time the case remained open, which would be ninety days, case to be dismissed at the end of that time. This would be an extremely lenient disposition.

Again, my client demurred, and I am unable to give the "are you crazy" speech in which I start screaming at my client that she is going to go to jail if she persists. I hate to admit that this was in large part because ever since the "Mr. Dangerous" case, I had a feeling I could win almost anything. The case then proceeded to trial, and some testimony was taken. Since we had a late start, the case was continued to the following day.

The next day, the case resumed. The previous afternoon, I had asked my client to bring in the weapon, the bat used to "allegedly" smack the child. I did this because I knew the bat in question was a plastic bat, not a Louisville Slugger type, and probably not very imposing. I recall standing in the parking lot while my client opened the trunk of her car to reveal an enormous plastic bat, the type a circus clown would have, and I also remember slamming the trunk shut very quickly on the off chance that a passing juror might see it. It is always amazing to me how fast one can move if the occasion calls for it. So it was hasta la vista to the bat, and there it lay while the case continued. In court, the exasperated judge made one more attempt at ending the matter, which didn't work. I remember little of what the evidence was or how the case was presented except that it came out that the victim child was a terror. He hit the other kids, threw toys, threw his food, and was defiant about quiet time.

My frustrated client finally took the bat in question and gave the kid a tap and admonished him: she just wanted him to know what it felt like when he hit the other kids. Of course, this was guilt, and there was the note and the interviews as part of the mix. Also, as part of the government's case, the conniving mother had produced a photo of a scratch on the kid's bum. This was bogus, of course, because obviously a bat does not make a scratch. The trial continued, and at length, the case was submitted to the jury, and in fairly short order, the jury came back and astonished everyone with a not-guilty verdict—except for my client, of course, and also me, the lawyer who was used to trying cases with long odds.

Just like most of my other cases, there had to be some bizarre element that took the case out of the ordinary. To that end, within seconds of the verdict's announcement, there was a loud "Oh, fuck!" coming from somewhere among the assembled onlookers. Now this occurred in the courtroom, and in a courtroom, there is an expectation of some sort of decorum. People spun around, and the judge craned his neck to see who could have said this. But I didn't have to look because I knew who it was. It was the child's mother, who had just seen that civil case that she had dreamed about pursuing go into the toilet. I was, of course, happy, as was my client, and we left the courthouse walking on air, as it always feels like when cases go the right way and against the expectations of an opposite result.

And the question is, is it right that this woman should have been acquitted? She had, after all, smacked the child with the bat. She had admitted it in a note to the parent and admitted it to the investigators from the license people. She was, in fact, guilty. And the judge understood this, as did I, and yet the case went to trial, and she was found not guilty. And yet who would say that the verdict was wrong? The child wasn't injured, and maybe the child learned a lesson. At the very least, order may have been restored at her day care. But the judge knew that technically, the defendant was guilty, and that's why all those "Let's get rid of this" bench conferences happened.

This is the beauty of the jury, in my opinion. Justice is delivered as the jury sees it and out from under the "everybody is guilty" disease, which infects the judiciary and the prosecution. This is something desperately needed if the defendant population is to receive true justice.

Weeks later, I was back in that same court before that same judge on a different matter. He is looking at me with a puzzled expression as if to ask how I could possibly have won that case. Although my efforts were the greatest part of the acquittal, the judge helped manfully by the charge he gave the jury. He was a practical judge, and his charge to the jury contained the definition, naturally, of assault and battery. He defined that crime and then added that this had to be without justification or excuse.

Plainly, the jury thought that even if the episode was not justified, they were able to excuse her and thus the verdict of acquittal. What the judge meant, but did not elaborate on, was "legal" justification or excuse. Put the word *legal* in front of anything, of course, and one is off to a galaxy far, far away from the world of common sense, which somehow only juries can grasp. In Massachusetts, without going into it in detail, *legal* justification or excuse in assault and battery cases barely exists, and so we were most grateful for the judge's omission and thus his unwitting contribution to our winning effort.

# 33

## I Receive a New Name

**As these cases demonstrate, I** had by now long since become among the most resourceful of lawyers, even though I was not always successful and knew I was battling tough odds every time I tried a case. I had not, however, been recognized publicly as such, even though I was aware that the clientele, which kept an informal box score, had me at the top of the batting order. From that vantage point, I was in good standing. I had expected that this would be a well-kept secret known only to the defendant population, which seemed to be generally happy with my representational efforts. I was yet to be recognized openly and had no particular expectation that it would happen.

Still, it was annoying that, given the results I was getting, I was not publicly acknowledged in some way. At long last, it did happen, although in a small way, and yet it was heartening, to say the least. There were no announcements on the evening news, no Internet virality, no biplanes pulling streamers. It essentially went unnoticed, but it was a special recognition nonetheless. And this is how it came about.

I had been assigned to represent a young man who had three cases in the municipal court—a wonderful man. I had occasion to represent him on future occasions as well. One of these three cases had been dismissed, and one I had tried and he was acquitted. That was a disorderly person case, and that case had special merit. It survives in the folklore of the municipal court as "The Case of the Pink Boot."

The defendant in this last of his three pending matters had been arrested as a result of those stings periodically carried out in the downtown Boston area. Calls would come into the police station about the presence of so many prostitutes that they were becoming a nuisance. Typically, an undercover cop approaches an apparent prostitute who gives her menu of services and a price list and then is arrested and charged with prostitution. My client was offering the services, but unlike the women in the net stockings and the tight dresses, he was a he and was soliciting for I don't know what since I am not hip. He is arrested in his lovely dress and wig. Police reports are made out and later a supervisor heads to court and applies for complaints. By now, my client, appearance to the contrary, has been discovered to be and is listed as a male.

The crime of prostitution or sex for a fee as it is called has been on the books in Massachusetts since before the *Mayflower*. As time went on, as I'm sure everyone knows, the prostitutes cried foul. If the girls were to be punished, how about those lascivious guys? The so-called John law was passed, which made it a crime to offer to pay for sex as well as to offer to sell it. (Stings are also carried out where undercover female cops are deployed to catch the men.)

The clerk in the hustle and bustle of issuing complaints first thing in the morning sees the defendant's sex listed as male and assumes that my client is one offering to pay for sex rather than offering the sex and issues a complaint for that crime instead of a complaint that he "did offer pruriently his bodee for sex against the peace by force and arms" or whatever the silly legal lingo is. This brings into play a feature of the criminal justice system, which is that nobody reads the complaints to see what the actual charges are except for the small cadre of lawyers who are looking for every edge, no matter how small. If I learned anything at Harvard Law School, and there is a good argument to be had that I didn't, it was that it might be of benefit to check out the complaint. So I did that and saw that my client was charged with offering to pay for sex rather than get paid for sex.

Realizing this, I tell my client that he should go to trial. But I don't tell him why. I also notify the assignment session that the case is a trial, and the case is sent out to a judge. I also tell the session that it will be a jury-waived trial. I have convinced my client who, unlike many clients, trusts me and has agreed to the waiver.

A note about jury-waived trials: under no circumstances should any defendant ever—I mean ever—agree to a jury-waived trial, except under the rarest of circumstances. A jury-waived trial is nothing more than a plea by another name. Some lawyers who don't like to try cases, particularly cases like *Burgundy v. Red* and *Seal v. Dove*, talk their clients into going jury-waived if efforts to get fired don't succeed, so they can quickly conclude the case without going in front of a jury and be done with it. A colloquy precedes the waiver request in which the judge wants to be sure that the defendant knows what he or she is doing before approving the waiver.

A sigh of relief from those lawyers when the defendant's waiver is accepted by the court. One of the exceptions to the non-waiver rule is if the issue is strictly legal, then a jury waiver makes sense. And that being the case here, the defendant filed for a jury waiver.

My client is now before the judge, and a colloquy is held. The judge is satisfied that the defendant knows what he is doing and accepts the waiver, whereupon the non-jury trial commences. We have a new DA who is bucking for advancement, and she starts laying it on thick. She has her cop on the witness stand who has spent a thousand hours at the police school learning how to pose as a sex fiend and has participated in the arrest of hundreds. A description of the defendant, his attire, and his list of services, which I have conveniently forgotten what they were, is testified to. Another witness testifies to various things the defendant has in his possession upon being searched, including a hefty supply of condoms.

In the meantime, I am asking few questions and making it clear I'm not making this much of a contest. The judge has apparently made the assumption that this case is only being tried because I have a defendant who refuses to make sense and plead guilty. He goes into a reverie and waits for the parties to say they rest, and then he can enter the guilty finding and impose a penalty. My client, who is not embarrassed by much, is sinking into his shoes as all this testimony comes in and is thinking I have no idea what I am doing. Eventually, the case wraps up. Both sides rest.

The judge now asks if I want to be heard, thinking I probably don't or at best will have some sort of lame argument that amounts to a concession. I point out to the judge that the evidence shows the defendant is offering the sex and not offering to pay for the sex. He is charged as the sex buyer when the evidence shows he is actually the sex seller, a different complaint. At first, the judge doesn't get it. I ask him to read the complaint, something the DA never did, and it finally dawns on him what is happening. It is also dawning on our valiant opponent, who is having apoplexy.

The judge says, “Oh, so they got the wrong complaint.”

Right-o, Judge. He then looks at the DA and says, “I have to find the defendant not guilty, don’t I?”

To which the DA, choking back her fury, agrees. My client now gets it also, and his cringe disappears, and he lets out with a belly laugh. The joke is definitely not shared by the opposition as the not guilty finding, a happy event, is entered on the record.

A while later, maybe weeks, maybe months, I’m in the security check line at the courthouse. The line stretches out into the street. I am nowhere near the entry point, and I have a long way and a long wait before I’m to be let in. The judge from the above case comes by, sees me, and motions me aside. The judges and other court personnel are exempt from the security screening and have a separate entrance and an elevator that takes them to their respective offices. “Come on,” he says, and I gratefully leave the line and go with him toward his special elevator. He’s going to get me in through the judge’s entrance so I can avoid the silly security check. We proceed in the direction of the elevator.

Arriving, the elevator is crowded, and as he steps aboard, he turns and asks with a laugh if enough room can be made for this “shifty lawyer.” Everybody else laughs. I laugh but I love it. And that’s it. I am crowned, renamed, titled, outed, whatever. I felt as if the queen herself had laid the blade on my shoulder and named me a peer of the realm—Sir Shifty? And I ever shall be the shifty lawyer. And better than the queen, it was the chief justice of the municipal court, a man of wisdom and perspicacity. Who better to know what shifty truly is?

# 34

## Shifty Is as Shifty Does

**Being called shifty and actually** being shifty are, of course, two different things. But as I thought about it, I realized that I was already accomplished at that kind of behavior long before I actually earned the title. Now that I had been publicly anointed, it was important that I work hard to maintain that status. And here is a case where I was able to do just that and burnish my reputation to an even greater degree.

I had been assigned a case in the municipal court that ultimately required the utmost in shifty behavior—footwork that, in the end, even the most accomplished would have had difficulty emulating. My client had been charged with failing to register as a sex offender, second offense. Since it was a second offense, the penalty was substantial. You couldn't have those sex offenders running around unregistered and thumbing their noses at the authorities. Once was bad enough, but twice? I had no idea what the underlying sex offense was, but the charge was that he failed to report timely to the local police department as required, having been designated a sex offender by the sex bureaucracy. Since he was homeless, he was required to register often—something like every forty-five days. I forget the actual time period.

There had already been a trial on that second offense charge, on which he had been represented by someone else. He had been convicted and, after many hearings and motions, his request for a new trial, surprisingly, had been granted. My assignment was to represent him on his new trial. A review of the case showed that there was some technical reason why the new trial had been ordered, and it looked to me that on his new trial, he would be found guilty. It's been a while, so I am not up on the current complexities of the sex offender laws. My recollection is that anyone caught up in the sex offender maelstrom might as well cease to breathe.

My new client was serving a sentence on another matter out at the supermax, about forty miles outside Boston. I went to pay him a visit. Quickly, I discovered this client was what can best be described as a screamer. This is not meant to be a derogatory assessment. He was kind, dignified, and wise beyond his years, but he had a high-pitched voice and complained loudly and nonstop about whatever was currently bothering him. Attempts to have him turn down the volume were futile. First, he was upset he couldn't have a contact visit, and he was off to the races about that. His chief complaint was that he was about to be released from his current sentence but that bail would be imposed on the new trial issue, and he would be held at the supermax, where they had soundproofing. I was able to wedge in an occasional word and returned, by some miracle, still on the case.

Soon, his matter was on for a hearing in the municipal court, and he was brought in from the supermax. His sentence was about to expire, and he was extremely anxious, which meant a concomitant increase in volume. The issue before the court was the matter of setting a trial date and bail. I contacted the chief DA for the court, who I knew to be seasoned and, from time to time, allowed something approaching common sense to enter into her thinking. I persuaded her that if my client ever saw the inside of a courtroom, it would be a mess, and we would all have to wear earplugs. I suggested that the best way to handle this was to ask the judge to file the case without a change of plea. This would dispose of the second offense case, and the possible disaster of a no-win trial would be avoided. It was essential that the presence of the defendant in the courtroom be waived or else there would be a three-ring circus.

Sometimes shifty behavior requires that a few corners be cut. The crucial part, of course, was that I was not going to ask the defendant's permission. I knew he would never agree. One of the few good decisions the appellate courts had made was that in these filed cases, there has to be a limit as to how long cases are available for removal from the files. Placing a time limit meant that cases could not be removed from the files years after the filing and a defendant be prosecuted long after the criminal charges were brought.

The case was called, and I gave some story to the court about how we could do this in the defendant's absence, and shortly, it was done. It took a few minutes because it was clear the judge was of the opinion we were trying to get something by her, which we were. The best part of the result was that the judge ordered, at my suggestion, that the time limit for removal from the files was only the next sixty days. After that, removal from the files was barred.

With some anxiety, I went down to the holding cell to see my client and told him what I had done. I explained in detail what had gone on in court and that soon he would be a free man. And this is what happened. He opened his mouth to speak, and no words came out; and that was because all the things he might want to scream about had just been eliminated. He realized what I had done for him, and his silence spoke of the depth of his appreciation.

There were a few loose ends to tie up. I was receiving calls from the CPCS high command, which had been contacted loudly, along with a few other organizations, by the defendant. CPCS was doing its usual dump job on the overworked bar advocates, so it had to be assured I was handling the matter appropriately. Also, the prison was having a hard time believing his case had been disposed of. I needed to send it certified copies in order to expedite placing the disposition on the defendant's official criminal record so that his release date would be honored.

A few weeks later, I was in Boston and had just finished my early morning breakfast. I had been commuting to Boston at an early hour to avoid as much of the congestion as I could. I was on my way to my office, and the sun was just coming up. I bumped into this client, who had been released from prison just a short time ago. Now that he was out, he had turned down the volume. He had been living at a shelter and had been rousted out early, as was its practice. We spoke for a few minutes, and I knew how much he appreciated the work I had done because he didn't try and hit me up for money, even though I was sure he would. I wished him the best, and we parted—quietly. The moves I made in this case resulted in freeing my client despite the combined efforts of the court, the prison, and the self-defeating moves my client was prepared to make. This was a very special and very rewarding case.

# 35

## A Different Type of Case Altogether

**So it must be abundantly** clear by now that the job of a lowly public defender is to represent the hopelessly guilty and make excuses for all kinds of bad behavior. The beacon that shone like a bright light and led one to begin this thankless career in public defense is all but extinguished, and the Perry Mason dream has been dashed on the rocks of ongoing reality. But I had not been long into that career when a case came along that resurrected the entire Perry thing in all its splendor. I was called upon to represent one of that virtually extinct breed—an unjustly accused person.

I was little prepared for this because this client came along during my stint as the defender in the major violator cases, the cases where the evidence was supposedly overwhelming and the defendants possessed of lengthy criminal records. This was a special case and the rarest of the rare, but as I was to learn, one that occurs every once in a very great while, and it is the case where your client is innocent.

This is a type of case that any lawyer dreads because of the pressure that builds up. This is the type of case where you, the attorney, must win or else there has been that most horrible of consequences, a miscarriage of justice, and no amount of mental gymnastics can cure the remorse that would follow such an event. The first thing that is hard to do is to be able to spot this type of case. Since most clients claim they are innocent and sometimes wishful thinking can lead one to think that a particular client is innocent, it is important to be able to spot the real thing so that in the end you don't look like you've been had.

It would seem that an innocent man or woman would sparkle like a shining star and that these cases would be easy. A mere mention of your client's innocence to the prosecution and the case would be dropped, one would suppose, since the government has an obligation not to prosecute innocent people.

But here is the truth which I learned early in my career, and that is this: nothing whets the appetite of the government to get a conviction more than the suggestion that the person being prosecuted is innocent; and the more obvious the claim of innocence, the greater the government's efforts to secure that conviction.

Here is how I learned this. I had just finished another one of those bruising trials in the "violators" session. The jury had departed after another difficult loss when I was told I had to report to another courtroom. It was a different judge but just as whack-prone as the regular one. Apparently, the major violators had become so popular that an extra session was needed. Reporting, I was told I was to start my next case the following day. I had been busy with other matters and done next to nothing for my client. I protested that I couldn't possibly start that soon and further there were matters that needed looking into. My request to have the case continued was denied, and I was met with the usual "Yeah, sure, it's a major violators case and there will be no defense, so let's move forward."

The judge reluctantly gave me all of one day to make any preparation and investigation I needed. The client in this case had a long record, but it was all for one crime: drunkenness. No violence, no stealing. He was charged with home invasion, a serious charge which carried a twenty-year minimum. A couple maintained that they were at home and someone broke into their house and at knife point attempted to rob them. The putative victims resisted and in the ensuing struggle, the wife received a knife wound. The assailant fled. Some time later, the couple reconnoitered the area, saw the defendant and identified him as the perpetrator. He was arrested and charged.

My client said he had no memory of anything he might have been doing on the day in question. Great but not unusual. Many clients often have some difficulty recalling their whereabouts at virtually any time. But he did say he was often in detoxes, and there was a possibility he might have been in one of those. The office had one investigator whom I sent out to check the area. He came back with the astounding report that on the very night the defendant was alleged to have committed the home invasion, he actually had been in a detox. He had been there so many times he was well known to the staff. The nurse on duty remembered him and could testify to his continued presence from the frequently required bed checks. There was also copious documentary evidence in the form of detox records supporting the nurse's recollection.

*Obvious* is not a word used by lawyers because nothing is obvious in the legal profession. Since, as I have postulated from the beginning, I was only an approximation of a lawyer who somehow slipped through the net designed to keep pretend practitioners such as myself out, I can use that word. Obviously, this defendant was innocent, and a mistake had been made.

The day of the trial, I had the nurse in court along with the detox records, and before the trial was to start, she first had to be interviewed by the government. The purpose of this type of interview, conducted normally by hard-ass investigators, is to convince defense witnesses that they are making a big mistake and that if they testify, they will not be believed and shortly will be indicted for perjury. The nurse stood her ground and held fast to her records and said she was going to testify.

It is written in the Hansel and Gretel part of legal mythology that the prosecution has an obligation not to prosecute innocent persons, especially "obvious" ones such as this defendant. So do you think the Commonwealth dropped the case? Do you think the DA sat with his victims and said, "We have reviewed the evidence and are aware that a mistake has been made"? Not at all. To repeat: nothing stinks in the nostrils of the prosecution so much as a suggestion that a defendant, any defendant, is innocent. Efforts were redoubled to convict the defendant. The case was tried to a jury, and the government had the temerity to argue, among other things, that the detox had made the whole thing up so as to pad its attendance records and obtain more state and federal funding. This was after suggesting that the defendant had somehow escaped the facility, run the four-minute mile, and committed the crime in between the frequent bed checks.

It didn't work, although the jury was out a little longer than I had expected. Finally, after a few hours of deliberation, the jury returned with a not-guilty verdict, something it should have done after about ten minutes. So maybe the government's ploys had some effect. I had been particularly worried about this one juror in the back row who sat with her eyes closed during my summation. Probably saying a prayer in hopes I didn't screw up.

Fortunately, justice, such as it is, was served. But there is a lesson here—an important lesson. I think it might have been Lincoln who said that it was better that ten guilty people go free than that one innocent person be convicted. Think of that. Defendants going to prison and possibly even executed for things they didn't do. Our wonderful legal system is supposed to prevent that. What this case shows is that maxim has been stood on its head. Not to worry if innocent people are convicted as long as we can be sure that not one guilty person is set free—that's the government's slogan. And that means that every defendant is prosecuted with the utmost vigor, even the obviously innocent. Or maybe this, something that I had often heard said—the defendants wouldn't be there unless they were guilty. And what happens when twenty years later it is confirmed that some unfortunate person is innocent as that person has been saying all along and finally after numerous post-conviction court appearances is freed? The government celebrates and has a little party and says, "See, the system works, even if it takes a while!"

Suppose in this case the judge had reviewed the evidence and said, "It is clear the defendant is innocent, and in the interest of justice, I'm dismissing the case."

The government objects, and the judge says, "I don't care. I'm not going to let you have a shot at convicting an innocent man." He dismisses, and the Commonwealth appeals.

Not allowed, rules the Massachusetts Supreme Judicial Court. The opportunity for the government to screw the defendant shall not be abridged. It decides, in essence, that the government controls what is prosecuted and what is not, and the charges are to be reinstated. The Commonwealth has the final say, and the judges have no power over what goes to trial.

This is another facet of a system which is heavily weighted in favor of the government and why the ability to try cases is so important. Think of this: establishing the innocence of clients is solely the responsibility of defense counsel. The judges have no say, and the government prosecutes everybody, even when the evidence, as here, clearly shows innocence. Don't you love it?

Years later, I was at some sort of annual gathering of the public defender troops where awards were to be given out for what was determined to be public defender merit. I knew I needn't worry that any of these honors, such as they were, would fall in my direction. One of the speakers mentioned that he had been talking with another of the guests, a currently sitting justice on one of the Massachusetts courts. The two of them recalled that at one time or another in the distant past, they had each been supervised by me in the short times they had worked at the public defenders. He recounted how he was representing a court-appointed client and that he came to speak to me about the case in my capacity as his supervisor.

During the conversation, he recounted, he had made the observation that the prosecutor seemed to be a reasonable person. "I had become agitated," the speaker said, "and got in his face loudly with the pointed suggestion that this lovely, most reasonable prosecutor was trying to give his client two years in the house of correction."

I had not remembered this event but was glad to see where I was even way back when. For this is the lesson of that case, and that is that the government has only one objective, and that is to convict the defendant—any defendant—in any way possible. If this lesson is forgotten for one moment, I guarantee something, some event will come along which will remind one of that fact. Never forget. That home invasion trial was a standout case which helped me learn that important lesson.

I continued on my merry way, trying cases in my own unorthodox way—unusual way, whatever one wants to call it. Many years passed, and the Perry part of criminal work, which had been resurrected for that one case, had apparently disappeared for good, I thought. Until one day, a man came to my office and wanted to retain me,—actually pay me, and I should have given pause before I took his case. And this was because after talking to him for a few minutes, I knew he was one of those feared clients, an innocent person. It had been what seemed like eons since I had seen this type of client and thought that they had become extinct, and I was unsure I was up to handling this sort of case.

The pressure I had experienced in that long-ago "violators" case was reignited in spades. What happens if the case is lost? Do you resign from the bar? You tell an appellate lawyer that your unfortunate innocent client has been convicted, and he or she says, "Yeah, yeah, we've heard that before," and he or she goes through the motions on the appeal? And only because I am a certified crazy person, and in need of some cash, did I agree to accept the retainer.

This client had a good job—a state government job—and no record of criminal behavior. He had just been married, and he and his wife were looking for an apartment to share, but for the time being, they were living separately. On the night in question, he went over to where she was living, a rooming house. While dating his wife-to-be, my client had come to know her landlady, with whom he had developed a friendship. He and his wife were going out for the evening, and while he waited for her to get ready, he sat and chatted with the landlady. At some point, the son of the landlady appeared and begged my client to give him a lift to a place close by. He had some story about why he needed a ride. Since it would be a while before his wife would be ready, my client reluctantly agreed, told his wife what he was doing, and that he would be back shortly.

He drove to the spot but not before the son produced two friends who climbed into the back seat. At the appointed place, an apartment building a short distance away, the son disappeared, then came back to the car. Just as he was about to enter the car, numerous police officers showed up, and my client, who was dressed in a suit and tie, found himself on the ground, his shirt ripped, and a police-issued firearm pointed at his forehead. A quick search of his car yielded a baggie of drugs which was found in the footwell of the front passenger seat. Drugs were found on the passengers. The seat with the baggie was the seat that had been vacated by the landlady's son. My client had no contraband.

Since the passenger—the landlady's son—had not made it back to the car at the time the police intervened, it seemed improbable that those drugs could have come from him. My client ended up being charged with possession with intent to distribute a class B drug—cocaine. So where did the drugs come from? My client didn't know.

During my interviews with him, I impressed upon him the importance of an explanation for this, but he couldn't provide an answer. He was emphatic they didn't belong to him.

Finally, after a few months of the usual backing and filling, we are in a trial session. The case is ready for trial except that the government is now complaining that I haven't let them know that the wife is going to testify. They object, and there is a hearing. There was no reason to object except for the usual government attempt to obstruct defense efforts to present its case. I tell the judge they can't really think they are hurt by the lack of notice and say she is available to be interviewed. The judge reluctantly okays the wife as a witness and gives the government ample time to interview her.

There are many cases in the session, as is usual, and there is a lot of talking going on about settling cases. The possibility that there might be a trial causes many defendants to think about a resolution, particularly if the judge has a reputation of being a little heavy on the sentencing end. This was a county I didn't often appear in, so I couldn't advise my client one way or another on the sentencing propensities of our judge. For some reason, the DA comes over and offers my client a continued without a finding for six months and dropping the charges down to mere possession—a hell of a deal if he's guilty.

I bring this to my client, as I am obligated to do, and he surprises me by saying that maybe he should think about accepting the DA's offer. My response? "If you take that, you are chickenshit!"

I was upset. This is not on the HLS-approved list of manners in which to counsel one's defendant. Maybe I explained that he would have to admit the charge in order to get that disposition and that might pose a difficulty in view of his professed innocence. And maybe I should also have explained that intemperance frequently gets the better of me. Anyway, he decides he doesn't want to be chickenshit and opts for cannon fodder instead. I tell the judge we are going to trial. This infuriates the government, so naturally, it sets about trying to find a way to see that the defendant is convicted.

A jury is selected, and the case begins. And it goes badly, the whole thing. The Commonwealth produces its policeman who testified to the circumstances of the arrest. The drugs are produced with the analysis which says that they are crack cocaine. The defendant testified, as did his wife. Both told consistent stories about how the defendant happened to drive the seller of the drugs to the sale point. Their testimony was not particularly great but honest and believable, I thought. The case went over to the following day.

Odd what one remembers about a case. The next morning, the prosecutor showed up wearing a tie with tiny Mickey Mice on it. I felt we had an advantage because he was not appreciating the seriousness of the case. The testimony was finished about lunchtime, and instead of a recess, the judge made us argue. He was clearly in the Commonwealth's corner, and I was sure the defendant would be jailed if he was convicted. The jury was charged, and we waited and waited and waited. I was out in the corridor, anxiously contemplating resigning from the bar if my defendant was found guilty. My client was so thoroughly upset with me—he thought for certain he was going to jail—that he wasn't speaking to me.

Finally, the jury came back, and I heaved a sigh of relief when the not-guilty words were spoken. My client burst into tears, I'm guessing from the tension. The judge, who was obviously displeased with the verdict, had to have the last word. In giving his unenthusiastic thanks to the jury, he had to mention the defendant's "excess of emotion," as if he wasn't allowed to show it. My client hurried out of the courthouse and never thanked me. But he didn't have to. His tears told the story, and his record could now be cleared. He could have everything connected with the arrest sealed, and a record search on him would show "no record." An emotional but rewarding day.

This was not a big case as cases go. But serious consequences may have followed if he had been convicted. His state government job would have been in jeopardy, and future job prospects would have been impaired; and what if he had gone to prison? I hate to think. Months later, I was thinking about nothing in particular when it occurred to me that very likely those drugs came from someone in the back seat. I had tried to interview the other people in the car, but their CPCS lawyers wouldn't allow it. They told me that if I summoned them, they would take the fifth, even though their cases had already been disposed of. The reason? They might be indicted for conspiracy and therefore were entitled to plead the fifth if called. This was the usual CPCS dodge because that would never have happened as an actual matter. Their cases had already been disposed of; they were doing time, and no further charges would ever have been brought.

So here's another example of how the system works. The Commonwealth knew that the defendant had nothing to do with this drug deal. Even the other three at the station told the police he had nothing to do with it. The case should never have been prosecuted. Instead, the DA's office sent down one of their top lawyers to see if they could stick it to the defendant. The government always wants a piece of the defendant. Even though they knew they were prosecuting an innocent man, no one can leave the courthouse without getting marked in some way. They hoped that the offer of the deal would do just that. And if I had not been stupid enough to do what I did instead of saying, "That's a great deal, you should take it," it would have worked. It's the courage—or is it pigheadedness?—to try cases that prevailed, and I thank all the years of preparation and all the dead-end cases that I had previously tried. It was a moment to savor, even if my client had no inkling of what a success the case had been.

But maybe he did but couldn't show it in the emotion of the moment. So there it was. The defendant avoided what the government tries so hard to dish out—a screwing. And that's what the defense has to do—push back hard.

I remember a case I had in the Boston Juvenile Court. I was representing a juvenile who was charged with using a motor vehicle without authority—joyriding in the vernacular. He had been walking back from school, and some of his friends stopped by in a car and offered him a lift. He knew the driver, knew he had a license, and had seen him driving cars previously. So he accepted. In fact, the car was stolen, something unknown to him. The car was later stopped by the police, and all four occupants were arrested and charged.

My client is absolutely innocent, as everyone knows. The prosecutor knows it. The codefendants know it. The police know it. My client is a clean kid who has never been arrested for anything. I am retained by the family, for whom I have done some work, and we go to court. I tell the judge I am ready for trial. The judge will not give me a trial, and I continue the case to another date and get the same judge. He will dismiss the case, but I can't get a trial to clear my client's record. Note that dismissed cases cannot be sealed by right as they can in the case of acquittals. I offer to waive the jury for the case, and we will be done in five minutes on a stipulation of facts. The judge won't do it, and the defendant is deprived of a "not delinquent" finding.

As I have mentioned previously, a case cannot be dismissed over the objection of the government. But the defendant? Different story. The court can do what it wants. The court just wants a piece of every defendant. The prosecution can compel a defendant to go to trial, but the reverse? It is this disgusting cynicism that so often prevails and is part and parcel of the tremendous power the government has over the criminal courts.

# 36

## The Government Never Rests

**Here's another example of how** the government never rests in an effort to convict innocent defendants. How this case ever got to the point of being in the government's sights is a little hard to believe. This client was charged with indecent assault and battery. The defendant was someone who worked at a hair salon. The victim, if he can be called that, was a client at that salon. The defendant gave the victim a shampoo and a haircut. In giving the shampoo, the defendant apparently splashed water on himself and on his pants. The shampoo had been given with a certain amount of vigor, resulting in the splashing. After the shampoo, the defendant sees the victim staring at his pants onto which water had been splashed. The defendant looks at his pants, sees the splashed water, and says, "I made a mess."

The victim paid and left the salon. Now absurdity took hold, and a case began to be manufactured in the diseased mind of the homophobic "victim." The defendant was gay and effeminate in aspect. The victim told his girlfriend about the incident at the salon, and then she told her mother, and then the victim's mother was also brought in on the story. The story grew and grew, and outrage developed, and everyone was sure that what had happened was that my client had rubbed his penis against the arm of the victim during the shampoo and then ejaculated into his pants. Really. Note the fact that this salon was a part of a national chain, and it was crowded with customers and employees when this nonsense was alleged to have occurred. A trip to the local police station produced a police report, and this being the legal system where daffiness reigns, a complaint was somehow obtained.

It was then investigated by detectives from the sexual assault unit of the Boston Police. Two detectives descended on this unfortunate and bewildered client, grilled him, and searched the records of the salon to find evidence of the victim's visit. They obtained a saliva swab from the defendant to test for his DNA on the victim's clothes. They gathered clothes from this supposed victim in an effort to determine if they could locate semen stains which, of course, they couldn't. And so was this absurdity going to result in a dismissal or a dropped prosecution? It's the government; it prosecutes everyone, no matter what the evidence.

Instead, they assigned a top prosecutor to the case and proceeded to trial. The victim and girlfriend testified and were cross-examined. The defendant testified, as did the woman who had the chair next to him. In my closing argument, I spent most of the time explaining the definition of the word preposterous as descriptive of the government's case. Thankfully, after a wait, the jury had little trouble with the case, and the defendant was acquitted. This is just another example of how the government tries to convict any defendant, and the more obviously innocent that person is, the more it tries to win.

Another case, an extraordinarily difficult case, caused me no end of anxiety, but fortunately, it all came out as it should have through a lot of work and also some good fortune at the end. I apologize in advance for some impertinence in the recounting of this case. The memory of it still rankles. It was nothing more than a vicious prosecution of a patently innocent defendant. A young man from a foreign country had a job as a security guard in a local town. He heard that a woman from his home country was working at a garage just a few blocks away. He went over after his shift to investigate. He sees her and realizes she is someone he had known slightly from the school he attended. She has a job as the garage cashier. She collects the fees and opens the gate. They have a conversation which, in time, turns acrimonious.

Infuriated, she suddenly dumps her unfinished soda cup onto my client and skulls him with one of those heavy plastic desktop tape dispensers. My client is aghast and leaves. The next day, he is on his way to get together with a friend and decides to swing through the garage to see if this person has calmed down. He just wants to be friends. They are from the same country, and there are not that many of them. The woman sees his car come into the garage on the security camera and immediately assumes that he has come to retaliate for the day before. She becomes hysterical, shuts the booth, and raises the gate and hides. But she peeks enough to see that the defendant is holding a what—a handgun? She calls the police.

The defendant, who does not know that the police have been alerted, leaves in exasperation. As he goes, he crumples up the parking ticket and throws it in disgust against the now-closed ticket booth.

The police arrive and take a statement about a firearm, look around the area, and can't find the defendant. However, they have information from the victim that he works security in a nearby building. They continue their investigation and locate my client at a business a few blocks away where he does work. They arrest him and charge him with stalking, three counts of assault (assault and battery by means of a dangerous weapon, assault by means of a dangerous weapon and simple assault), and threats. A stroke of good fortune was that the booking was videotaped. At his arraignment, he is assigned a CPCS attorney, and he does his job well. The defendant is held for a hearing on the dangerousness bail statute, which allows judges to deem a defendant a danger to the community and hold him without bail for sixty days. The hearing is held, and of course, the defendant is so deemed and sent to jail for sixty days—no bail. This result is part and parcel of what permeates the criminal courts—the presumption of guilt, which is shared by the court, the prosecution, and, unfortunately, his defense counsel.

I had previously successfully represented a man from this country, and he calls me. "Of course I'll take the case, and don't worry about the money." I go to see my new client, who is not held in the local jail but is held in a distant prison where they keep federal detainees and defendants awaiting trial on the most serious state charges. I interview my client, and I quickly realize that he is utterly innocent. I can't do anything about the bail for the sixty days in view of the dangerousness determination, which is not appealable. But I do schedule the case for a bail hearing at the end of the sixty days. In court on that day is his extended family and a representative of his country from its embassy in Washington.

This was a court I didn't appear in very often. Some of the judges I knew and some I didn't. It really didn't make any difference in this case because I would have to deal with whoever came out on the bench. The judge for this hearing was a man I knew from Harvard College. He had been in the class ahead of me, and we were in the same social club. Good news? Not exactly, since we had never been friendly.

At the conclusion of the hearing, the bail is set at $10,000 cash—an exorbitant amount, even considering the charges. On the other hand, considering the bias that exists in favor of the government, the bail was, in some sense, reasonable, and it was at least a bail as opposed to the previous no bail order. Fortunately, the Washington connection had some money, and the bail was posted. There was a joyous moment when he was released from custody. Lots of hugs and smiles. A happy occasion.

The case dragged on, but for sure, it was going to be a trial. I took a different approach from the outset, which was to get in the prosecutor's face and point out, at first gently, that my client was innocent and then a little more pointedly as time went on.

Since I was getting nowhere, I took a step that I don't often like to take but one that seemed necessary under the circumstances. Reluctantly, I went to the clerk's office with the defendant and sought complaints for assault and battery by means of a dangerous weapon (the tape dispenser) and assault and battery (the soda) against the victim. These complaints were granted after a short hearing. The DA's office was now in the position of representing both sides of the case. Ordinarily, this would mean the end of the prosecution of either side. Both sides take the fifth, as they are entitled to do, and there is thus no case against either defendant, and all the cases are dismissed.

I was prepared for what my experience had been, which was the government is insulted by the very thought that anybody can be innocent, and it would do its best to get a conviction. But I thought that at least the government would play by the rules. But it didn't. It cheated.

So here's what the DA's office did. They took another DA from their own office who sat and interviewed my client for a few minutes. Then, without so much as a word to me, that office, the same office, filed a nolle prosequi on the charges my client had obtained. This was a clear conflict of interest. The case should have been referred to another county DA's office for prosecution. My client was deprived of his day in court on the assault by the victim. I thought of referring the matter to the Board of Bar Overseers but concluded it would be a waste of time and it just wasn't my style. Instead, what I did was lose my temper, and for the first time in my career, I cursed the prosecutor in the middle of a lobby conference.

Fortunately, the judge on the case was well acquainted with my unconventional behavior, and I was able to get away with it.

Preparation for the case took forever. I spent weekends preparing a handwritten transcript of the booking videotape. I was able to obtain phone records to prove what I already knew, which was that the alleged firearm was nothing but the defendant's cell phone, which he was in the process of talking on as he passed the ticket booth with the woman cowering in a corner. Allegedly, he made a statement to the police: "I could have killed her."

His command of the language wasn't the best. What he was trying to say was he had the opportunity to kill her, and since he didn't, it meant that he didn't have a weapon. No matter. The government sought to twist this statement and use it as evidence of the defendant's guilt. You could hear him on the booking tape asking incredulously, "Weapon?" when the charges are explained. You can also hear the officers laughing at him when he tries to explain his innocence. I was getting nowhere with the opposition, and they were redoubling their efforts to convict this defendant.

Eventually, the trial date was approaching. I had subpoenaed the phone records, and they verified the cell phone was in use at the time of the imagined assault. I had obtained the tape dispenser from the garage and had the cell phone itself ready to introduce into evidence. In this particular county, one could expect government-oriented juries, which I knew would be part of the problem in the case. The judge was one I had tried in front of before, so I knew him—a former prosecutor. We empaneled a jury, and this case above all was bothering me. The victim perjured herself, as I had expected. She was unbelievable, I thought. She, of course, denied the incident of throwing the tape dispenser and dumping the soda on my client. The assault and battery by mean of a dangerous weapon was supposedly that the defendant threw a lit cigarette at her.

Of course, that didn't happen, and she forgot to tell the police about it during her first interview. It was only when they were fishing for additional charges that this came up. The cigarette had been extinguished by the flung soda and was merely tossed aside, but of course, this became an assault in this deranged woman's mind.

The defendant took the stand, and I wasn't about to let anything go unsaid, so I had him testify as to the nolle prosequi on the complaints he had obtained. The defendant testified to the entire proceeding, right up to the time of his arrest, the booking procedure, and the Commonwealth's behavior afterward. This, in the judge's mind, opened the door to the broadest possible cross-examination of the defendant. Unfortunately, although I can't blame him, the defendant became sarcastic with the prosecutor when he was allowed to ask questions about his religion and whether he went to church. The trial was a mockery, although I had succeeded in entering everything into the record. There was one unfortunate aspect to this case.

It was tried in a small courtroom. The jury box was against a wall whose other side fronted on a corridor leading to the judges' chambers. Every time someone went down the corridor, they had to pass through a heavy door which slammed and consequently shook the wall behind the jury. The jurors would wince every time they heard the door open, and this put them in a nasty mood.

The case was argued and submitted to the jury. Again, the prosecutor was allowed all sorts of leeway in closing, much of which I objected to. The jury came back, and thankfully they acquitted my client of the three felony charges—stalking, assault and battery with a dangerous weapon, and assault with a dangerous weapon—but incredibly, they convicted him of simple assault and threats. How these charges were supported by any view of the evidence is a mystery. The jury blew it. I had seen plenty of jury compromises, and usually, the defendant benefits. Not this time. The defendant's bail was not revoked, so I didn't think he was going to be jailed.

After the verdict, the prosecutor went before another judge on another floor in the same building and obtained an ex parte restraining order against the defendant, despite the fact we were in the building and could have appeared in opposition. That judge was never told that the defendant and his counsel were available. This was the depths.

The next day, since the "victim" would be in court, I advised my client not to go to the courtroom as he would be in violation of the order. When the judge came out, he wanted to know why my client wasn't there. He was about to default him when I offered my explanation. Finally, at last, the judge reprimanded the assistant DA for his unethical behavior. The defendant was allowed into the courtroom for sentencing. His punishment: a year in the house of correction suspended, two years' probation on each charge. The defendant immediately filed his appeal. So the government succeeded. It convicted an innocent man. Fortunately, he was not jailed.

But it wasn't quite over yet. The appellate lawyer assigned to this case, and I conferred. She moved for a new trial on various grounds, and miraculously, the trial judge, who is required to hear new trial motions, allowed the motion, and the verdicts against the defendant were set aside. I would like to think that the judge saw the light and realized my client's innocence. Not likely. The threat of a possible reversal in an appellate court was probably what was working. But a happy result either way.

I told my client that I wasn't able to handle the retrial. A note to CPCS about the importance of this case and my client's innocence was sent along with my case file. The result? The case was dumped through a plea deal. One charge dismissed, and the other continued without a finding, which meant he had to admit he had committed a crime.

My client was able to finish his courses at a neighboring community college and, most important, achieve citizenship. Last I heard, he was doing well. A conviction of any one of those felony charges could have meant deportation. So ends the saga of this case, which shows that in its zeal to convict, cheating is not ruled out. A lot of hard work went into the final exoneration of this client and the successful resolution of his case. I look back on it with pride.

I repeat: what these cases represent is the new theory that the government wants to be sure that no guilty person ever gets away with it. And what difference does it make if a few innocents wind up with convictions and jail time? This places a heavy obligation on the defense bar and results in pressure to take deals even when cases should be tried.

The second case of these four is an example of how the client even considered a guilty plea, even though he hadn't committed a crime. Will this ever change? Of course not. What needs to be kept in mind is the importance of being able to try cases and to recognize that one has to deal with the tremendous power of the government to convict anyone, whether guilty or completely innocent.

So I had my chance to play Perry Mason and work for those unjustly accused defendants who come along ever so once in a while. There were others along with these four, but not many. I am happy to say that my conscience is clear; I am confident that no innocent client of mine ever was convicted. That is something for which I am immensely proud.

But what about those myriad not-so-"obviously" innocent defendants, or may I dare say, those nearly obviously guilty defendants who have, with my help, been acquitted? Should I take equally as much pride in the results of those cases as I do in the "obviously" innocent cases I have just described? I am happy to say that I do—possibly ever so much more.

# 37

## The Government Fights Back

**The government is now faced** with a dire situation. The government can't get convictions in some of these "easy-to-win" fish-in-a-barrel type cases. Shifty lawyers like myself are getting people off, and the guilty are going scot-free. Fat people with tattoos are not receiving the full measure of justice. People are stealing the MBTA blind, and sex non-reporters are walking out the door unpunished. Worst of all, it is becoming difficult to convict those most egregious offenders of all—the defendants who are innocent. This is a big problem for the government, which believes that the defendants, all defendants, are guilty and should be appropriately punished, which most often means being sent to jail. This is happening despite well-trained cops and prosecutors mounting their best efforts and the cooperation of the judges and the appellate courts.

An early move to shore up the system in favor of the government and also to whittle away the effect of those dumb jurors sympathizing with defendants was to eliminate the rule of unanimity required for jury verdicts. I had a number of cases where there was a hung jury. Many times, the government would back away from a second trial and offer a disposition that was favorable to the defendant, and the case would be ended. The government would not want to go to the expense of a second trial or take the risk of a loss—a not guilty verdict.

Often, I would be told by the DA in the hung jury cases that there was a holdout, that the case was eleven to one for conviction. I never knew whether to believe this or not. The government's premise was that hung juries were the result of one or two jurors refusing to join the majority and convict. I was gratified to learn that this obvious attempt by the government to make it easier to convict failed when our high court correctly ruled unanimous juries were part of a defendant's Sixth Amendment rights. This was a significant victory.

The failure of the move to eliminate the rule of unanimity has only made the problem worse. There still is the jury, unanimous or not, assisted by those shifty lawyers, a group of which I consider myself to be a prominent member, that is screwing up the government's ability to stuff defendants into jail. Those lawyers have been able to convince juries that their clients should somehow be let go. Those canny lawyers are going to hopefully stay, but the jury, that is a different matter. If somehow the jury could be avoided in the process of attempting to jail defendants, the government would be left with the judges. They are ever happy to send people away and administer true, "unstupid" justice and pay no attention to the shifty attorneys, same as in the old days in the district courts. And to that end, the government was not going to take this appalling state of affairs lying down.

Instead, the government came up with an idea which has only one objective: to deprive defendants of their important right to have their cases tried by a jury. The idea of a jury trial is embedded in the criminal justice system inherited from our British forebears but, of course, that is a right that can be waived, and a way was found so that most, if not all, defendants would find it most compelling to forego that important right and plead guilty. And so was introduced into the criminal justice world the most pernicious idea ever: the minimum sentence.

This idea had its genesis from something that was already on the books: the habitual offender law. This law, little used initially, was that if a defendant had twice before been convicted of a felony and served separate sentences of three years or more, he could be deemed a habitual offender. A person convicted as a habitual was required to be sentenced to the maximum term prescribed by statute. For instance, if the habitual was armed robbery, the sentence would have to be life, the maximum. Burglary was twenty years, the maximum. Parole possibilities softened the blow only slightly. Life terms had a fifteen-year parole eligibility. Terms of years had parole available at half-time, but parole was never a certainty.

Initially, the habitual offender law was little used. There was some reluctance possibly because the penalties were so draconian. In addition, record-keeping was in the Neolithic stage, and it was difficult to determine who had been convicted of the predicate offenses. Records were kept on little three-by-five cards, entries were made by hand and were notoriously inaccurate. This all changed with the advent of the computer, and it was now possible to more accurately track prior offenses and prior prison terms. And there was a further impediment to the use of the habitual offender process, and that was that the predicate convictions had to be separately charged and proved. The defendant could demand a separate jury for proof of that issue, an expensive and time-consuming undertaking.

Gradually, however, it dawned on the Commonwealth that this could be used to bypass those "stupid" jurors who are setting those guilty defendants free and, particularly upsetting, acquitting innocent defendants. The way it would work is an indictment is obtained charging under the habitual offender statute where the predicate offenses exist. Then, if the defendant is facing a ten- or twenty-year minimum sentence, the government offers something less, and the defendant shrinks from putting himself at risk for the minimum sentence. No jury trial and no stupid jurors reaching those silly verdicts which result in those unbelievable acquittals. Instead, the frightened defendant gives up his right to a jury and takes the deal. The result is that the government gets its conviction, and the risk the defendant will be freed by those jurors is avoided.

These minimum prison terms initially applied only to habitual offender cases, and the number of defendants who had accumulated the requisite underlying sentences were few. But it seemed to be such a good idea in principle that it then began to spread to other situations as well. New minimum penalties were enacted for crimes already on the books. In many crimes, these sentences didn't require the predicate offenses in order to be put into effect. Second offense laws for many crimes were on the books, and for these, also, minimum sentences began to proliferate. The most egregious of these were the mandatory sentences for second offense drug dealing.

These cases almost always involved hand-to-hand sales to undercover officers. Proof of these cases was an exercise in simplicity. Let's say your client has one of these charges and is in the superior court. The DA almost always—really always because if he doesn't, there will be a trial—offers less. So your client facing five years, the mandatory penalty for a second offense drug violation, is now offered three, and the second offense portion of the charge will be dismissed. Considering what he is facing, what's his answer going to be? He's going to accept it and not risk going to trial on a case that he has little chance of winning. Minimum sentences proliferate in other crimes as well. I had a defendant charged with a twenty-year minimum on a burglary case, and the DA offers ten. It was a tough decision. Ultimately, he pled out to the ten rather than take the risk. The defendant's case ought to have been tried. Risk of twenty years as opposed to ten? Guilty plea and no jury trial and no chance for an acquittal.

Here is a disgusting example of how the three-strikes law worked to deprive a client of a jury trial in a case that ought to have been tried. This case involved another habitual offender charge. The underlying offense was assault and battery by means of a dangerous weapon which, coupled with the habitual, would mean a ten-year sentence. Parole eligibility would be at half the time or five years. The defendant had a long past and had the requisite two sentences of three years or more. He was now older and had put his life in order. His sister had taken him in and helped him stay out of trouble. He was working steadily for the labor pool and was contributing to his sister for household expenses.

On the day he was arrested, he had just been to the state income tax office to pick up some forms for his income tax. He had a valise with him that contained the forms and some other personal papers. There was a place near this office where there were benches, and he stopped to have a smoke. Suddenly, there was a commotion, and he went over to see what it was. He was immediately bearhugged, and another person grabbed his valise. The two of them took off down the street. There was an intoxicated man off to the side who was part of this group, and my client, enraged, went over and tried to ascertain who the culprits were. A couple of passersby saw the confrontation and mistakenly thought a robbery was in progress. When the police arrived, my client was furious and attempting to explain he had just been robbed and demanded the police go after the culprits.

The police buy into the observations of the witnesses, and my client is arrested and charged with unarmed robbery. Eventually, the robbery charge is not indicted, and the final charge is assault and battery with a dangerous weapon, the weapon being a shod foot.

I interview my client. He is held on bail, and there is little I can do about that because of his record. His sister won't put up the high bail imposed because the case has the habitual charge. In the interview, I realize that my client is a hothead, and likely, his interaction with the drunk may have involved the shod foot. He denies it, but I have the testimony of the witnesses who will say it did happen. The victim is a habitual drunkard. I review his hospital records, which consume hundreds of pages. I do not expect him to appear as a witness. So I am representing a defendant who was a robbery victim and lost his temper and may have committed the offense charged. He has a case that begs to be tried.

The case moves closer to a trial date, and soon, we are in a trial session. The DA comes to me and offers time served on a plea. Her witnesses are out of state, and she would bring them in but has decided to negotiate the case out. My defendant reluctantly, and with the encouragement of his sister, accepts the time-served disposition along with a few years of probation. The defendant had spent almost a year waiting for trial. I hated myself for even bringing the government's offer of disposition to him. It was hard to gauge the risk that he would be convicted of the assault and battery with a dangerous weapon, but it was a reality that had to be faced. Without the three-strikes statute, this case certainly would have been a trial, and if he were not acquitted, I can't imagine a judge putting him in jail given the facts of the case.

So another example of how these mandatory sentence schemes operate to deprive defendants of jury trials. It's a win for the government as a jury does not have to be dealt with, and the defendant can be appropriately punished without risk of those "miscarriages" of justice.

# 38

# Those Evil School Zones

**Defending cases involving second-offense drug** cases was one thing, but first-offense drug distribution was a different matter. No mandatory sentences there, so those cases could be tried to a jury without the risk of a heavy mandatory sentence being imposed if there was a conviction. Jurors were looking askance at these types of cases where there was a suggestion that there was entrapment. So what to do in order to continue with the plan to stick defendants in jail?

A new invention came along, which was the school zone violation. This violation was punishable by a minimum mandatory sentence of two years in the house of correction—no good time, no parole, no work release, no concurrent sentence, and yes, do all 730 days; and it was mandated that this penalty had to be from and after any sentence on the drug distribution charge. This requirement was so draconian that most judges, forced to impose the two-year penalty on the zone violation from and after the dealing conviction, only sentenced a day on the underlying distribution charge.

The object of this was to keep the prisons full. It certainly wasn't going to stem the flow of drugs into the city nor stem the flow of suburbanites coming into the city to get their needed supply. As fast as defendants were stuck in jail, there was someone else jobless or making a few dollars an hour who was willing to chance it and make a few hundred for an evening's work. The school zone charge worked so well that soon the jails were so full that prisoners had to be sent out of the Commonwealth to a place where space was available, like Texas, where there was a thriving private prison industry. I had a former client who told me about being flown down to some remote place in Texas on a 707 jetliner, which, when it landed, was surrounded by shotgun-toting Texas Rangers on horseback.

But here was the most pernicious thing about the school zone charge. The zone was a thousand-foot circle, and it would be hard to find a spot in Boston that wasn't in a school zone. If that didn't work, there was the park zone—a hundred feet for that. And just to make sure that the net spread wide, there was the invention of the secret school. It was called the University High School, and it was centrally located in downtown Boston—the "zone"—where much of the drug trade seemed to take place. This was a school for kids who had been kicked out of the regular high schools and was run by a group called the Action for Boston Community Development or ABCD.

This so-called school was buried inside an ordinary-looking office building, which used to be the home of the Boston Edison Company. The building had a large sign on the exterior that said "Boston Edison Company." The only people who knew this school existed were ABCD, the people who went there, and the police. There was nothing on the outside of the building to indicate there was a school inside. Avoid the school zone? This was impossible with the secret school because nothing showed that it even existed.

I had case after case involving a school zone charge with this school, and it would proceed like this if the case were to be tried. I would show the police witness—the undercover—a picture of the building. He would admit—had to admit—nothing to show a school at that address. I would then produce a phone book and ask the witness to look up a phone number for the University High School. No listing. ABCD? Not there either. Suppose you wanted to call the school? Didn't know how to do it. How did he know it was a school? Because he knew. What courses were taught? Didn't know. Did the school have sports teams? Didn't know.

There was some litigation on this school, and the Massachusetts Courts have told the government not to worry. First, the evidence needed to establish the existence of a school goes this way: "I know there is a school there, I saw two kids with bookbags." Good evidence, nothing more is needed to establish the existence of a school. And whether our self-respecting drug dealer needs to have an even chance of knowing whether he or she is within a school zone? We go to the Latin dictionary, which all lawyers carry around with them to look up their secret language. And this is where pat in Latin is superior to distinguished English, and so Latin it is; *Scienter* not required. The statute is *Malum Prohibitum*. Here is the translation straight from the Latin: "The defendant is fucked."

A more expansive translation is that knowledge that one is in a school zone is not required. This is the ruling from the great liberal judicial system of the Commonwealth of Massachusetts. The secret school wins, and your client gets the two years and does not pass go.

I tried this approach, that this secret school wasn't, couldn't, be a school within the meaning of the statute, in innumerable cases, and I was laughed at. I seem to remember one judge getting tired of the argument and giving me a directed verdict on one case, so that was something.

Of course, the government has to prove that the incident took place within the thousand-foot zone. To that end, the police have these little orange-colored wheelie things that they use to make the thousand-foot measurements. You can see them in the streets of Boston, pushing them along and taking measurements. They go to court and testify that they are experts in the use of the wheelie, having gone to wheelie school in some faraway place at government expense, and also that they have had their wheelie checked at the National Bureau of Wheelie Standards, which just happens to be located on the east coast, close to a resort community—also at government expense. In practice, this is the way these cases work themselves out. The government will drop the mandatory school zone if the defendant agrees to plead guilty and take a short sentence or probation. This way, the case is not tried. Most of these cases appear to be of the open and shut variety, so they would most likely be pleas, one would imagine.

But as I've demonstrated in the cases I did try that resulted in a hung jury, these cases are most definitely not of the open and shut variety on account of the hint of entrapment, a suggestion which juries found abhorrent. It's just that with the mandatory sentence possibility attached, defendants were afraid to take the risk. And so the plan worked. Cases that juries might entertain favorably for defendants now became pleas, and the risk to the government is eliminated.

So there it is. Jails stuffed with inmates for selling an infinitesimally small amount of narcotics despite the skepticism of reluctant jurors. I had a client who went to trial, lost, and received a four-to-six-year sentence on a distribution charge where the amount was 0.01 grams. Does that weigh more than an atomic particle? I wonder. How many years for 0.02 grams? I hate to think. Easy to see how these cases were almost always pleas.

If the distribution charge was a second and subsequent and also committed in a school zone, then the penalties were even worse. School zone two years, and the dealing offense five years, and they must be served consecutively. DA says, "We'll drop the school zone and the second offense if the defendant pleads guilty to a first offense and accepts three or four years."

Since most of these cases were of the hand-to-hand sale variety, the defendants would fold and take the deal rather than be looking at seven. So the mandatory minimum sentence regime essentially eliminated trial in cases where there should have been or at least could have been trials. In addition, mandatory sentences leave no room for the sentencing judge. Defendants who in some cases should be dealt with some leniency are now stuck with whatever the government offers or else face a heavy and arguably unfair sentence. And a corollary to these mandatory minimum cases was this: heavy bail requirements because judges setting bail for certain knew that the cases would be resolved with the defendant serving time.

So let's be fair. Get rid of the mandatory minimum sentences. They have done nothing but fill up the jails and compromise defendants' right to a jury trial. Allow the defendants to exercise those rights. Years ago, the issue of the legality of the mandatory sentences came up before the Massachusetts Supreme Court. They were validated. And who wrote the court's opinion? A former prosecutor. Let's give judges back the power to decide what punishments are appropriate. How many times have I heard judges say reluctantly they have to impose certain harsh penalties because their hands have been tied by the legislature? This reform is urgently needed if the criminal justice system is to regain its credibility and any sense of fairness.

# 39

## So You Want to Be a PD

**So despite all the pitfalls,** the intrigue, and the forces arrayed against you, you have decided, against all advice to the contrary that you want to be a public defender. It looks to you as if being a public defender would be a gas. You win cases and are hugged and cheered by your clients. You have that good feeling when you win and the jury says, "Not guilty." Sure, you lose a few, but those are cases you didn't expect to win, and at least you helped your client through the process. You are able to do many good works for people who, in the eyes of society, don't deserve it, and you get to stick it to the government on a regular basis.

This is nothing more than a legal life of Riley. Of course, there is no pay to speak of, but your wife, husband or partner realizes the great work you are doing and gladly bears most of the burden of paying for all the expensive things that life requires. But before you rush to fill out those applications for a job at the local defender agency, it might be well to let me fill you in on some of the hidden realities of the public defender business. True, it has its rewards, but it is an arduous life, filled with minefields and cross currents that can easily test your mettle in unexpected ways. So here it is—the reality show of the public defender business as I experienced it. Bear in mind some of my previous comments and remember that my approach was somewhat unique.

I started my career in a way that likely would not be possible in today's amped-up and politically correct world. I jumped in with no experience, no training, and probably no sanity. But here are some of the things that you have to put up with that will make you even crazier than you initially thought possible. I found various ways of dealing with the many obstacles, some of which I have already described. As I said at the beginning, a sense of humor is required, and shiftiness is an absolute necessity. Remember, my frame of reference is the Massachusetts courts, but in general, I'm sure that the experience is similar elsewhere.

One thing that's good about the public defender business is that one doesn't have to hustle for clients. No golf dates, no cocktail parties, no trying to please in whatever way possible. Considering my previously noted lack of social skills and my ability to put my foot in my mouth, chasing clients and keeping them happy would have been tough for me. Most of the clients I had were perennially unhappy anyway and not capable of being pleased, so an inability to charm them made not the slightest difference. Even if they were found not guilty, they were often still unhappy.

The way the organization I worked for, the Suffolk Lawyers for Justice (yes, that's what it's called), had it set up was to assign its attorneys to different courts so that coverage was complete throughout Suffolk County. I was assigned to the Boston Municipal Court and the Suffolk Superior Court. Each quarter, I would be given a number of so-called "duty" days so I could pick up new cases. I was grateful for my court assignments because this would involve the least traveling as those courthouses were within walking distance of my office. Since my home was located in a faraway place, parking was an issue. I managed this by parking in an expensive garage near the courthouses, which put a big hole in my meager paycheck. This gave me a parking pass, which allowed me to come and go as I pleased. This was a blessing in case I had to go somewhere during the day, such as visit a prison, most of which were a distance away.

These assignment dates were absolute musts on the calendar because they meant picking up new cases, and new cases meant money. It also meant meeting new people who had a different outlook on life than my colleagues at Harvard, something I cherished. It was often difficult to keep these dates if one had a busy trial calendar, and conflicts would frequently arise. A visit to the organization's website would involve an attempt to trade one day for another so that one of the duty days would not be lost. It was all very complicated, and as a result, many billing issues arose. There were complex rules in the billing process, such as maximum times for certain activities and also rules limiting how many hours could be billed per day and also for a year. Some defenders figured out how to max out their annual hours over nine months and then go on vacation for the remaining three. I never knew how they did it. Over the space of twenty years, I only reached the maximum once, and that was on the last few days of the year.

A duty day arrives, and experience tells me that the closest thing to complete chaos is about to begin, particularly if it is in the district or municipal court. Handling one of these duty days takes a special skill and a determination not to go mental at all costs. On arrival at the courthouse arraignment session, one is presented with a list of the people in the lockup who may need counsel. This is usually just about all of them. There are three of us assigned to this appointment day, and we divide up the cases among the three of us, but one of us hasn't shown up, so we give him or her a third of the cases anyway.

Has anyone heard from this person? No, so it is assumed he or she will be there. Later, that person sends in a message he or she is busy somewhere else, but that message is not received until after the two of us who are there have been yelled at by the court for not talking to that lawyer's clients.

It is most important to put yourself in a position to get paid, and that means the absolutely necessary form called the notice of assignment of counsel, the NAC. That form requires information such as the charges and the bail status, which can't be added until the arraignment is over. Then the form has to be countersigned by the court, and all this has to happen while the court is in session.

Sneaking, bent over, up to the clerk's desk to obtain a copy of the complaint or to offer the form for the judge's signature is frowned upon. Each one of these forms has a serial number of about fifteen digits, which identifies the case and will be the controlling entry in the computer. I was in the habit of filling out the forms in advance and jotting down the serial numbers. Back at the office, the cases could be opened in the CPCS's payments portal with those numbers and the defendants' names. Getting this paperwork done is a major victory. You hope that when all the dust has settled at the end of the day, you have all the forms, and you know who your clients are and whether they have been released or are in custody. How many times have clients been released, and I have no contact information? Very embarrassing.

A frequent occurrence is running after a just-released client to get a telephone number and having the judge yell that the next case is yours and asking, "Where are you going?" Also, it is important to bring a lot of cheap ballpoint pens. Clients who are released have to sign what's called a bail warning. The bail warning tells the client that they can be suspended from the human race if they fail to show at the next hearing. Since it is very hectic, and your new client is in a hurry, and the judge is already starting the hearing on your next client, he or she somehow often manages to walk off with your pen. Originally, I thought it was impressive to have nice pens for clients to use, but after some went missing, I switched to the cheaper variety. I considered creating a pen warning, something like, "That pen you are writing your signature with is mine. Please return it to me after its use"—but I never got around to it.

Assuming there are a few minutes left after dealing with the NACs and gathering other related paperwork in order to actually represent someone, the prisoners need to be interviewed. There are a lot of people in the lockup and limited space to speak with clients. Fifteen people may be there with only one small window available to conduct interviews. A hazard of the business is that when your client comes to that small window to speak with you, it is almost guaranteed that he or she will find an excuse to cough or sneeze. It is not wrong to come to these assignment days with plenty of cold medication. The court is in a hurry because the transportation people want to get going to have their morning coffee break. The purpose of these interviews is to prepare for the next event, which is a bail hearing.

Getting ready for a bail hearing usually means getting a copy of the police report and a copy of the complaint. The complaint has to come from the clerk, who is busy, and the police report has to come from the DA, who is also busy. The client wants to see both because they frequently haven't the faintest idea why they are there. It is normal for a prospective client to tell you that the complaint is "fucked up" and they are innocent. You attempt to get as much background information as you can, such as which choir they sing in and how many sportsmanship awards they have won. Sorting all this out takes some doing. The case is called, and you have also had a chance to review the criminal past—the rap sheet—if any as part of your preparation. With some of these, you try not to let out an audible gasp.

Now you are ready to make a pitch on bail. The government goes first and reads the police affidavit. This usually takes some time because the court wants to hear every word of the damning report. This is followed by the prosecution's usual astronomical bail request, to which the court has said, "That's all you're asking?"

This police report, which you have hopefully already seen, usually buries your client. I see lawyers at these bail hearings telling the court that their clients say they are innocent, which means what? Why say it when it will not be believed. It is a good idea to refrain from stating that your client has roots in the community because it is trite and also because the clearest evidence of roots is often time spent incarcerated. A frequent request from your client is that he needs to be free because his baby's mother is about to have the baby, and he needs to be back at the bedside. Probably good to resist the temptation to say this because the client is usually charged with some conduct clearly not performed at the expectant mothers bedside.

Prior to the hearing, the client is brought out shackled and handcuffed. No grooming facilities are available, so your client does not look like he or she has recently been to the salon. Also, belts and shoelaces have been removed, so your client is holding up his pants, hopefully, and walking gingerly in his laceless high-tops. Your chance comes to ask for your client to be freed on his own recognizance, which may or may not be reasonable. While you are speaking, your client is often coaching you in a low voice but loud enough to be heard by the judge and also recorded on the courtroom tape system. That tape system picks up everything, and one needs to be careful what one says.

I was involved in a bail hearing once where the defendant kept interrupting me, and finally, I said, "Look, I know what I'm doing, and this is working" before the judge assured me that it wasn't. You have done a good job if your new client doesn't say at the end of the hearing that he wants a new lawyer. After the hearing, follow your client back to the lockup, if you are still on speaking terms. He or she is either on his or her way out or bail has been imposed. Counsel your client on what the next move will be. Find out if there isn't someone you can contact who can come up with the bail money if bail has been ordered.

In Massachusetts, there is a right to appeal the lower court's bail order to the superior court. Exceptions are on probation surrenders and orders that defendants be held without bail after a so-called dangerousness hearing. Advise your client regarding a possible bail appeal. Often, that depends on which judge is sitting in the superior court where the appeal will be held. If the defendant insists, schedule the hearing, which may take place as soon as the next day. Finally, after the place clears out, which may be as late as five or six o'clock, you get a chance to go back to the office where you collapse with the paperwork and maybe get the new cases into the computer and files opened before heading home. If you get this all taken care of right away, you can start thinking about how in hell you are going to defend the cases. It is a fact that any one of these can end up being a trial. For sure. While thinking about that possibility, it is a good idea to try not to run off the road.

# 40

## Preparing for Trial

**I have a habit, which** comes naturally, to start thinking about how the case can be defended from the get-go. I never think in terms of winners or losers but how to handle the case if the defendant refuses to plead, as is his right. A quick review of the police report gives me a good idea of where to start. I always make sure my client has a copy of the police report, usually at the arraignment, even if it means giving him or her my own. I know I can always get another copy from the clerk's office. At the first sit-down, whether it is at my office or at a place of confinement, there is a basis for discussion.

Let's say that you are trying to make an appointment for someone who has been released. And let's say your client has, as often happens, given you a telephone number that's disconnected, or you reach a cell phone with a mailbox that is full or one that has not been set up yet. Learn to deal with the frustration when you get any of those messages and make a note in the file in case CPCS or BOBO levels an accusation that you never spoke with your client. Or suppose you reach the mother who says, "I haven't seen him in weeks, but if I see him, I will tell him you called."

Something tells you the client is standing right there. In any case, it is important to document this call as well. "Called client, 2:15 p.m. Client's mother says client is looking for a real lawyer."

If you are successful in making the appointment, be sure and have plenty of other things to do, because some clients have a rather loose idea of what time 2:00 p.m. is. Try and be flexible if the first client shows up an hour late and at the same time as the second client, who now has to be asked to go have dinner while you interview the first client. Also, be prepared for the unusual that occasionally happens.

I had an office interview with one client who was extraordinarily difficult. She just went on and on about her case and was making no sense at all. Finally, she left. I had tried to be understanding of her predicament but let out a sigh of relief when the interview was finally over. I was about to be on my way, but I wasn't fast enough. The client reappeared in my doorway in crisis mode because she had parked next to a hydrant and her car got towed. I had to help the poor dear, which meant locating the tow lot and driving her to it. Did I lend her money? Memory is cloudy here.

Once your client has made himself comfortable in your well-appointed office, you can begin the interview. You go over the charges, the possible penalties, and you discuss with your client his or her version of what happened. I try and take a careful longhand writing of that because if the defendant testifies, I will use it as a guide in my direct examination. The interview ends, and another interview is scheduled if necessary; investigation is arranged if needed, and the client should be reminded of the upcoming court date and what that date is for—trial, motion hearing, court conference, or the like. A reminder of what time the court starts is useful, and a note in the file that you told him is good. Also mention that late arrivals are sometimes assessed fees and even, on occasion, jailed. I try to contact the client the day of court because I often get, "It's today? I thought it was next week."

There is something else worth mentioning, and that is that clients on the street often show up for office interviews smoked. At this point, the best that can be done is to attempt to get an interview and no aspersions. Just try and understand it's a wild world out there.

Supposing your client actually appears at the next court date and it is for a pretrial conference. That pretrial conference is a necessity. It is stated in some court handbook that these conferences must be held. There is a form that must be filled out and submitted to the court. Most pretrial conferences never result in anything resembling an actual conference. The client wants to get out of there as soon as possible. Try to have the pretrial conference form completed by the first call, and then have a date in mind. Hopefully, that date will be agreeable with the government so that the case can then be continued. In the rare case where the client is amenable, the case can be negotiated with the government, and the case can be disposed of. Normally, this does not happen because the client doesn't want to accept the outrageous offer from the Commonwealth.

There is also the possibility of delaying the day of reckoning by asking for a further pretrial conference date. This can be done by telling the court that some piece of discovery, unnecessary to the case, has not yet been provided by the Commonwealth. A good excuse is that there is somewhere a security camera which recorded the entire event and that the discovery of the same will exonerate your client but that the government has failed in its duty to locate it. Depending on the judge, this may go on for some time until eventually, the case must be resolved or tried.

Let's say the case has been forced, at long last, into a trial session. Usually, this brings some kind of reckoning. Many cases are dropped because witnesses don't show up. In the eventuality that the witnesses are there, this usually works to put your client into resolution mode, and the case can be concluded. But remember, the cases that get tried are not necessarily the ones that you would like to have tried. If there is a trial, a group from the jury pool is brought in, and the case begins.

Suppose that your client has not been released. Then the client must be seen at the place of confinement. Normally, this will be the jail, but in the case of women, they are held at the house of correction, which is someplace else. Assuming you know the sex of your client, you know where to go. The jail is very busy with visitors. Afternoons are crowded with family and friends who want to see their loved ones. Negotiating the visitation process takes time, and eventually, a lot of experience will make the process easier and faster. A pass must be filled out, and a token for the locker obtained. Everything not relevant to the interview must be locked up. There is a metal detector that probably does work that one is required to pass through.

Once this is accomplished, then the thumbs up for the gatekeeper, and you are in. All inmates are on even-numbered floors two through six. Each floor has four units. Your pass will have the unit number marked. You show it to the guardhouse. This is necessary because the elevator that takes you to the proper floor is not operated by you but remotely by the guardhouse person. The elevator door opens, you get on, the door closes, and then nothing happens. There may be two reasons for this: something has come up, and they have forgotten about you, or they don't like your face, and they are sitting there laughing their asses off while you stew.

When this has happened to me, I have opened a file and started to read. That's because there is no way to communicate with anybody. If the delay is lengthy, pushing the fire alarm button will usually get someone's attention. After a wait, the elevator will move, most often to a floor you don't want to be at. The door will open, and a guard will get on with fourteen prisoners who are being transferred to other units, two of whom you have previously represented and have not been pleased with the results. Stand close to the guard. If you explain your situation, the guard will get on his device and tell the controller to send you to the right floor.

Arriving at the right unit, you have been buzzed in and are now in the small, tight space where the interview will take place. You sit in one of those grade school chairs that has that special extended arm for writing notes, and you wait for your client to show up. The door to the unit has a large glass window in it, and you can see what is going on. I often have a thought about this. I walk to the jail, and people are about their business, scowling, hollow-eyed, bent over with the cares of the world. I look into the unit, and it is electric with happiness and joy. People are working out in the corner, playing cards or board games, and plotting their next move once they get out. Maybe they're over by the phone bank, calling their girlfriends or giving shit to their lawyers. Once in a while, a fight breaks out, and they get to mix it up with the guards. And there are three squares a day.

What could be better? I wonder about all the gaspers who are complaining about the prison population. I knew a client who used to tell me, "Doing time is easy. It's living on the outside that is tough." He had a fairly easy life.

These interviews are usually fruitful because your client is going to be straight, although not necessarily straight with you. There was a ukase put out by CPCS one time that said clients must be seen within three days of arraignment. This was never obeyed, at least not by me, because so many clients come off the street "messed up" in the vernacular. There can be reasons to see a client quickly but not as a general rule. I take notes and try to reassure my client that even though I am paid by the state, I have his best interests at heart. You hope the client has appreciated your visit. You also hope that the three other clients of yours who are banging on the glass and wondering why you have not come to visit them will not hold it against you. You make your exit from the unit by telling the guard whether you are going to another floor or leaving the building and would they *please* call an elevator. Now a different procedure is in play. The elevator arrives so quickly that by the time you get to it, the door is just closing on your outstretched arm.

Eventually, you have come to know and love your client and are ready to do battle for him or her in a place akin to the lion's den. I've already talked in detail about the forces arrayed against you in your attempt to save your client from getting it in the neck. In most cases, your client will realize that there is only so much you can do, and the case will end up peacefully with some kind of plea. You will play on the redeeming qualities you have found in your client and achieve a decent disposition.

Many of the offenses are minor and will not call for incarceration. The DAs are very busy and don't have time to prosecute everybody to the limit. So, everybody is fat, dumb, and happy. Most bar advocates prefer to confine their efforts to the district court for just that reason. Little stress and, therefore, not much in the way of aggravation. That's in the district court. A different animal is the superior court, big time.

# 41

## The Basics

**Before talking about life in** the superior court, there are some practical necessities a public defender—bar advocate—needs to know about. It is a special life and different from anything one could possibly imagine. I will start with the office and some of the basics. The office is the epicenter of your existence, where you go to cool down and shout obscenities at the treatment you and or your clients have received at the hands of the evil forces arrayed against you or, on occasion, to exult over a hard-won victory. In either case, it is a chance to shape your environment in a way that is comfortable and also, one would hope, comforting.

My last office space I had for maybe all of ten years, and it was definitely the best of the many different ones I had through all the time I practiced. But the office is where you will only have to spend some of your time. The rest of the time, maybe the bulk of it, will be in court or visiting clients in prison. In my case, time spent in the office was a welcome respite from those activities. You therefore need to have that comfortable place be like a home away from home. Since as a public defender you aren't making any money, it is important that the rent be as low as possible. The rent problem limits your possibilities and normally you find yourself in an old, dilapidated building shortly to be scheduled for demolition. And true to this thought, I was forced to vacate two of my last four office locations because the buildings were going to be rehabbed.

An elevator is also a nice thing to have. I did have a client who was afraid of elevators and had to walk up all eight floors to my office. She was extremely cheerful about this. Since most clients can manage the elevator, it is not necessary to insist on space at street level. You will most likely not be meeting with high-end clientele, so you need not worry about decoration. My final office resting place was about a hundred square feet. Much of this was taken up by the four five-drawer filing cabinets, which contained twenty years' worth of files. I had a desk, a few chairs, a hutch with a matching bookcase on top, and a "some assembly required" computer stand with casters. I had a telephone, which is a necessity. I had an inherited rug of the grossest color, which had, I imagine, been on the floor of that office since the Stone Age. A lot of stains do not a rug pattern make.

It is worth considering the layout of one's office. A suggestion might be that it would be a good idea to place your desk so that it is between the door and the area where your client is to be interviewed. My office was set up in such a way that it was virtually impossible to achieve this objective, and, fortunately, I never had any difficulty. Just the same, there was an occasional client who made me a little nervous, and I often thought a different office arrangement would have made for a more relaxed interview.

I had one thing I did not like, which was people in my office after I left for the day, which meant essentially the cleaning service. The result—a lot of dirt and dust. So okay, it wasn't the neatest, and an accumulation of dust bunnies didn't seem to bother people. It wasn't State Street after all. The door had a lock on it, which could be picked in no time, but at least it kept the other suite members out. Down the hall, there was a basket for the mail. I had a couple of windows, which made for a nice, light, and breezy place to work and meet with clients. If I leaned way out of one of them, I could see Chestnut Hill in the distance.

Across the street was the Old Granary Burying Ground, which gave the office a certain gallows dignity. Also, I had a potted plant with no plant in it, which lent an air of I don't know what. I had hung diplomas from every school I had ever attended, my bar admission certificates from the Massachusetts and Federal Courts, plus some diplomas that were not mine—my father's graduation from law school and college. The more the merrier. A large photograph of uncertain vintage, which was of an intramural college football team I once played on, dominated one wall surface. A pastime for clients was to guess which one of the dozen or so players was me. Prizes were given for correct guesses.

Many would ask what position I played, and I would always answer "drawback." This would get a laugh, and then we could relax and go about discussing the subject of my client's innocence and how we were going to establish this obvious fiction.

The computer cart held a computer which I mostly did not know how to operate except to play card games and other rudimentary forms of entertainment. The computer only became necessary with the advent of computerized billing. Toward the end of my career, discovery was often furnished by disc or direct email. I was baffled. I could never play the discs. I often had to go to the DA's office and have them play them for me. One feature of my office that everyone noticed was that my desk had nothing on it. I had at some point been at the detective bureau in a local police station and noticed that all the detectives had nothing on their desks except for a telephone. I was impressed and ever since had kept my desktop clear of all paperwork and assorted paraphernalia. I did the detectives one better by not even having a phone, which I placed on a low side table. I thought that this would show that my clients would have my undivided attention. All my files were put away, the closed files in the five-drawer cabinets and the files of current clients in the "This is America" filing cabinet. Then I began to worry that prospective clients might think I had no clients and therefore was not much of a practitioner, so I put a stack or two of files somewhere where they could be seen.

One of the most important things about an office is the telephone. It is a necessary means of communication with the outside world. The next most important thing is the type of phone you get. Most bar advocates, such as myself, are operating on a shoestring and can't afford secretaries or receptionists who can answer the phone and say we're not there when we really are. It is therefore important to have a phone that will take messages that you can listen to while you're sitting next to it. That way, you can decide whether or not to answer. This means that one has to wait for the announcement that says that you are not there to listen for who is calling.

I had my line of "Oh, I just walked into the office" down pat if it was a call I wanted to take. As a general rule, it is important to set the phone this way because if there is one rule that should be followed it is never, never under any circumstances to answer the phone unless you know who is calling.

Here is an example of how this works. You forget the never-answer rule, and the phone rings or beeps or lights up if you have the ringer off, and you imagine your ship has come in and you are about to get the big retainer you've always wished for. Instead, it is something else, something that is the bane of lawyers in the public business—a collect call from the joint. It goes something like this: "This is a collect call from (institution named)," and then a blank spot in the recording to let you know that "aaarggh" has called you. You don't know who this is because the name is unintelligible. The only thing I have never figured out is when you slam down the receiver does the calling party know that and take offense.

Worse, if you accept the call, it is often from someone who is not your client who wants to ask you a question about his case. You have to gently tell him to speak with his own lawyer. Or it is your client and he doesn't want to talk about his case. He just has nothing else to do and wants to converse. Otherwise, it could be a court clerk that is telling you that such and such case is in the trial session, and the judge wants you to come up and empanel in ten minutes. Hard to dodge that, but at least you have enough time to figure out your excuses.

Over time, the collect calling business became more of a business. You knew a call charged to you was coming because a robot would announce that some outer space telephone company was holding a call for you. I was supposed to have set up an account with my credit card so that these calls could go through. I never signed on, and so the calls didn't. But I never had any complaints to speak of. One client told me he could never reach me. While my mind turned a cartwheel, I explained that was because I was very busy.

That worked, and I heard no more about it. This would have given an aneurysm to the CPCS hierarchy. I had seen letters sent by fired CPCS attorneys in which clients were encouraged to call, and they would of course accept the charges. Better to have a loving phone confab than get up and go see the client. Also worth noting, these calls are extraordinarily expensive, and you, the advocate, are picking up the tab as opposed to the CPCS-ers who seemed to have unlimited phone funds.

The other means of communication with the outside world is the mail. Your clients want you to send them a copy of every document pertaining to their cases. This builds up copying expenses and postage expenses, but it's worth it because this is one thing that will help to keep clients happy, and a state of happiness for a client in custody is not an easy thing to achieve. One could bill for costs, but there was a complex billing procedure that had to be followed that I could never figure out. Adding in an extra quarter hour to some activity was an easy way to cover them. But it's the mail, and you have to make use of it. Use a nice-looking and good-quality manila-style envelope to send out copies of court papers because that will later become your custody client's briefcase. A common sight is handcuffed clients coming into court with the same, now-rumpled envelope you originally sent out.

That's one part of the mail. The other important part is correspondence. Since it is impossible to make enough visits for each client, letters are normally sent in between those times. Letters from clients are normally in longhand; if they are typed, you are in trouble. It is usually a motion to have you removed as counsel or to otherwise complain about your representation. At the bottom, there often is a note intending to be ominous—"cc filed." Fortunately or unfortunately—it depends—I didn't receive many of these letters. A good rule of thumb I had with these typed letters is not to open them for a week or two until their radioactivity had diminished.

Typed letters were pretty easy to figure out. Not so easy were the longhand letters. A good guess as to the state of your client's feelings is how many times the letter has been folded over. If an eight-and-a-half-by-eleven piece of paper has been folded so it is the size of a pencil, watch out. Three folds is okay, and you are probably still on good terms. Also beware of letters that start out by saying that the writer hopes you are in good health and spirits because by the time you get to the end, you likely won't be.

I, early on, was in the habit of writing letters to clients in longhand. Mistakenly, I thought this put me on a par with my clients. It was also due to the fact I didn't have a so-called word processor, although after a while, I got hold of an old typewriter. I could never straighten out the margins or learn to type more than ten words per hour, so I went back to longhand. An advantage of this type of communication was that nobody could read my handwriting, so there was little to criticize. I could always do a translation when I made a prison visit.

I had one client who wrote me and provided me with a script of what I was to say to the judge next court date. Literally, it was like the script for a movie. We got that straightened out in a real hurry. I had occasion to represent this bad actor a second time. I received a letter (longhand and copiously folded) from him blasting me for not scheduling a bail appeal. It was a screed about how he had no defaults and his codefendant, a woman, had a bail review, and had been released. Shifty is as shifty does. I checked the docket (they actually had dockets for the bail review hearings) and found out the woman codefendant had her bail review and that her petition had been denied, and she was still in custody. Further, this defendant had defaults.

I obtained a copy of the docket entry showing the denial and a copy of his record and sent them to him, making liberal use of my trusty Sharpie, the one with the blunt tip, for emphasis. Included was a blast in my usual longhand, written in block print so it was legible. I had no problem getting down to the level of my clients and sending off unprofessional squeals of the type which would have given the CPCS people a hemorrhage. Later, in court, this is what I got from this client—an apology. I was touched. He became only a semi-bad actor.

The mail can only go so far, and it is necessary to make visits to the place of your client's custody. I have talked about visits to the jail. Visits to prison facilities are much different and require a far different approach.

# 42

## Prison Visits

**Your client is going to** be held most likely in one of two places: either the jail, the visiting procedure for which I have already discussed, or, if there has been a previous state incarceration, which is often the case, then at the prison in Concord. This prison is about twenty miles and what seems like seven hours of driving time away. Occasionally, a client is being held at another of the myriad prisons throughout the Commonwealth, and these vary in the time required to get to them. You are allowed to be compensated for driving time, but this has been reduced to a formula, so you can't bill for the actual amount of time. Presumptively, you are deemed to be going no less than thirty miles per hour, which is a joke.

This means that prison visits at midnight or five a.m. are recommended when traffic is light. A trip to the prison at Concord, the one most frequently visited, requires negotiating something called the Concord rotary, which even at normal times takes at least a half-hour to get around.

The prison at Concord presents a far different situation, as do the other prisons in the system, from the jail. I will talk about the visiting procedure to Concord since it is the one most frequently visited, although it is basically the same for the others. The parking lots for these prisons are far enough away so that if the weather is bad, you get soaked or frozen. All the close parking spots are reserved for the guards and other prison personnel. Occasionally, there are no spots available at all. One of the things to never do is to call in advance to schedule a time to see a client. If you do this, then the institution just gets extra time to figure out how to screw you over before you even get there. On your arrival, if you are asked if you called to schedule and a problem arises and you are denied the visit, take back the visiting request and send a copy to your client with a note that you tried to see him but were denied by the authorities. This puts the blame for lack of a visit away from you and onto someone else.

Generally, the prisons don't care if you call ahead. They can give you a hard time just as easily without a lot of planning how to do it. Upon arrival, it is important to stand in front of the guardhouse window until someone recognizes that you have arrived. Usually, you will be ignored. The reason for this is that the staff is engaged in one of the day's most important events, which is either ordering a pizza, awaiting the delivery of a pizza, or actually consuming a pizza. In any case, your arrival has interrupted this very important activity, and no attention will be paid. Stand at the window long enough, and you will see the arrival of a pizza delivery person with one of those zipper cases designed to keep the goodies piping hot. A side door will open, and this person will be welcomed like the prodigal son, and you will be attended to only when there is a break in this most important process.

Let's say you are there to visit a difficult client that you are not particularly anxious to see. You can only hope that that person has been transferred to another institution or that he has been taken to court that day on another matter and is therefore not there to be seen. Then the above procedure is to be followed, namely to send out a copy of the visit request and explain that you tried. Not a good idea to intentionally go to the wrong prison and then try to claim that either your client or the prison system gave you the wrong information.

The first thing that has to be done is to get the visit request. Some prisons have them available on shelves or tables in the prison anteroom; some do not, in which case you need to go to the guardhouse and ask for one. Frequently, you are ignored. I try to bring along some paperwork and begin to read while I am standing waiting. Some of these places are encased in glass so thick that they could withstand bazooka fire from close range. The glass is heavily smoked to boot. Is someone actually in there?

At length, someone will acknowledge your presence, and you now have your chance to say who you want to visit. You find out that your client hasn't been transferred to some other institution or gone to court, so you will have to face the fact that the visit is going to take place.

Next, the visit request must be filled out. I have never understood this, but the visit request for attorneys is the same as it is for the general public, so you, the attorney, who very likely would not be practicing law if you had been convicted of a crime, have to state for the umpteenth time that, no, you have not been convicted of a felony. Your name, your residence (always your business residence unless you are out of your mind), your date of birth, and usually your license number, which in my case I could never remember since my state was one of those that didn't use the social. Upon completion, the visit request, your ID (your driver's license in most cases), and your bar registration card are presented to the authorities who carefully check everything. You now have your pass, and you are halfway to seeing your client.

You are not going to just walk into the prison with whatever you have, so you are warned you can only bring in what is necessary for the interview. Unless you left everything in your car or back at your office, there are going to be things you need to lock up. Forget about locking up a coat because most lockers are the size of a breadbox and will barely handle a pair of gloves. If you travel the way I do, which is with my office in my coat pockets, I have a lot to lock up and a lot to forget to lock up.

If it's pouring outside, bring a folding umbrella, or if it's regulation size, just leave it somewhere and hope it's there when you return. Everything inside? It is now that you discover that you forgot to bring a quarter, which you need for the locker. If you are like me, you have stashed about fifty bucks' worth of them in your car's ashtray, only to forget to bring any because you are so preoccupied with the upcoming visit. If you are resourceful, there is usually a candy machine in the vestibule, and a dollar will get you a nut bar and a quarter change.

Other options are to panhandle the families waiting to see the inmates—not recommended—or to ask the guardhouse for change. Usually, it's a turn down with, "What are we, the Transit Authority?"

Once you have the quarter, placing it in the slot enables the key to turn and be removed. So you have chosen the locker that swallows your quarter and doesn't lock, and now you discover you have forgotten to bring extra quarters to cover this eventuality. It's back to the candy machine, and now you have enough nut bars to cover you in case the interview goes long, and you are late for dinner. You move your stuff to another locker, and hopefully, you are done. Remember, only things for the interview: glasses if needed, writing instruments, client files. It's a good idea to bring two pens. I don't know how many times I've run out of ink in the middle of an interview. I've also forgotten note paper. Take some extra visiting request forms if available and write on the back. That will work.

Next, it's into the prison. I'm glad to report that of the hundreds and maybe thousands of visits I've made to various lockups, I've always made it back out, but there's a feeling each time I go inside. Before you are admitted, there usually is a wait while the staff gets ready to clear you for entry. You have a seat; the door opens, and a CO calls you or your client's name. You hope you don't have to wait too long. I was at the supermax one time, waiting for my name to be called. I waited and waited and waited some more. I just thought they were giving me a hard time, so I just kept waiting. Finally, the CO behind the desk comes over and asks me what I am doing there. I tell him, and he asks me if I had filled out a visit request, and I tell him, "About an hour ago."

He says, "Well, we don't have one."

I fill out another pass and go in to see my client. What happened? The first pass, when completed, was placed upside down on a nearby shelf by the officer taking the visiting requests. The backside had the request in Spanish, I discovered. Apparently, a Spanish speaker had seen it, taken it, and filled it out, unaware that the other side had been completed. You can figure the rest. A delay.

Next, it's through the trap and into the prison. Jackets off. All jacket pockets searched. Pants pockets must be pulled out and shoes removed. Sometimes you are permitted to try the metal detector with shoes on, so I try to wear shoes with no metal. On rare occasions, I've been told I have to leave my necktie and also my glasses case. On one occasion, I had to open my mouth for inspection. You've got to respect this because ingenious are the ways in which contraband is brought into prisons, and once in a while, a lawyer is involved.

In my first incarnation as a public defender, I represented a woman who was charged with bringing a prohibited substance into a county prison. She had brought in a pair of jeans for her boyfriend to wear to court. Heroin was discovered sewn into a seam. The case was won because the government could not prove my client had knowledge of the contraband. It was a directed verdict of not guilty, one of the few I ever achieved. Even though my client was cleared, it shows the ingenuity that is used to smuggle contraband into the joint.

By this time, you have had enough time to view some of the discovery that you would have received at the time of the arraignment. This would be police reports and grand jury testimony, if there was an indictment, and you would have had a chance to see how bad your client's case was or rarely how good it was. Your initial interview is just the beginning of what may be a long process. You will have to work with your client and get to know him or her as you go along. It is a good idea to try and impress upon your client how delighted you are to be taking his or her case. You might tell him (I'll use "him" to shorten this up as most defendants are males) a little about how experienced you are and try to impress the idea that you will work the best you can for his benefit. You already have one strike against you because you are being paid by the Commonwealth, and he didn't choose you to be his lawyer. Maybe that's two strikes.

Have copies of the discovery material for him to look at, even if you have already mailed it because your client may not bring it to the interview. I like to be sure that the client is furnished with copies of the indictments in addition to the discovery. It is extremely important because this is the basis of the criminal case against your client. I'm always surprised at how many cases where I have been successor counsel and there are no copies of the indictments in the file. It also shows a certain professionalism that you are working on preparing to defeat the allegations surrounding those charges. Ultimately, if jailhouse lawyers become involved, that will be an early complaint if the indictment copies have not been provided.

If you are giving him copies of anything, be sure that you ask permission from the CO present in the interview room. I was once nearly thrown against the wall by an angry guard because I had given copies of a couple of motions I had filed to my client without his, the guard's, permission. It looks good. It avoids an issue with staff and it may impress your client as being professional. And it may avoid trouble for your client who will be searched upon exiting the interview.

In general, be polite to the prison staff. It can't hurt. In talking to your client, try to get a glimpse of what the possible defense to the case might be. Make sure you explain the charges and work into this explanation the maximum and minimum sentences, if any, particularly mandatory minimums. A little experience, and you will learn how to earn some confidence from your client in your first interview. Upon leaving, explain when you think you will next be out and what further discovery you might be sending and any motions you are contemplating filing. In addition, it is important to discuss bail possibilities, such as anybody you could contact who might be able to post bail or whether or not a further bail hearing should be scheduled.

If you have done the right thing and gone over what the charges are and what the possible penalties could be, you can get some sense of where the case might be going. It is premature, but from a caseload management standpoint, a sense of whether the case might be a plea or a trial early on cannot hurt. Stressing the maximums is essential, especially for the client but also for yourself in judging how the case will be handled, and to repeat, particular attention should be paid if there are minimum sentences.

Another important thing I do is to start thinking about a closing argument. Every case, no matter how bad, has the potential to become a trial—"taking it to the hoop" in the vernacular (this is amended every fourth year to read "going for the gold"). This habit helped me to be ready when the time came to actually give a close. As the case went along, my closing argument idea for each case was continually being shaped by new developments as more evidence was discovered. One of the oldest downsides in a trial is to reach that point where both sides have rested, and the judge looks at you with a smile and asks, "Ready to argue?" and where you, the defense counsel, look as if you have just received a death threat, and the judge says, "Would you like a few minutes?" and you have to say yes.

You have half conceded your case at this point. If, on the other hand, you have been preparing for that moment all along, you can confidently say you are ready, no need to wait for your chance to pummel the opposition. Another trick is sometimes you are following the clock and think that the lunch hour is approaching or you expect the court to recess for the day, and you will have additional time to prepare.

Judges who are pro-government will sometimes make you give your closing during the luncheon recess just to throw you off. So you need to be prepared for the wrap-up speech, which is one of the most important parts of any criminal trial. Some have said that closings don't necessarily win cases but that poor closings can lose them. As important as it is, it is also one of the most difficult. You stand in front of fourteen people (usually twelve, plus two alternates) and have to sum up for your client. The stress is remarkable. You think that one false note may be the difference. Remember the case I talked about earlier where the respected clerk told me that he didn't know what my client was thinking, but he was going to do a lot of time? Pressure.

Thinking back, I still don't know how I had the nerve to try that case. I've found that a certain devil-may-care attitude is helpful. Let the prosecution have it. Nothing to be gained by holding back.

The hardest thing about these interviews with your client and case preparation is sort of the psychology of the whole thing. Your client is in a jam. He or she doesn't know what to do. Clients often want you to make decisions for them, and this can be for a variety of reasons. Maybe they legitimately don't know what to do and want you to call the shots. There are some who have been around who want to trap you into making the call on how the case proceeds. so if it doesn't go to their liking, you can get blamed.

In all cases, it is important to let the client make the final decision on important matters in the case. Should the client plead? Should the client go to trial? Should the client testify? All important decisions. Here is one I get frequently after the first interview. "Do you believe me?" This is usually asked after some lame account of what amounts to no defense to the charges. I always answer with this: "I am not in the belief business. If I was, I would be doing something else. My job is to represent you to the best of my ability."

If you say that you think the client is a liar, as I have seen some lawyers do, you will be off the case. Similarly, saying you do believe him makes you look gullible. And by all means, do not say to the client that you cannot help him or her unless they tell you the truth. Every client has a story which is consistent with innocence. There are good stories, lame stories, impossible stories, and yes, true stories. That story that you have is your brief for the case, and you must live with it. It's a hard business.

I used to treat every case as if there was a possibility that the story I was told by my client might be true and did the best I could with what I had. I have found that the most important thing in criminal representation is the ability and willingness to try the case to a jury. If that can be communicated to your client, you are on solid ground.

# 43

## More Preparing for Trial

**Preparation for trial is the** space of time after the initial interview and concurrent with subsequent interviews. In Massachusetts, cases are put on the clock, and various events are scheduled at the time of arraignment with a tentative trial date picked months or even a year in advance. There is some flexibility in these schedules, such as if you get married or have extended recuperation from surgery, but generally, these dates have to be followed. A death in the family? Well, maybe, but only if it's a close relative. Conferences are scheduled. Motions have to be filed by certain dates and so forth. The idea is to keep the case from disappearing from sight, and that's why the authorities have invented this thing called the tracking order.

My own personal feeling is that the discovery process is overblown. You really don't need much to prepare for a criminal case. The police report is totally necessary, the grand jury testimony not so much unless it is a complex case, which most are not. The issues are simple, and not a lot of research is required. It is possible to overprepare. I see lawyers who have these snap ring binders which contain everything in the case and then some. I walk into a courtroom, and

I hear the snapping as another document is added to the binder. Maybe it works for them, but I have my doubts. Best keep it as simple as possible. Another thing is motions for discovery. These don't need to be filed unless the DA has refused to give you something that is critical to the case. Otherwise, it is time wasted.

Most discovery can be obtained by a simple phone call. Just ask, and you can usually get what you need. The DA doesn't want you going to court complaining that you are being stonewalled on something you should have as a matter of right.

One motion that is an absolute necessity is a request for an order to probation to furnish you with criminal records, if any, of all civilian witnesses. It is surprising what can turn up. Criminal records can be used to impeach credibility, but there are statutory strict rules that must be followed for their use. Knowing the ins and outs of what can be used is a necessity. Even if the record cannot be put in evidence because it does not meet the statutory requirements, you have an edge because you have knowledge that the witness had prior bad behavior. Also, be sure and figure out what can be used against your client if he or she wants to testify and be ready to object. If the impeaching convictions are of the same variety as the case charged, those priors can be excluded as prejudicial.

So the trial date is approaching, and there are those last-minute things. Usually, an interview with the client shortly before is a good idea. Always explore, where possible, the possibility of a resolution short of trial, but with care so the client doesn't accuse you of selling out. Get ready any motions needed for trial, which in my case are only two—a motion to sequester witnesses and a motion for a required finding of not guilty. The first is always granted as a matter of course, the second almost never, but it is absolutely necessary that this be filed for any appellate purposes. If there is more than one indictment, prepare one for each in case one or more of the indictments are dismissed or there is a not guilty verdict on just some of the charges. This is necessary to preserve rights of appeal.

Motions are the bane of this lawyer's existence. Motions are a large part of every lawyer's weaponry, except for mine. I long ago concluded that motions were a waste of time. Let's say you are in the middle of a case and you have a bunch of motions. There is a hearing date, and you walk in with your motions and hand them to the clerk, who would then turn and hand them to the judge. The judge would then smile and say those are denied before he or she even looked at them. This was a joke, of course, but then the judge would look at all your motions, and he or she would now for sure in real time deny them all. This would give the judge an opportunity to say his or her favorite word to the defense, which is *denied*, and it would put him or her in a good mood at least for the start of the hearing or trial, whichever.

I was in the habit of not filing any motions unless absolutely necessary, and when I got to trial, I would sit back and watch while the government filed its stack of motions *in limine* (Latin), the object of which was to strip the defendant of any defense whatsoever. These motions were always dropped on the counsel table minutes before the hearing so that defense counsel has no opportunity to review them. After this initial skirmish, it would be the defense's turn for motions, and what a shock. I didn't have any except one—a motion for sequestration of witnesses. This would put the court in the bad position of having the only defense motion being one it had to allow. There would be a sort of low-voiced (Latin: *sotto voce*), "Oh yes, I have to allow that one."

The fact that the judge had to mutter the word *allowed* and had no defense motions to deny would put the judge in a bad mood and covertly and conversely put me in a good mood, and I'd be off and running in the right frame of mind.

There is an exception to this general practice which I early learned to follow, and this was when the time for the attorney evaluations drew near. I would get a call to schedule a time for my evaluation by a CPCS mastermind, and I would be reminded to bring along a few of my case files. I had made the mistake in one of my early evaluations when I was asked to show motions I had filed of saying, "What motions? I don't file motions. They're a waste of time." With reluctance, they still allowed me to practice. So now what I would do is take one case and file all the motions I could think of, have a hearing in which, as expected, they were all denied, but at least I would have them for evaluation day and the knee jerkers who insisted that the waste of time paperwork be filed. Motions "*in limine*"? Just object to whatever evidence you don't like at trial. It is just as effective, and the jury gets to see you shot down and can conclude the judge is against you and be on your side.

# 44

## A Little Law Required

**There are rare times when** motions do have to be filed, even if the thought gives one hives, as it does me. Frequently, this involves so-called legal writing, which is different from everyday writing in that it is largely incomprehensible. This is something to be avoided at all costs. I could never figure this out. I could get on my feet and argue a case at trial, but I could never write anything considered to be legal writing. If there was a legal argument, and there was almost always a legal argument, it would start with a heading: "Question Presented." I never knew what the question was. The words that struck terror in my heart were for a judge to say, "I need a little law" on a certain point. At all times, it was a necessity for me to avoid legal writing, but sometimes I just couldn't.

One of these times came up in a trial. The defendant had been convicted of distribution of a controlled substance. I had filed a required finding motion at the appropriate times. By the way, this has always been a mystery to me. One moves for a required finding of not guilty at the close of the government's case. This is a motion that asks the judge to find for your client because the government has not met its burden of producing enough evidence for the jury to even consider a guilty finding.

Now suppose that the defendant has decided not to put on a case and rests after the prosecution rests. Do I need to move for a required finding a second time? Nothing has changed. No evidence has been added. But apparently, I need to file two motions, one at the end of the government's case and one at the "close of all the evidence," even if there has been no further evidence. Anyway, I had filed both motions, and the judge floored me by saying she would give me a few days to file a brief as she was considering setting aside the verdict and allowing the defense motion for a required finding at the close of the evidence. I knew the issue was that where it is inconclusive in a drug deal as to whether the defendant is the seller or the buyer, the defendant was entitled to a verdict in his favor on the dealing charge.

I went to the library to look up some case law. The library in Boston is called the "Social Law Library." Don't ask me why it's called that. What is social law anyway? I have no idea. No socializing is going on there, and usually, the librarians outnumber the library users two to one. The library is connected to the courthouse or at least it used to be. You now have to go outdoors for a few steps to find the library entrance. The library is expensive to belong to, about dollar sign five zero zero dot zero zero per year but worth it in my opinion. Its worth is twofold.

It is a good place to go in case you are trying to hide from a client or also a judge who might want you for a hearing or a conference or maybe a probation officer. The other is to use their facilities instead of the grubby ones they have over in the courthouse. I mean, they are the best. At the courthouse, there is an unfortunate dearth of those ubiquitous restroom signs which say, "We aim to please. You aim too, please." Also, it is extremely restful and quiet if you feel like nodding off.

The furniture is good, and the place is deserted. If one of those court people finds you at a later time and demands to know where you have been, they will be mollified when they learn you were at the library, boning up on legal points rather than at the movies. Just don't tell them you were crouched low over behind the Nevada Reports. There are some rooms and spaces between the shelves where if you were *in extremis*, you might never be found.

Anyway, I found some law that supported the defendant's position. So here's what I did. I wrote a motion captioned "Motion to Set Aside the Verdict" and then wrote that "in support thereof," the defendant cites the following cases, put in the citation for four cases, and then concluded that "on the basis of the foregoing," the defendant's motion should be granted. The entire motion took up about a half a page, and no "memo" of law was attached.

Days later, there was a hearing on the motion. Prior to this, the government filed its standard fifteen-page missive in opposition. This was done with the usual government ploy, which was to give you, the defense lawyer, a copy of its brief two minutes before the hearing so you are still reading it when the case is called. I don't know whether the judge appreciated the brevity of the motion or what, but this magnificent judge, who apparently had not gotten the message from judge school which was that the only word ever allowed in a courtroom when speaking to the defense was "denied" (okay, "maybe objection overruled" are another couple of words), but she granted the motion, and my client walked out a free man. As can be expected, the Commonwealth representative was extraordinarily unhappy. This was a very nice day, and I had succeeded without laboring through the terrors of brief writing.

Another case was a lot more complex. It involved a charge of a second offense weapons violation. There were several ways in which there could be a first offense, which if committed again became a second offense with an enhanced penalty. The government had tried to allege that this case was a second offense except that this offense was of a different kind than any of the enumerated first offenses in the second offense statute. Most importantly, this kind of weapons violation was invented ten years after the second offense statute had been enacted, and there was no suggestion that this new weapons violation be made a part of the second offense law. I didn't quarrel with the offense itself, just that it could not be a second offense, and I filed a motion to dismiss the second offense portion of the charge.

A hearing of sorts was held, and I was astounded that the judge was leaning in the direction of the government. The case was taken under advisement. This is often done because the judge has no idea what anybody is talking about and has to do some research or farm the thing out to a law clerk. Now I'm thinking I better file something. So I made this huge mistake, which was to ask one of the appellate guys in our office to write a memo—yes, that's what they're called. I have no idea why they are called that. Maybe so that the person who gets the memo is to be reminded of some law they forgot.

A few days later, I was handed something which, on reading, I realized had absolutely nothing, I mean nothing to do with the "question presented." And I actually paid this guy for this nothing. I filed it anyway since I had nothing else to give to the court. Later, after a short hearing, the judge informed me she was denying my motion to dismiss. I was now doubly astounded and had to regroup.

I gave as much thought to the problem as it deserved—maybe more than it deserved—and began to realize I was not really dealing with a legal issue but with something else, which was that the judge had a thing for this assistant DA. I don't mean that, but that she liked or maybe we can go with was fond of this DA.

As soon as he came into court, this judge would give him the big hello and exchange pleasantries, even if it was in the middle of a hearing. I knew that I, a stooped, balding, seventy-something could never compete with this fair-haired legal wizard, but I couldn't let this go. I don't mean to put this judge down because she was a great jurist who did so many really good things for a lot of people. But she was going to make a mistake and likely get reversed on appeal, even given all the nuttiness in the appellate courts. This meant that I was going to have to try my hand at legal writing, a definite anathema. I put together something of a few pages and did something that was not on the approved list of legal writing norms at HLS, which is that I used a tool known as a Sharpie and highlighted the text that was important and also the sections of the applicable Mass. General Laws with arrows and underlining. It was a black Sharpie, not one of those lame yellow highlighters fancied by people who read in cafeterias. Also, that damnable little blue book—*A Uniform System of Citation*—was given a furlough for this venture. The caption was "A Motion for Reconsideration," and I filed it.

The next thing that happened was the occurrence of a minor—no, a major miracle. The judge reversed herself, said she was convinced, and allowed the motion for reconsideration and also allowed the motion to dismiss. A great piece of work was done when the judge gave salve to the disappointed DA by iterating that she was doing so "but that it was a close case," which it wasn't as she and

I both knew, and maybe the DA did too. But it was something of a breakup. And my client was very appreciative, as he should have been. I had followed my rule, which was never to contest unless you really had something.

# 45

## You're Going to Trial

**All attempts at resolution in** your case have failed, and the day of the trial dawns bright and cheery. You go to court with your heart in your throat, having gotten no sleep the night before. Your client is brought down from the lock-up, and his handcuffs are removed. Usually, your client will show up with that moth-eaten manila envelope which contains the copies of the discovery materials you sent him or her months ago. It's a good idea to have that stowed away before the venire comes down for selection. There may be several lobby conferences beforehand, and pressure will be applied to your client, such as if he doesn't plead to the very generous government offer and gets found guilty, he will regret it.

Your client is not a part of lobby conferences, so it is imperative that their gist be communicated as completely as possible. More importantly, stay away from making up your client's mind as to whether to accept any offers of resolution suggested by the court. Your client may want guidance as to whether he should consider pleading out and may ask your opinion of the case. I sometimes say that the case looks like a tough one, but I'm quick to add that tough cases sometimes win. Never guarantee a victory or even suggest that you are pretty sure you can win it. It is always better if the aftermath is unfavorable that you were pressed by your client to go to trial. Some lawyers insist that you prepare a written statement that the trial is the result of the defendant's decision and his alone and that the client has been advised of all possible outcomes and have the defendant sign it. For me, not a good idea. It suggests a lack of trust between you and your client. Treat his word as being trustworthy. I've never had any trouble with that.

Attempts at avoiding a trial have failed, and, gulp, your client is set at the bar for trial, as it is said. The doors are flung open, and a panel of prospective jurors is brought in—many dozens or just a few dozen, depending on the complexity of the case. You are now on stage, and it is important to remember this, and it is also important that you explain this carefully to your client. My normal procedure is to give my client some paper and a pen and have him write down suggestions he has for me while the case is ongoing. If it is necessary to confer at length, I will ask for a recess. Always be respectful when speaking with your client when the jury is present, even if the request from your client is sheer lunacy.

Often, your client suggests you ask questions about something that is inadmissible, or worse, questions about something which will help the government's case. Treating your client with respect is most important. This does not mean holding your client's hand or rubbing his back or patting his arm. Lay off the touchy-feely stuff.

The questions required by statute are asked, and there is a show of hands as to whether any of them apply. Usually, the judge has briefly outlined what the case is about, so the jurors who have a particular antipathy to a certain type of crime can express their doubts as to their partiality. They do so by holding up their number cards they have been provided in the jury room. These jurors will then be spoken to at side bar when necessary. Normally, jurors are called in numerical order, and those expressing no reservations about serving are seated. The court gives you a form to try and keep track of what number is seated in what seat.

This is a personal predisposition of mine. I rip up the preprinted form provided by the court and throw it in the trash. I use a sheet of my own paper to keep the box score on the jurors. Somehow, using the government's form makes me feel as if I am in league with the Commonwealth. All psychology, I know, but I need as much of that as I can use.

Your client has the right but not a requirement to be present at sidebar when there is questioning regarding the impartiality of a prospective juror. I always recommend to my client that he or she be present. Input by the client is vital for the main reason that it is your client's case and your client's jury. I am not afraid to make suggestions, but I always defer to the client's wishes even if they are only operating on hunches. This will save possible disputes later on. Also, pay attention to the mechanics of the sidebars where these juror examinations are taking place. There is you, your client, the DA, the prospective juror, and sometimes a stenographer, all whispering. Have your client stand back so that he or she does not physically intimidate the prospective juror.

Finally, sometimes it takes hours—and if there are multiple defendants, days—before a jury is assembled. The object is to arrive at a panel that excludes those who believe that the only reason the defendant is there is because he is guilty of something and those who believe in the violent overthrow of the government as presently constituted or assert they were victims of police brutality.

About the time I left on my first burnout, I had signed up for a two-day seminar sponsored by NACDL (National Association of Criminal Defense Lawyers). Jury selection was a cutting-edge topic. Several big criminal cases had been won where teams of jury selection experts claimed substantial responsibility for the results. These teams had used psychological techniques and other tools to assure that the jury selected would be prone to an acquittal. I was there to learn, and although I doubted I would ever have the type of case which would allow for the high expense of one of these jury selection experts, I might still gain knowledge which could help. But I would have to be persuaded because I had my own jury selection technique, and it was this: "Gimme any twelve." That was because I was convinced there was absolutely no way to determine if a juror would favor your cause or not, and if I couldn't convince the average juror, then I wasn't doing my job.

I have to qualify this because years later, I was empaneling a jury in a certain town where virtually everyone on the prospective jurors' panel was either a neighbor of a cop or was a relative of a cop or was a cop, and if it wasn't cops, then it was FBI agents. So maybe not those twelve. There are always exceptions. And in another case, there was a prospective juror who was a lawyer employed by the very office that was prosecuting my client. Normally, this would be an easy challenge. However, he also happened to be the grandson of the most notorious criminal defense lawyer of the previous thirty years. What to do? I tried to suggest to my client maybe we should consider keeping him, but he wouldn't hear of it, and with great reluctance, I challenged him.

The final day of the seminar, the two expert camps were to be put to the test. A number of people were rounded up and brought into the conference hall to play the role of prospective jurors. They were vetted and questioned by the expert panels, and here is what happened. The expert camps couldn't agree on who should sit on the jury in the fictitious murder charge which was drawn up especially for the exercise. The arguing and the name-calling became intense over which prospective juror was best. My "gimme any twelve" theory had weathered the storm, and I'm still convinced that that is the best approach. There are other things that can be accomplished during the jury selection process, but they have nothing to do with guessing who is going to go your way in their deliberations.

Just because I believe in the "gimme any twelve" theory does not mean that I am not aggressive in challenging jurors—not because I have any expertise in jury selection but because it helps me to get into trial mode and calm the butterflies that go with trying a criminal case. The reality is, in virtually all cases, the defense has very little, and the evidence against is overwhelming. And there is always the remote possibility, if the jury selection process drags along, that something will happen and you won't have to try the damn thing.

Eventually, the box is filled with jurors considered to be unbiased. Before they are sworn, the DA is given the opportunity to have a messenger run down to its offices and run a record check on the prospective jurors. It has been decided by the higher-ups that this information should be available. We don't want the venire to be dirtied by anyone with a past association with the criminal justice system. This gives the court a chance to ask a prospective juror, "How come you didn't tell us about the fifteen years you did in Georgia for cattle rustling?"

Eventually, the dust settles, everyone is happy, and the jury is sworn: "If he is guilty, you will say so. If not guilty, you will say so, and no more." I suppose that's because the jury can be polled after a guilty verdict to be sure it is unanimous. I've never done it but have been tempted on occasion.

The judge will, at this point, make some preliminary remarks. These remarks are usually to educate the jurors but also to let the jurors know that he or she is a smart and decent person—marrying the jury, it is called. This works to varying degrees. It is important to pay attention to this process so as to have a read on how the case might proceed. The interaction between you as counsel and the judge is extraordinarily important. At the beginning, be sure if the judge tells jokes that you laugh at them. It can't hurt, and sometimes they are even funny. The judge is establishing that he or she is the one in control, and you, the counselor, better believe it.

Never, never, never take on the judge. Even if the jury does not particularly like the judge, the respect is still there, and you will lose face if you are disrespectful to the court. And remember, if you, the lawyer, go off the rails and lose it over what appears to be the obvious partiality of the judge, the judge can impartially put you in jail. It doesn't happen often, but it does happen, and guess who gets backed up on an appeal to the single justice. So be respectful to the court at all times. The jury will get the idea if the judge is trying to steer the case.

# 46

## The Trial Begins

**The trial is about to** begin, and there are certain things I usually like to do. You will be sitting facing the judge with the jury off to the left or the right, depending on which courtroom you are in. It is important that you, the lawyer, always take the seat closest to the jury. You are handling the case, and you are in charge, you hope. Keep the client in your shadow so the jury can't see what kind of miscreant he or she is. You are able to provide some cover for your client in case he wants to clear out his nose or scratch himself.

I once had a client lean over to say something during a trial, and he drooled on me. It was hard to be surreptitious about this, and I'm sure the jury noticed. I certainly did. I didn't win that case. And always speak to your client respectfully. Your client may come up with an idiotic suggestion during the trial. Try not to say audibly "Listen, stupid" or "You should have pleaded this case out." I always give a pen and paper to my client and suggest that he write down suggestions. This is so that he doesn't engage you in conversation when the testimony is ongoing and cause you to miss what is being said.

Another habit I had was to try and look small. This took some effort since I am a fairly big person. I could usually find a chair with broken springs to make use of. This made me a little lower than the other people in the courtroom and enhanced the aspect of being picked on. This is very important. It is like hiding behind stone walls the way the colonists did when facing the British or maybe more like the famous cartoon of "Kilroy was here," where the edge of counsel table is about nose-level.

Another helpful thing is if the government shows up with a ton of evidence. Boxes and boxes of stuff that the government plans to put into the case to bury your client. I call this the wheelie advantage. It is where the government has so much evidence they have to use a wheelie to bring it all in. The jury is likely to think the defense is being overwhelmed, hopefully unfairly, and will lean in your direction. To reemphasize this, I usually take the discovery material I have been provided and reduce it to as few pages as possible. I've mentioned that I usually only have a few motions. They might be in one file, and the police report and grand jury testimony in another. That's it. That's all you need. I see those lawyers who have now deployed their three-ring binders. I have found that in the heat of a trial, where you are trying to listen to the testimony, make objections, make faces at the jury, and scowl at the judge, there is no time to consult binder number three to see if the witness said something slightly different three months ago.

I also keep a pad in front of me and try to make a note of what I want to ask on cross-examination. I am prone to that thought that when I sit down, it is, oh shit, I forgot to ask something important or my client will scold me for not asking about something he thought was crucial to the case. After a cross-examination, I always, before ending, ask the court if I may have a moment and check with the client and also look at my notations to see if there is something I have missed. It's a good idea. It saves trouble later if the client tries to accuse you of ineffective assistance of counsel. "I asked you, and you didn't bring it up."

I have said that sometimes, the "No questions, Your Honor" is the best cross. That usually works well if the witness is duplicative of other witnesses, and it can point out that the government is just wasting time. But sometimes, it is good to fill up some space by asking a series of dumb questions just to show you are not rolling over and playing dead. I've already mentioned the case where I was able to establish that the ballistician wasn't able to see the projectile leave the gun at the time of the test fire. These types of questions may possibly develop sympathy for the client by showing that the defendant's lawyer is incompetent. It is important to be respectful to the witness. Some irritation is okay if you keep getting the amnesia responses "I can't recall" from the cops and unresponsive answers from the witnesses who want to fill in their own irrelevant views of the case. Control is important, but you can't always have it.

One thing about cross-examination: you see ads for textbooks about so-called "Killer" cross-examination. Keep your money. The best cross is ordinarily low key, and the best cross you ever gave is one you didn't even know was effective. Also, don't worry about questions that get answers that appear to be damaging to your client. Even with the greatest of care, some question will result in an answer you might regret. Pretend it didn't happen, hope the jury was napping, and move on to the next question. Everyone puts his foot in it from time to time.

So now the Commonwealth has rested, and it is time for the defense to put in a case if it wants to. Frequently, you don't have any witnesses, and even if you do, there is the very important question of whether the defendant will testify. The judge has likely given the instruction at the beginning of the case about the burden of proof and that no inference can be drawn from the defendant's non-testimony or failure to present evidence. Recently, it has been ruled that this instruction need not be given if the defendant opts out because it highlights the issue. My druthers? Always, always ask for the instruction. I can't give a reason. It's just the way I like to do it.

You probably will have explored the question about the defendant taking the stand before trial. Occasionally, the defendant will be sure he will not testify. So that usually ends it, but it is very important to keep a little corner of your brain open in case there is a change of mind. You don't want to be caught flat-footed in case the wind shifts.

Many pundits think that having the defendant testify is the worst thing that he or she can do. I am very much of the opposite opinion. It is important that this be understood: these cases are the defendants' cases, and as much as possible, what takes place in the trial should be with the defendant's advice and consent. You will never win them all, and if your client winds up in the jug, your client will at least feel as if he got his best shot. I can't tell you how many times I've been thanked after the client got sent away, and conversely, how many times I've received no thanks for a job well done on an acquittal.

Another reason is, why not? Your client has probably been buried by all that evidence they've unloaded from the wheelie. Maybe the defendant can charm the jury and get out from under. A second reason is the DA's office. DAs have no experience at cross-examination. More often than not, the DA makes the defendant look good. They yell at the defendant and insinuate that the defendant is lying and wind up generating sympathy for your client. Most important is that the decision be completely your client's. Most clients want to box you in and make it your decision.

I have developed a usable patter to keep the defendant on track for making the decision his own. You should too. It will avoid problems later on. Anticipating the possibility that my client might testify, I usually have prepared a separate sheet or sheets of paper which contain what I expect to be the defendant's testimony. I then ask questions designed to elicit his or her version of the case. I just hope the defendant is able to follow along and not say something like "I never said that" or "What are you asking me that for?"

Before the defendant has an opportunity to testify, the court will occasionally ask if the defendant intends to do so, either at a recess or at sidebar. If the answer is yes, then the judge will sometimes excuse the jury (if the question has been asked at sidebar) and engage in a colloquy with the defendant as to whether he or she understands what they are doing. Normally, the defendant will be warned that he will be subject to cross-examination. This will now be on the record in case the defendant later says you never told him he could be questioned by the DA. The purpose of this colloquy normally is to talk your client out of it and get on with it. Hopefully, your client will pay no attention to this, but an emphatic warning by the court as to possible cross-examination by the DA will go a long way to avoid future problems and also ready your client for that eventuality.

# 47

# The Close

**Assume that you have survived** the evidentiary part of the case, and it is now necessary to go to the next phase. Remember that you have to say that the defendant rests. Many times, I have forgotten this in the heat of a trial and looked like an idiot. The judge says, "Are you resting?"

"Oh yes. I forgot."

Laughter from the jury.

This next part is the closing. Sometimes the judge will give a little speech informing the jury about the function of the closing. "It's not evidence, blah, blah." This gives you a minute to compose yourself and vanquish the butterflies. Occasionally, there will be a recess for a few minutes. Since the defense goes first, the judge frequently asks you, the defense counsel, with a smirk on his or her face if you would like a little time to polish up the BS. Sometimes the judge will just go into the closing argument with no fanfare. This is the best because it means the closing will be over sooner rather than later.

I repeat, on a rare occasion, the judge will cross up your expectation that there will be a recess when you have reached a late hour and expect the court to recess for the day. The idea is to catch you flatfooted. You need to be prepared for this possibility.

Arising from your low seat and thinking, *What the hell am I going to say?* you begin your summation. Don't say, "May it please the court"; that's for high echelon stuff. I don't even say, "Ladies and Gentlemen of the jury." Too stilted. Get up slowly and stand about ten feet from the jury box, even though you would rather be ten miles away. Start off with something sensible like, "As you are probably aware, I am the defense counsel, and I have the difficult job of defending my obviously innocent client." That's always a good start.

I usually have with me a short list of the points I want to make. There's never time to refer to it, so the function of that list is to remind you of all the things you meant to say but didn't after you sit down. Try to engage the jury with eye contact, especially that person who is scowling at you and that other person who is holding onto his neck. And never pace back and forth. The only reason to ever do this is if you want the jury to pay no attention to what you are saying. I have developed the ability to speak while another part of my mind is thinking about what I am going to say next. There is also a small part of my brain, a very small part, that is astonished at what I actually am saying.

I am usually aggressive in my presentation. A little emotion on behalf of your client can never hurt. When the closing is over, you will feel better, and so will your client, if you have let the prosecution have it. I have always felt there is nothing to be gained by holding back. Conclude by asking the jury to find your client not guilty, but be sure that you include the word *not* in there. At long last, the ordeal is over, and you can sit, or more likely slump, into your chair. The deed is done, and the case is over. You can now watch as the DA gets up and excoriates you and your client while you surreptitiously try hard not to shake your head in disagreement. The judge is already doing the opposite.

This part is finally over, and you have objected to every word of the prosecutor's closing and moved for a mistrial. Now comes the judge's charge. The judge's charge is pretty much cookie-cutter. There are some general remarks—burden of proof, presumption of innocence, reasonable doubt, direct and circumstantial evidence, as well as the elements of the offenses charged. The courtroom is sealed off more tightly than a COVID-19 hospital room. That is so that no one will disturb this part of the proceedings. This is important because, as a general rule, the judge's charge is incomprehensible, which is an aid to your cause. The jury can only think, "We have no clue," so it can do what it wants.

Some of these charges go on for hours. Look for that juror who is dozing. He or she is probably on the side of the defendant. Some have said that some charges favor the defendant and some favor the Commonwealth. Truthfully, they all sound to me like they all but say, "Find the defendant guilty." The judge then calls the two sides up to the bench and asks if there is anything he or she has missed, and if they have, I never know and say, "No, Your Honor."

Now the jury is sent out. Not a good idea to write in large letters on a legal pad, "My client is really a good guy" and put it where the jurors can see it as they pass by on their way to deliberate. The courtroom opens up, and the waiting begins. I usually congratulate the opposition on what a fine job it has done. If I win, this will just be salt in the wound. If I lose, at least I have been a gracious loser. Sometimes, after the rare occasion when I do win, I go up to the prosecutor and remind him or her that he or she never had a chance.

While I'm waiting, a lawyer that I know might happen by and ask if I have a jury out. I tell him I do. He asks how long the jury has been out, and I tell him ten minutes. "Wow," he says, "that's a victory in itself!" Indeed. A lot of waiting goes on while the jury is deliberating. I have a good record of convincing the jury to at least think about it, as they say, and so I have probably had more than the ordinary share of waiting. If my client is in custody, I periodically go up to the lockup to reassure him.

"You never know" is usually about the best I can say. In many cases, the jury is out for a while, and then you are summoned to the courtroom for a jury question. There is a delay normally because the prosecutor can't be found. If the jury has to be brought in to have the question answered, I try to look anxious but hopeful. I have spent many hours at home perfecting that look. Some of the questions can give a hint as to which way the jury is leaning, but not always. Eventually, a court officer will come out and tell you that a verdict has been reached. I have already explained to my client what will happen when that occurs. There will be a lot of court muscle standing behind him because some defendants have acted out to an adverse result. I ask my client to take it matter-of-factly if it's bad and remain calm.

There is still the issue of disposition, and a stream of profanity or wrestling match with a bailiff will probably not help. And on the other hand, dancing and war whoops if there is a favorable verdict is probably not a good idea either. I've had clients who collapsed on the rendering of a guilty verdict and clients who didn't know what happened. I've had clients who were so nervous that they didn't know they were acquitted until I told them. Sometimes the foreperson who delivers the verdict gets a throat frog, and there is a delay in the verdict announcement. The jury gets nervous too.

If the verdict is not guilty, you get the hell out of there, unless your client has been in custody, in which case there needs to be a check to see if there might be a warrant outstanding from another court. If your client is already serving time elsewhere, off she or he goes to that place, usually so fast you don't have time to accept the thanks you expect from a grateful client. As the jury files out, you smile sweetly and mouth "Thank you." Air kisses are discouraged. If the verdict is guilty, then you need to hang around for the disposition, which may be right then and there or at a later date.

Right then and there is usually better, unless the jury has decided to remain for the sentencing. A later date gives more time to wind up on your client, and you'd rather just close the file and not have to go back and be reminded how you blew it. And if your client does time in the state's prison, remember the sentence appeal. That way, you will have an opportunity to have your teeth kicked in all over again.

Years ago, public executions were dispensed with, but that doesn't mean that all the bloodletting has been abolished. In Massachusetts, it has been decided that the course of justice is best served by extending an invitation to the sitting jury in the case of a guilty verdict to attend the sentencing. This, of course, amps up the possibility that the disposition may be on the heavy side. Even though there is an obvious drawback to a later sentencing, you can say you need time to prepare for the sentencing event because you were sure your client was going to be acquitted. A delay usually means the jury, which has had enough taken out of their lives, will not return for a postponed sentencing hearing. If the sentencing takes place immediately, the jurors might give you that look after you have spent time building up your client and claiming he is innocent in your closing, only to find out that your client is a habitual offender and has spent half his life breaking into houses. You can ignore them. The case is over, and there is no further need to charm them.

You do the best you can at the dispositional hearing and hope that your client receives a sentence that he or she can handle, and you are done. Papers should be filed for an appeal on the merits, as opposed to the sentence appeal, which is different, and most important, you need to withdraw from the case. If you don't, you will be getting a notice from the appeals court asking if your appellate brief is ready. Be sure the case is referred to CPCS for assignment of the appeal matter to appellate counsel. Keep the file in readiness because there is always the chance there is some complaint that something wasn't handled appropriately, and you will need to explain the action you took.

And that is pretty much how it is, at least for this practitioner. An arduous time with all its twists and turns, but for me, fulfilling nonetheless. And what helped make the journey through all of those on-again, off-again forty-six years so worthwhile were the clients for whom I never felt I could do enough in guiding them through their time before the bar of justice.

# 48

## Those Lovely Clients

**So now you've learned what** it takes to handle criminal cases in the upper and lower courts of the Commonwealth, and you have already concluded—not so fast—about becoming a public defender. If further urging in that direction—a final convincer—is necessary, then I must remind you of the clientele and the truly amazing individuals they are. As I mentioned, I used to look forward to my court appointment days because it would give me the opportunity to meet many new and fascinating people. There are some clients, and that's most of them, who exist on the very edges of the sane world, and I can't help but have a small place in my heart for them. I also think that I have, at one time or another, represented most of them.

This lovely man came into view on one of those days when I was the duty person. I was always on the lookout for something new and interesting, and I took as many cases as I could so as to maximize that possibility. I get word that there is a man in the lockup who is acting a little strangely, the type of person I automatically gravitate toward. So I make it a point to talk to him. He was charged with indecent assault and battery. The allegations were that he was at the

Boston Medical Center for some unknown reason. As he was passing a woman waiting at an ATM, he had, for some further unknown reason, been moved to gently place his forearm against her posterior. This quite naturally upset the victim, who reported the incident. A search for the perpetrator was conducted. The medical center treats some rough customers and so has a large and aggressive police force. The place is also wall-to-wall surveillance cameras. It was not long before the defendant was located and arrested.

This charge, of course, brings into play the sex police and the attendant requirements of the sex registry, and he had to be warned about all of that. A preliminary interview indicated to me that everything didn't seem to fit together, so I asked the on-duty psychologist to conduct an examination as to mental state—competency, as it were. I don't have to be present, but I almost always stay for these examinations for reasons I'm not entirely clear about. The questioning is schematic but enough to determine whether a full-blown examination at the State Hospital is needed. The questioning takes place after the "Lamb" warnings—I always thought an odd name for the warnings that anything that is said is not confidential as far as the case is concerned.

The examination for this client proceeded, and he is at first a little unusual in his answers but not seriously so. At a later point in the exam, the defendant is asked about drug usage, and he responds that yes, he has taken drugs. He is then asked what drugs these were, and he replies, "The kind that make you want to have sex all night" (I paraphrase here).

So now we are alerted that we are headed down a path, and as the exam continues, it develops that he wants to be sure that we understand he is a member of the national security team of the

George Bush White House. Follow-up questions about his White House participation are answered with the assertion that this can only be disclosed "on a need-to-know" basis. This earns him a State Hospital trip.

The result of his examination at the hospital was that he was mentally ill, and he was committed for treatment. He never forgot the kind and thoroughly professional representation I had given him, and I received many letters informing me that I was being fired, but since there were no hard feelings, would I be kind enough to make a contribution to his canteen? I received many engaging letters of this sort. Holidays would arrive, and I would receive a note wishing me felicitations for the season and also a reminder that he had informed George Bush that "I was a good guy." I've often wondered if our national security team, such as it is, couldn't have used a contribution from this wonderful man.

Another client I met I was assigned to on one of those duty days in a district court. He had been arrested and charged with burglary. He had been found sleeping (passed out) in an upstairs hallway of a secure building in downtown Boston. Nobody was sure how he got there. The defendant had a previous record and was ordered, after a hearing, held on bail. Since there was no intent to cause any mischief, I was able at a later court hearing to gain his release and have the charge reduced to a misdemeanor.

While that case was pending, he came to my office for an interview. He told me that he had recently done time for bank robbery. We had a little chuckle over the fact that one of the banks he had knocked over was in the same building as my office. He had been arrested for that, and it was one of the offenses for which he had been sentenced to prison. He had been a model inmate and worked a prison job that paid him a small hourly wage. He had saved his money, and by the time of his release, he told me he had a stockpile of something like seventeen hundred dollars. Happy to be out, he had gone to one of the local casinos, got drunk, and blew it all in one night, he claimed. He came back to Boston, and with no place to stay, had managed to find his way into that building where he was arrested on the burglary charge.

He tells me that he has a problem. When he drinks, a metamorphosis takes place, and there is a risk he will become a bank robber. He knew that staying dry was of utmost importance lest the changeover began. At length, his open case was dismissed. He would stop by my office from time to time to talk. He was a shy man, good-humored, and industrious. Wherever he worked, he worked hard and was appreciated by his employers. Time passed, and then one day, I receive a call from the court. Mr. Bank Robber has emerged, and he is in the lockup and in need of my services.

At court, he sheepishly informs me that he had started drinking and he went big time, robbing two banks on successive days. These banks were across from each other on Freedom Corner at State and Congress Street. I agree to represent him, and sometime later, I receive the discovery package. Photos of my client leaving each of the banks with the loot had been taken by security cameras. And what was that he was wearing? Was it a sweatshirt? It was. And what was that on that sweatshirt? Could it be a shield—a coat of arms? And could it be crimson-colored? It was. Robbing a bank wearing a shirt emblazoned with the Harvard coat of arms? Priceless.

On another case, I was assigned to represent a defendant charged with possession of obscene material, three counts. The case was complicated by the fact that he had similar cases in a different state where he had been on probation, and that state wanted him for violating that probation. As a result, an interstate rendition warrant had been lodged against him. If he made bail, the rendition warrant would take him to that other state. His ploy was that he would plead out the present case if the rendition warrant was dropped, something that was not going to be done. This meant a probable trial on the obscene materials charges since he wouldn't plead. I obtained the file from the last of the five attorneys who had previously represented this defendant—thousands of pages in three file boxes that I could barely lift.

This defendant had managed to tie up the judicial system for four years. He had been in jail for so long that he had preprinted address labels, minus the name of the jail, of course. This was handy because, as I soon found out, this defendant was a furious letter writer. The files I received were filled with correspondence with previous lawyers, most of whom he had been displeased with. For some reason or other, we got along just fine. This meant I was to be the recipient of many, many letters.

One of the reasons the case had gone on for so long was because of a motion to suppress that had been filed by a previous attorney. A hearing had been held, and some of the material to be used as evidence was suppressed. The government, naturally displeased and aware they have a friend in the appellate courts, appealed. This was an interlocutory appeal, which is accepted according to the discretion of the appellate courts. When the government appeals, this appeal is almost always allowed because to let the suppression ruling stand would mean the end of the case. Can't have that, so the appellate court takes the case. This takes time. Briefs. Counter-briefs.

Extensions. Arguments and time to mull over a decision and then write and publish the decision add to the delay.

By the time a decision was rendered, years had gone by, and you can guess what happened—allowance of motion to suppress reversed, and evidence will be permitted against the defendant.

I pay many visits to my client, who for some reason is being held in a remote jail in the middle of the state—a two-hour drive. He is likable, but he's wired, and he is going to drive me nuts, although I don't have far to go. These visits are necessary in order to prepare a complex case for trial. On one occasion, I go to see him, and I have been sent a bunch of letters. This time, three arrive on the same day. I have received so many letters, many of them pages long and all handwritten in hard-to-read handwriting that I've given up reading them. I'm in the parking lot of the jail, and I don't much feel like seeing this man at this point, but I think I better look at the three before I see him. I glance through them and see he just wants some document or other among the hundreds he already has. I leave with a sigh of relief and mail him what he wants.

On another occasion, I go to see him. I am rattled at the prospect of talking with this wild man. I lock up my belongings and make the visit, and it goes okay or as okay as these visits can go. I go to my locker, and it's empty. I'm trying to explain to the staff that someone has stolen my belongings and receive the usual, "Why bother us?"

I go back and make a further check. What an idiot. I put my stuff in a locker and then absentmindedly locked the one underneath. This was the state I was in with this client.

Eventually, his case goes to trial. I know what the evidence is going to be, and I am not describing it for this family magazine. The DA shows up with his equipment to display the obscene pictures. Normally, the government rolls in some rickety old projector and fires it up. Then the first picture displayed is the hand of the prosecutor trying to get that picture into the machine. The pictures are so small they can only be seen with the aid of a telescope. Not this time. They have brought in a specialist who knows how to run the machine, and it is displaying pictures in the same size as a large-screen movie theater. The first picture is being shown, and it is of a woman in some form of undress. I know that the pictures are going to be shown by this crafty DA in ascending scales of shock value.

The jury suspects this, and for sure, no one on this jury is going to ask me out. Finally, after a day's worth of trial, I explain to my client that each one of the three indictments carries a possible five years, and we have a judge who is capable of imposing from and after sentences. Since the DA is still offering concurrent sentences, maybe a plea would be wise—especially since he has about four and a half years of jail credits for time awaiting trial. The plea is offered and accepted, and I have survived. He does a few weeks and is then off to that other state. I wish him well, but that doesn't stop the letters. I receive a few more—pencil-sized.

I mentioned previously the group I have called the gang of twenty-two that apparently has check-cashing privileges at the appeals court. I have to discuss this episode very carefully because, obviously, members of that group are very serious people. It started off this way, as near as I can determine. A very well-dressed and well-groomed man walked into a gang office and asked for so-and-so at the reception area. It was the day before Thanksgiving, and not many people were around. He assured the receptionist that he was there on legitimate business and was allowed back into the office area.

Soon he left with salutations to all to have a nice holiday. What was not known was that he had not left empty-handed. He had also left with a few checkbooks belonging to others, and he had managed not to take the ones on top of the box but ones on the bottom where they would, he hoped, not be missed. This well-dressed gentleman, in order to keep himself well-dressed and fed, then proceeded to write checks on those accounts and then deposit them into an account that he had opened in a new identity he had created for himself. His hope was that enough money would be going into the purloined accounts so that as fast as he drew on them, they would be replenished, and thus the outflow would not be discovered. At some point, a large check was written by Mr. Twenty-two on one of the accounts such that, as a consequence of the fradulent withdrawals, there were not enough funds to cover, and the embarrassed victim received a friendly letter from his bank that his check had been dishonored.

There was an investigation, and it was discovered that the losses were substantial and involved more than one individual and more than one firm. Through a set of circumstances too lengthy to go into, the culprit, now discovered to be the defendant, was apprehended and prosecuted. I was assigned the case. I wish to assure all and sundry that over the years, I have not borne the slightest resentment toward any of that group. They are, after all, the most honorable of men and women and are pillars of the legal community, as is well known in the appeals court. Nevertheless, I did notice as I went along with my representation of this client that there was a spring in my step that I had not noticed previously. It wasn't as if I had done the thing myself, after all.

I had said earlier that the people I met in my job search knew how to add, subtract, multiply, and divide. Maybe forget the add and subtract because apparently, this was not being done in any checkbook register. Is it wrong to ask? Are there some people who have so much money lying around they don't bother to keep track? Business must be good at those firms.

My representation of this client resulted in a plea. A stay in one of the prisons rubbed off a little of the charm, and he was a letter writer, so I heard a lot about the discomforts of prison life. His brother was an upstanding citizen who ran a large Midwestern company. We were in touch, and he sent me a small fee to see if I could do something to have the sentence reduced. I couldn't, which further irked my now ungrateful client. This wasn't quite the end of this. I left my office one afternoon a few years later on my way to lunch. No sooner had I stepped outside when a cab pulled up and out hopped this client, whom I had largely forgotten about. He had just finished up his time and had managed to wangle a cab ride to my office, which was forty miles from the prison. After salutations and "What are you doing here?" he proceeded to tell me he needed some money because he wanted to travel to New York. He knew about the fee I had been paid by his brother, which he felt I had not quite earned.

I should be given the keys to the city for what followed. My bank was right there, and at speed, I had the requested $100 in hand along with a bus schedule, which had somehow appeared. He departed with his many thanks and my best wishes for a safe and prosperous journey. I had obtained the money so fast that I had forgotten to remove my ATM card from the machine and had to go back later to get it.

In a week or so, I received a note from him that he was, in fact, in New York. And, yes, even though he is in New York, I still check my bank balance regularly. Soon I received a letter from him. And for sure, the world is flat, and if you sail out of Boston Harbor, you will fall off the edge, for the letter concluded with the news that he was being considered by the Trump organization for a position managing one of its properties. Who knew? I never heard whether he was hired, but of course, kudos to Mr. Trump for offering to help the criminally besmirched get a new start in life.

# 49

## I Know What I'm Doing

**By this time, I had** a lot of experience, and I was beginning to get the feel of how things worked. I could go to a courtroom with a client and know what to do and when to do it. It was sort of a sixth sense of when to make a move and when to be quiet. It was a good feeling, like I knew without thinking about it. It was instinctive. It had been a long time in coming. I had handled thousands of cases and many, many trials. I was no longer doing the silly things I did at the beginning, although I could still make an ass of myself. But those times were now few and far between. I felt like I knew how to get the most for my clients.

One of the things I enjoyed was going to courts I hadn't been to before or at least appearing before judges I didn't know. There would be the moment when I first appeared when I knew the judge was sizing me up to see if he or she could put something by me. It was that first feeling out of the opposition that I enjoyed.

I had one of those rare cases where I was actually hired, and it was in one of those courts where I infrequently appeared. I had done some work for a man which took me to a court I had never been to previously. I had achieved a successful result, and he had recommended me to this new client. He was a hardworking, good-looking man with no previous record who had a landscaping business. He was charged with possession with intent to distribute a Class D substance—marijuana. He had been pulled over by the state police for a traffic violation. A search of his car had produced an object wrapped in tinfoil that was about the size and shape of a regulation NBA basketball. The object inside the foil was enough gage to turn on half the town where he lived. He was originally from a southern island clime where that, rather than a Beefeater martini, was the preferred form of relaxation.

I wanted to do something for this man in the worst way. We went before a judge that I was not familiar with. He was friendly. There was a little repartee, and the case was put over for the filing of a motion to suppress. Motions to suppress I regarded essentially as losers. I had won a few, but these things involved law and briefs and memoranda, things that were abhorrent to me. In this case, the reason for the stop was that the deck light was out—that third light that every car manufactured after a certain year has. There is a Massachusetts statute that says that the only lights that are required for a motor vehicle to be roadworthy are two red lights in the rear and two white lights in the front. I reasoned that therefore the third light was not a requirement and he could not be stopped for not having one, or as in this case, he had one but it was not working. I prepared a motion, and at the next court date, I filed it.

There was a brief hearing on the filing date, and the judge expressed interest in the contours of the basketball and the wording of the police report. There were some technical questions he had about some of the language of the report. I advanced the grounds of the motion, about which he expressed skepticism. Another court date was scheduled. In view of the judge's comments, I doubteds that I was going to have success, although I had not given up hope.

The next court date, we had a hearing on the motion. The judge asked a few questions and then took the matter under advisement. Another date was set at which time we expected a ruling. At that next court appearance, we were told that the judge was busy in another session, had not yet ruled, and the case was continued. This happened a few more times, and we were given the same excuse that the judge was busy in another session and also had not yet ruled.

A problem with motions to suppress in the district court is that the judges are often close to the local police. A motion to suppress, if allowed, is seen as a slap in the face to the locals. These are slightly different situations, but they illustrate the problem. Early in my career, I was in a district court where a judge decided that someone had not mistakenly walked into a police fist or doorway or fallen downstairs at the police station. A complaint for assault and battery was issued against a possibly offending officer. At arraignment, the entire local police force showed up in uniform to signal their support for the officer. While the case against the cop was pending, calls to the police department all too frequently went to voicemail.

Another example of the friendly judicial attitude I witnessed in the municipal court was when one judge, on spotting police witnesses in the audience, would invite them up for a friendly chat while the onlookers sat with their "What's going on here?" expressions. Still, in this case, it was the state police, so I thought the police pal syndrome might not be so strong.

After several continuances due to the "judge is busy" reason, we were in court early, and the DA came running in with the news that the judge was still busy in another session but had decided to allow the motion to suppress. Strangely, the DA seemed to be pleased with this result. There was no waiting for a judge to do the honors. The clerk told us the complaint was dismissed and read it into the record. Elated, we hurried out of the courtroom. As we entered the corridor, we saw Mr. Trooper heading up the stairs, toting his tinfoil basketball. His head was down as he was walking and hadn't seen us and was obviously unaware of what had just transpired. I was familiar with the building and knew there was another flight of stairs in the back. We didn't want to have to explain our early exit, so we bolted down those back stairs, whooping with joy like schoolkids when class is let out.

These are the magical moments that are hard to describe. Of particular happiness was that the weight was off my client. And the judge, in a different session, did not have to face the trooper's disappointment. I wonder what happened to all that magnificent Mary Jane.

This was not quite the end of the story as so often happens with so many cases. Later, a few weeks or months, whenever, I was leaving the Suffolk Superior Court and walking across the concourse in front when I saw the judge who had made the ruling. Too late for us to avoid each other, so we exchanged salutations. The court he sat in was about thirty miles away and in a different county, so I was curious what he was doing in Suffolk. He advised that he sometimes came to the library, which was adjacent to the superior court, to do research. He had a question for me, which was whether the government had appealed his ruling. I pretended to be astonished and said, "How could the wisdom of your ruling possibly be gainsaid?" or something of that sort. We had a good laugh about that. Hugging judges is not officially permitted, but if it had been, I might have done it. What he had done for my client, a good man, was immense, and he had earned a whole year's salary with that one ruling, in my opinion. This was real judging. Maybe I should have paid more attention to the judicial evaluations and given this judge a few compliments.

# 50

# I Sell Out and Still Win

**At the beginning of the** Mr. Dangerous case, the defendant accused me of being a sellout and attempted to discharge me. Being a sellout is a common accusation in criminal courts. I take a sellout to be a lawyer who does not attempt to pursue the defendant's case as the defendant gives it to him or her. Generally, I always went with whatever story I was told, and whatever it was, I would take it to trial if I had to. At long last, there was one case where circumstances made it imperative to do just that—sell out.

I was assigned to represent a client in superior court charged with breaking and entering a motor vehicle with intent to commit a felony. This crime is punishable by up to twenty years in state's prison. Because he had twice before been sentenced to state prison for three years or more, he was charged under the habitual offender law. Twenty years was the required penalty upon conviction, with no discretion for the court to impose less. The oddity in this case was that he was also charged with larceny of less than $250, a misdemeanor, and that's because what was actually stolen was property worth less than $250. So the government's case is that the defendant broke into a car with the intent to steal property worth more than $250, a felony, but only succeeded in stealing the lesser amount.

Here's what was so unusual: breaking and entering with intent to commit a misdemeanor, property less than $250, is only punishable by six months in the house of correction, and that crime is not a felony. The three-strikes law would not apply since it is only applicable to felonies. Larceny less, as it is called, is punishable by up to a year in the house of correction—again, no three-strikes application. Big difference in penalties depending on intent.

The government's case is that a man is up in his second-story apartment late at night and sees someone looking in his car and shining a flashlight into that car. He then sees the individual go into his car and rummage around. He calls the police, who arrive within minutes. They look for the culprit and find my client in a yard down the street, hiding under a bed of leaves. He is arrested, and on his person, he has some small change and lottery tickets, among other things, and a GPS device which, when a button is pushed, produces the name and address of the man who called and owns the car in question.

I visit the defendant at the place where he is being held on bail. We talk about the case. "I swear, Mr. Wood, I didn't do it." He was only in the yard to take a leak; the change was for the laundromat located ten miles away. And then, "Please, can't you get me out of here?" He needs to take care of his enfeebled mother, who has terminal cancer and who won't last much longer.

The leak story is standard stuff. I've represented enough leaking clients in yards in and around burglarized houses to have floated the city of Boston into the harbor with the tea leaves. So that's the story I have to work with, and I have a client who is facing twenty years mandatory. The no sellout rule means that's what I go with—the "I didn't do it" story—and if I lose, which seems likely, even with all my talents, it's too bad for him if he gets the twenty years. On the other hand, if it's breaking and entering with intent to commit a misdemeanor, he's looking at a maximum of eighteen months, six months plus one year, even if the judge imposes consecutive sentences, and not in state's prison but in the county house of correction.

I return to the office and call the wasting-away mother. I have to hold the phone well away from my ear while the supposedly enfeebled mother bellows at me for not getting her son off the hook. I prepare the case diligently, including having photos taken of the scene by my investigator. I see my client from time to time at the prison and go through the usual routine. He's going to fire me. I don't believe him. He has no faith in me. I expect to be fired, but it doesn't happen. I conference the case with the DA. She will drop the habitual charge if the defendant will accept a seven-year sentence (remember the how-to on the government's effort to sidestep the stupid jurors?). Seven years. He would likely have to do all of that, parole being out of the question. I am obligated to bring this offer to my client, who gives me the same: he didn't do it. We're going to go to trial.

The trial date arrives, and the witnesses are there—it's a go. We have a tough judge who would be more than happy to impose the twenty. There are several things that I think are helpful to the defendant. The first is that the government is going to introduce photos of the view from the victim's apartment, overlooking the spot where he saw my client reconnoitering his car. Those photos will show the expensive stereo equipment and his nice living conditions, which will contrast with my client's obvious impoverishment. In addition, it had been passed around that there were recent thefts in the area, and residents had been warned to lock their cars. This victim had not done so.

I'm wondering, as we empanel, how to approach this case. My brief from the defendant is he didn't do it. I've already done the red jacket versus the burgundy jacket and the bird tattoo versus the seal tattoo and other dead-end cases, so I can easily try the "I was only taking a leak" defense. In the end, the defendant loses and gets the twenty, and I can look at him and tell him I did my job and he should have taken the seven-year bid. But it just seemed that the misdemeanor angle was so promising, and I hated the idea that this man would have to swallow a twenty-year bid when, with a different approach, I might be able to do better for him. So now we are on trial.

The case goes along about as expected, and the evidence pretty much buries us. I'm up there, cross-examining the victim, and I still have in mind the intent to commit a misdemeanor as opposed to the intent to commit a felony. All the evidence shows is that my client's MO is that he shined a flashlight into a number of cars, and if he saw something, he tried the door. If the door was locked, he went on. No forced entry. No broken locks. No smashed windows. It transpires that the victim kept change for tolls, parking meters, handouts to panhandlers, whatnot in the console between the front seats. Now recognize I'm standing at the podium in a courtroom, trying to work for my client, and I can't help thinking it would be nice if the change were visible from outside the car. It wouldn't kill the case if it weren't, but it would help if it was. Ask the question in violation of the trial commandments? Sure, and the right answer was given. The console was open to view from outside the car.

My client is being a star. He is sitting quietly, paying attention, and acting interested in the proceedings. I'm getting to like him. This is a failing of mine, which is I begin to see redeeming qualities in my clients as my representation goes along, even if I am not charmed by the mother. No different here.

Now we arrive at the part where I have to give a closing argument. I know the judge will give an instruction on a lesser offense of breaking and entering misdemeanor. My brief from my client is he didn't do it, and that's what I should argue, and I should object to a charge of breaking and entering misdemeanor as irrelevant to our "he didn't do it" defense. When we probably lose, I tell my client, "Too bad, I did as I was instructed." I just can't do that.

Despite an occasional thought to the contrary, I still have my closely guarded humanity, empathy—whatever one wants to call it. I am going to go my own way and sell this client out, which means I am going to handle the defense the way I think it should be handled and not the way he has told me. So I do my closing and give a brief summation in which I argue that the leak story is gold and he didn't do it. Then I take out my cane and add lamely something like this: "In the utter impossibility that you, O dearly beloved jury, should think the impossible, which is that the defendant is guilty, it should be guilty of breaking and entering with intent to commit a misdemeanor." I hated myself and knew I was, for the first time, selling out my client. But I just couldn't go the non-sellout route. The judge charges the jury, including breaking and entering misdemeanor.

The hardest part of the case starts—the waiting. The jury is out a while, and we are told there is a verdict. The jury comes in and gives its verdict, and I was fairly confident it would go our way, and it did—breaking and entering misdemeanor. And now a remarkable thing happens. He is fully aware that instead of facing a twenty-year sentence, the most he can get is eighteen months and in the house of correction, not the state prison. So what does he do? He starts to cry, and he cries and he cries and he cries. Here is this man who has spent a large part of his life in jail, stealing from other people with the record to show it, revealing that underneath it all, he has some humanity. I just thought that this was a great moment.

But the jury was taken aback. They stood and watched the tearful reaction and couldn't understand because they thought they had returned a verdict that was favorable to him. They didn't know. They didn't know that these were tears of relief and not tears of anguish.

The judge took all of about half a second to impose the maximum: six months plus a year from and after. We didn't care. The defendant had waited for trial about fourteen months, which would be credited to his sentence, and he would be home soon and get howled at by his lovely mother.

I went downstairs to the lockup and spoke with the defendant briefly. I'm not sure he ever thanked me, but he didn't have to. His tears told me his appreciation. I had to wonder: is this the first time anyone had ever done anything for him? I thought about calling his mother, but my eardrum was still intact, so I forbore. Among other things, I'm also a realist, so if you live in the Boston area, lock your car.

# 51

## The Hard Edge of the Law

**This brings to mind another** case that I tried about a year earlier. Nothing particular about this case except the usual bizarre stuff and interesting with all its twists and turns. It's a little complex, so it takes some explaining. My client is arrested for a bunch of serious crimes: rape, armed robbery, assault dangerous weapon, and maybe some others. I'm assigned the case. It is held for a probable cause hearing in the municipal court. The bail is the usual astronomical amount, and the defendant is thus in custody. I see him at the jail, and we talk about the case.

Next court date, the DA moves to dismiss the charges because the victim has recanted, and the government now has no case. But while those charges were pending and before the recantation and subsequent dismissal, the government had obtained a search warrant and searched his room, looking for evidence in support of them. They didn't find anything to support those now dismissed charges but instead find ammunition and a high-capacity feeding device with which they now charge him. The ammunition charges are serious enough, but the high-cap case carries a ten-year mandatory sentence as part of the Massachusetts toughest-in-the-nation gun laws.

In court, after the earlier charges are dismissed, there is an arraignment on the new weapons charges and another high bail. Also, the defendant is on probation for something and owes a year on that. The weapons case is continued, and the probation matter is set down for a hearing at a later date. At the jail, I discuss the surrender hearing. The violation is the new arrest. The defendant was living in a rooming house owned by the mother of a friend, and he claims not to know anything about the new charges. He had been in custody and away from the room for about ten days before the room was searched, and anybody could have had access to his room and put the device in his closet, which was where it was found.

The probation hearing takes place, and we have asked his brother to come in to testify that the room was unlocked and that he had gone there to retrieve some poetry the defendant had written—seriously. My defendant was a self-proclaimed poet. We want to show that the room was unlocked and accessible to anybody in the defendant's absence. But the brother doesn't show up for the surrender hearing, so I put the defendant on the stand in an attempt to establish that fact, a very risky maneuver. We are having a mini-trial to try and beat the probation surrender.

"Look, Judge, he didn't commit the offense, so there is no violation."

We have the wrong judge, and it's one of those preponderance of the evidence type cases. The judge rules that the preponderance standard has been met, and so he's sentenced to the year. I think this is wrong, but there's nothing to be done since the weapons charges are still pending. He is now in the house of correction on the probation surrender but still has to face the weapons charges in superior court. That case rocks along, and there is more discovery provided by the DA. The high-capacity device was found in a jacket hanging in the closet in my client's room, and our crafty DA has had the jacket tested for DNA evidence.

The report comes back, and DNA was found on the collar, but it's not the defendant's. So I'm thinking that's the end of the case. But it isn't. Remember, where there is no case, this is taken as a personal insult by the government, and they ratchet up their prosecutorial armor. But the DA does show she hasn't completely lost her senses because she offers to drop the high-cap charge if the defendant will accept ninety days on the ammo charge, concurrent with the time he is doing. This is an early holiday gift and part and parcel of the goal in a weak case to at least get a piece of the defendant.

I visit him at the county lockup where he is now being held. I'm thinking this is a deal he can't refuse and the case will end. But he does refuse, and I now realize that the unpredictability that surrounds most of what I do is now back. He has confidence in me, he claims, and we are going to go to trial. Oh me, oh my! Finally, all the pretrial dance is over with, and the case is set for trial. We are in a session, and we have a judge known for his fairness, which is usually bad for the defense. I feel better when I am being picked on by one of the "Oh not this guy" judges. That happens a lot.

The case proceeds, and the testimony shows that yes, the weaponry was found in the defendant's room, but all those pictures of guns and the targets with bullet holes and the *Scarface* poster littering the wall belonged to someone else. So that was okay, and we're looking pretty good. The case goes on to another day, and I have the brother on tap, and he is going to come in with the poetry. He's late, and the session is about to start, and the jury is waiting. I grab the poems and find a copier somewhere, make copies, and give them to the DA because I know there will be a squawk if I'm trying to introduce evidence she hasn't seen. The jury files in, and I'm thinking maybe I better check out this poetry, and I do that as the jurors are taking their seats, and what did I just do? This poetry is great stuff, but it is all about my client in the act of coition with his girlfriend. I've just given the opposition a bunch of porno poetry! Am I trying to sink my client? I won't be offering the poems, and I don't know what happened, but the DA did nothing with them. Maybe we got lucky and she never read them.

Next, the DNA person testifies. This is going to be good, I'm thinking, because this will clear my client. The witness testifies and goes over the report in detail, which I am loving. And then there was this bombshell: the DNA, the expert testifies, belongs to a female. In my usual thorough preparation, I had failed to note this, and in fact, as I sat there, my reaction was I didn't know you could tell. You learn something new every day!

It now dawns on me what this crafty DA is trying to concoct in the way of a case. When the defendant had originally been arrested way back on the sex and robbery charges, there had been a woman in his room. I didn't know it at the time, but this is where I saved my client. At the probation surrender hearing during the defendant's testimony, the DA had asked for the name of the woman. I had objected for no particular reason, and the judge had excluded the question, and the defendant didn't have to answer. The DA was looking to learn the identity of the woman, and had she known who it was, could have investigated the weapon in the jacket. I had to marvel. Our dumb luck—dumb for sure. The probation officer was brought in at the trial and testified to my client's refusal to name the woman. This was a clever but thin attempt to suggest consciousness of guilt.

The case concluded, and it was time to argue. I lost it and was behaving unprofessionally, per usual, waving my arms and in the process knocking the open microphone on counsel table to the floor with what sounded like a sonic boom. And I concluded with my thought about the refusal to give the woman's name—"None of their damn business."

It didn't take long, and the defendant was, thankfully, acquitted on everything. The defendant had a nice way of putting things. He told me he was glad to see a little passion in the closing. He was particularly impressed with the "none of their business" quote. I couldn't resist. I went back to the district court and asked for a rehearing on the probation surrender. The violation had been those charges on which the defendant had been found not guilty. It was late in the year, and the defendant would be out early in January. I was asking the judge to reverse her previous ruling and let my client out for the holidays. Our unhappy DA opposed, and our heartless judge refused to alter the sentence. It was essentially the "have a heart" request, and our judge didn't have one.

In the administration of criminal justice, why must the hammer always be down? My thinking was that the judge's ruling was plainly wrong, in more ways than one, but there was no time left for an appeal. The request to reconsider was worth a try anyway. This was a very complex case but gratifying. One of my favorites.

# 52

## A Most Favorite Case

**I was well along in** this stretch of my practice. I was determined that I would keep going no matter how close I got to the edge of going dotty. Previous iterations of my "practice" had only lasted ten years. I was well into fifteen years, and I was pretty much on cruise control. I had tried a lot of cases since the days when I was Mr. Dangerous, and I was now more dangerous than ever. I was carrying a substantial caseload, although less than in previous years, and there were no real challenges on the horizon. But around the corner, there is always something unexpected. I recall a time when I was with the Defenders Committee, a judge had pulled me aside and suggested that maybe I should consider something else because the work must be getting boring. He was wrong. It's never boring. There is always something new. I was now, on occasion, close to behaving like a real lawyer. Well, maybe not.

Just when I think I am in my comfort zone and everything is second nature, something comes along that blindsides me, as this case did. I was assigned a case where the previous lawyer had been discharged, a usual thing for me. My client was in custody at the jail, so I prepared to visit him. The principal charge was serious—masked armed robbery, which had a five-year minimum. That sentence wasn't mandatory, but if imposed, it would be for a minimum of five years. Straight probation, which would avoid the minimum sentence, would be unlikely.

I read up on the case. Allegedly my defendant, along with four or five others, ordered some pizzas, and when the delivery man showed up, they took the pizzas and also whatever cash he had. I guess they were masked. This was at gunpoint—a rifle or handgun—I forget. It doesn't matter. The pizza driver was upset, of course, and the next day went looking for the culprits. He was helped in his search by the fact that his assailants, after they had eaten the pizzas, discarded the boxes into the trash in front of the house. The police became involved, investigated, and made some arrests, which included my client.

At the jail, I introduced myself. My client was delighted to see me. He was going to go to trial because he said this was a "beatable" case. I'm not sure if the word *beatable* exists, but on hearing this, any lawyer should immediately file a motion to withdraw. Since I am not any lawyer, I foolishly said, "Sure" with as much enthusiasm as I could muster. On looking a little deeper into the evidence, the case looked less and less beatable as it went along.

There was a codefendant in the case who was also looking at a trial, and there was another codefendant who had pled out and received a light sentence in exchange for his agreement to testify against the others. Trial time arrives, and I'm in the session with Mr. Beatable. The case has been sent to the session no one wants to be in because nothing in this session has been beaten for the last half-century, beatable or not. Waiting for us is the judge who has done her job and secured all guilty verdicts for the time she has been there. Lawyers were seen leaving the session shaking their heads in dismay, and others red-faced with anger with cries of "I can't believe what that judge just did." So this was going to be a battle, I was sure.

Both codefendant cases are in the session, and there is a problem. Because of something called the Bruton rule, the cases can't be tried together. Don't ask me what this is—you'll need a lawyer for that. This meant that only one of us was going to face the iron. In this modern day of fancified ways of decision-making, we went low-tech—we drew straws, literally. I lost, and my cocounsel, a man I knew well, wished me bon voyage through his combined guffaws, sighs of relief, and comments like "Too bad for you, pal."

The case starts, and everything is okay so far. A jury is selected. I am bowing and scraping and trying my best to stay out of harm's way. It is time for the opening statements, and there is some bit of evidence that I am wishing the DA to stay away from in her opening because I am going to be objecting to its admissibility, and it may be excluded. I am allowed to approach the bench, and timidly, I head up to sidebar. I state my case, and the judge rules. I head back to my seat, and as I do so, I feel the hot breath of the judge on my neck and a snarl that she doesn't want any more of these unnecessary bench conferences. I meekly turn and mumble that I thought it was important as I stumble back to my chair. What the judge didn't know was that this was music to my ears. I hated the things. They interrupted the flow of the trial. There was a lot of whispering, and it was hard to hear. I would raise my voice and get shushed. "The jury can hear you." So, good, I wasn't going to ask for any. And what happened? I'm guessing there were about forty bench conferences during the trial—all called by the judge. So it wasn't that the conferences were bad; it was just who was in control. I was more than happy to let her run the show.

The testimony begins and goes along in an orderly fashion. I had been provided with a copy of a taped interview the police had conducted with my client in which, to put it fairly, the police went amok when my client refused to confess or in any way cooperate with their investigation. They swore they were going to get him, and he was going to do a lot of time, and his kid wouldn't know to call him Daddy by the time he got out, which would probably be for the kid's graduation from college. It was so brutal that in my opening, with bravado, I said if the DA didn't play the tape, I was certainly going to. The prosecution's hand was forced, and they played it in all its obscenity.

In a nice moment, my client wept silently when the threatening parts were played. The government presented its lame coconspirator who had been given a sentence of only ninety days for his cooperation. He clearly was uncomfortable and did a good job of making it look as if the only reason he was naming my client was because of the extreme leniency he had been offered. It took five days of trial time for the case—an age for me since usually, I was good for just a day or two with my many "No questions, Your Honor" cross-examinations. Finally, the case went to the jury.

Now it is time for the closings, and I have to get up there and be stared at and hope I do a decent job. I have done this a lot, and so I know I can, but there is always a bit of—no, a lot of nervousness when the time comes. You're standing there, looking at people and trying to be sincere and not make mistakes. But sometimes you just know that you have hit gold. In this case, I was commenting on the police interview.

The interrogating officer kept saying to my client, "You are in a peck of trouble."

For some reason, I paused and said, "What is a peck anyway?"

At this, a juror in the front row became animated. She started waving and squirming and all but climbed out of the box because she knew what a peck was and was going to tell everybody. My follow-up line was that I didn't know, so I had looked it up. It was clear that we were now the only two people in the galaxy who knew. I gave the answer before she went to the chalkboard and wrote it down. The two of us had surely become fast friends. What a wonderful moment. I won't say this won the case, but it didn't hurt.

Soon the jury was sent out, and I whispered to my client that I thought they would be out for about two hours, but I expected an acquittal. About two hours on the dot, the jury came back—not guilty on all charges. I felt like such a pro—Babe Ruth and his called shot. I have thought often about this case, and although it was a while before retirement, this case represents to me the acme of what I was able to do. A serious case, tough judge, good jury, able prosecutor, many good moments. A case to savor. I left the courtroom to go down to the lockup to accept congratulations from Mr. Beatable. As I was headed to the stairwell, which would take me there, I ran into a half-dozen of the jurors. They had gathered their coats and were on their way out of the building. They were understandably excited and even exhilarated about their verdict in the case.

I stopped, and we spoke for a few moments. It was all smiles. I have had a few of these cases where I have seen the jury or some of the jurors after the fact of an acquittal, and I have a sneaking suspicion that they want to ask a question. And this question is, "Did he really do it?" or some variation. The jury wants some affirmation that their judgment was correct. This question was not asked, and I would, of course, have said he was as innocent as a newborn. There was a brief moment where the judge was discussed. I think I have a pretty good read on what is going on with people, particularly in these trials, but a comment from one of the jurors floored me.

She said, "That judge, she sure liked you."

Sorry, but I missed that. She "sure" had a funny way of showing it. Maybe it was all those bench conferences I never asked for.

So that was that, and I was now Clarence Darrow and a lot of others all rolled into one. This was the first loss in that session for the government since whenever—which helped make it a special victory. I was entitled to drag myself around downcast, and when someone asked how the case went, I could happily say, "I'll let you know after the funeral of a family member."

But that was not quite that, and depending on how one looks at it, there was something that made this case extra special, and that is that it reveals, at least to my way of thinking, the loopiness or perhaps I should say the absurdity of the criminal justice system. And that's because that defendant who was acquitted by that lovely jury that now knows what a peck is was actually, dare I say it, guilty. And that fact most certainly put a cherry on top of this legal sundae. Now I'm not saying my client was guilty because I thought he was guilty or it seemed like he was guilty or he told me he was guilty. I'm saying this because he absolutely was guilty, and this is how that is known.

After a few days of trial, the prosecutor comes up to me and wants to talk. I know the prosecutor and have had cases with her. She is capable, and she knows her stuff. She tells me she has evaluated her case and has thought carefully about it. She doesn't like how her case is going and wants to know if my client might accept a few years of probation in exchange for a guilty plea. I bring this to Mr. Beatable, and he is a practical guy and gives it about a nanosecond and says, "Sure." So now we are back upstairs in the session. We tell the judge that we have a disposition for her consideration.

A digression here is to explain the procedure under Massachusetts court rules. It is loosely referred to as the defendant's cap plea. The defendant offers to plead guilty, but the sentence that may be imposed is capped at the defendant's offer. If the judge wants to go higher, the defendant is told and has the option to accept, but the defendant also has the right to reject and exercise trial rights.

Here is what I could never understand about this procedure. Instead of there being a hearing on whether or not the judge will accept the suggested disposition before the plea colloquy, the judge goes right ahead and says, "Swear in the defendant."

Most judges follow this procedure. I know what's coming next, and on occasion, I have asked a judge, "Don't you think we should know what Your Honor will do before we go through the plea colloquy?" since the defendant will be required as part of the colloquy to swear under oath that he committed the offense. On the times I have asked that, I'm looked at like I am a space alien. So now the judge goes right into the colloquy with no preliminaries. I don't say anything because maybe I want the plea to work so I can finish with Mr. B. Or, more likely, it is a recommendation suggested by the government, so I'm confident the judge will accept it. Also, my client is in agreement.

The colloquy takes place, and it goes smoothly. There is a statement of the case and an admonition that he is admitting to the many pages of the police report that have just been read. And then there is the joke about how the only reason he is pleading guilty is because he is guilty and not because Mr. Beatable has some questions about how effective his counselor is or doesn't want to chance it that the case isn't beatable after all or wants to take the deal and eliminate the risk of what might happen when one is in a peck of trouble—like receive a stiff state's prison sentence. It is important that this is all under oath. This means that the defendant has now said under the pains and penalties of perjury that he did it, that he participated in the robbery of the pizza driver. And now we mention the suggested disposition of two years' probation and also point out it is a joint recommendation.

The government tells the court it would be most happy if the court would accept this proposed disposition. And then the hue and cry went up, and the fires burned bright, and no way was this acceptable—the defendant, rules the judge, has to do at least two years in prison. I didn't even try to convince him, but of course, he wasn't going to accept that, so he backs out of the plea, and the trial resumes. The case wraps up, and the defendant wins, even though he pled guilty and said under oath that he was guilty.

And I'm wondering, How does this work? Am I supposed to get up in front of the jury and announce that the defendant just pled guilty and please ignore this and find him innocent anyway? Can I say in front of the jury that he is innocent? What if the defendant wants to testify and say he was in the middle of the Sahara Desert when the thing went down? Can he do that? Was the plea a legal fiction? Is the whole legal thing a fiction? I'm thinking I'll need a manned spacecraft in order to return to my office.

So my most happy client walked, and shortly, his codefendant, whose lawyer thought he had dodged a bullet, had to face the iron. It was before a different judge. Seven to ten upstate. And my client? Probably enjoying a pizza somewhere—I'm sure it's one he paid for.

# 53

## Near Retirement

**More of the routine followed,** but late in this last run, I had a case that had been pending for a while. I wasn't in any hurry to try it because there was this heavy expectation that the case would be won. The charge was possession of a firearm and involved the usual mandatory sentence. My client was out on bail, and so the case did not have the priority of custody cases. There was a police chase, and the car being chased was pulled over at the end of a dead-end street. As the car came to a halt, a firearm was thrown out of the rear passenger side window, which was where my client was sitting. He was charged as a result. How much the police were able to observe was very much in question. The case eventually went to trial. The evidence was complex for a number of reasons, including the fact that there were others close by who also had guns—a lot of guns.

In the end, the jury agreed the defendant was not the guilty party, and he was acquitted. My grateful client was long gone before he had a chance to give me his many thank-yous. I did not realize it at the time, but this was to be my last jury trial. In retrospect, it was especially gratifying because it meant that this last twenty-year stint was bookended with not-guilty verdicts. An indication that I was slowing down and retirement was around the corner was because of what happened after the trial. The defense in the case was that the weapon did not belong to my client, and he did not throw anything out the window as he testified at the trial. The judge was the judge in the garage stalker case who had now shifted over to Suffolk County to make my life miserable there. The move, just to give that judge a little of a jiggle, would be to have asked to approach the bench after the trial.

Once at the bench, I should be telling the judge that I had just spoken with the defendant, and he was wondering if the court could give him some assistance in getting his gun back. This after the entire basis of the case was that the weapon was not the defendant's. Something held me back.

In earlier days, I would not have hesitated. Truly, I was getting mellow, and shifty was becoming a little worn around the edges. Thoughts of retirement began to preoccupy me from time to time, even though I had hoped to continue practicing until I could barely move. Maybe I was beginning to tire of tying the judges up in knots, going to prisons, and meeting many new and interesting people among the clientele. There was a feeling that the sharp edge had dulled somewhat, and the day-to-day enthusiasm was waning.

Toward the end of my run, although I was not aware I was drawing close to retirement, there was a course offered by Massachusetts Continuing Legal Education (MCLE) entitled "A Conversation with the Legends." Continuing education had become a major focus in Massachusetts. The forerunner was an organization called the New England Law Institute (NELI). It put out a small booklet on leading state and constitutional cases. It had a pink binding and was referred to as the "Nellie." That's all there was at the beginning, just that one booklet. Now MCLE has grown to be this ginormous organization which has its own building and produces enough how-to publications to fill an entire library.

Any subject one can think of is covered, including how to cough up a lunger while seated in front of a jury without its noticing. This course was on a much loftier topic, even though the last mentioned was of greater value for the kind of work I was doing. It was entitled "A Conversation with the Legends: In Celebration of the American Jury Trial." I knew a few of the lawyers who were featured on the panel. A course booklet was included in exchange for the substantial fee required to attend. The booklet was over seven hundred pages long and had transcript portions celebrating the juries which had been good enough to see things the way of the various panel members. Huge money verdicts were celebrated. It was a festive occasion.

As I sat there and listened or daydreamed or whatever, I couldn't help but recall a client I had previously represented. He was held at the jail on bail, and I had to travel there to talk to him about his case. He was one of those clients that I enjoyed visiting. A smart, hip man who was in on a drug dealing charge. I would sit in the small interview room waiting to speak with him. On one of these occasions, somewhere in a break in the conversation, he volunteered the following: "You know, Mr. Wood, you are a legend," after which we laughed so hard that we nearly fell out of our chairs. But I knew he meant it, and it was good enough for me. And the thought passed as I was listening to these big-time legends that they had missed out.

I couldn't care less about big money verdicts. I was a legend amongst these folks who were getting stuck in the criminal justice system, and that made me very happy. I didn't need MCLE or any other organization to tell me my worth. It came from the people who counted. I'm proud of the fact that I never was voted PD of the month or was accorded one of those MVP public interest awards that proliferate at year-end get-togethers of the public defender troops. One of those would have told me quite the opposite. Esteemed by my peers? I couldn't care less. Valued by the clients? Fantastic.

# 54

## Retirement for Sure

**A year or so later,** I was leaving the municipal courthouse and began to experience excruciating pain in a knee. I was able to make it back to the office with the aid of a cane I purchased on the way. I had had a successful hearing in which I managed to engineer a dismissal in a serious case and had pled out a man I was representing for maybe the sixth time to a short county sentence. A doctor visit resulted in the advice that I should stay off my feet for the next month. I called the court daily to arrange continuances on my open cases until I thought, maybe now is the time. I had spent the last twenty-one years flat out with virtually no time off, a murderous commute, workdays rising at 3:30 a.m., and I was tired, mentally exhausted. The decision was made, and I arranged to have my current cases reassigned.

So retirement came, not the way I expected, but as it turned out, it came in just the right way and at the right time. In addition to the medical issue that kept me away from the courts for a few weeks, there was also that feeling that I was having difficulty generating the get-up-and-go for my current cases. I had been at it a long time, and the decision to drop the baton and let someone else pick it up was easy. I called a lawyer I knew who relayed the decision to the court so other lawyers could be appointed. One judge, I was told, asked, "When's the party?"

Thankfully, there was none. If a few clients wanted to get together, that might have been different. Perhaps even a small send-off in an ante room of one of the prisons would have been appropriate. A regret that I had was that I did not have a chance to meet with a few special clients I had stayed in touch with over the years.

So I was out of there. I have gone on at length about the forty-six-year stretch from start to finish with many lane changes along the way. It was all the same. Go to court virtually every day with a bunch of cases and clients in it up to their eyeballs. Days I didn't go to court were days of boredom. I missed court and rubbing shoulders with one client or another even for one day. At least, if I couldn't get to court, I could go to some jail or prison to visit a client. There was always someone held on bail or someone serving time who needed attention. I was pushed to the limit and immersed in my work for the totality. It all stays with me, the memories of victories, of things well done, and of things not so well done, or maybe well enough done but thoughts that perhaps I could have done better. I was often helped by more experienced people who from time to time showed me the way.

I was lucky that in my first incarnation at the Massachusetts Defenders Committee, I had only a short taste of the supervisory role, enough to know that that was not for me. I recall a time in court waiting for one of my cases to be called. An attorney next to me asked if I had ever thought about being a judge. Not for one second. The person who asked me that question did become a judge, so that was what that question was about.

So I encourage all law students to follow into the public realm. Forget about money; there isn't any. You need a spouse with a good job in tech. Forget about moving on to high office and forget about accolades. The joy is in the doing. There is, however, one requirement for this type of job, and that is this: an understanding that anything you might have learned at law school is irrelevant. No, I mean it. For I tell you, that is the truth. As a neophyte, I used to spend hours in the library researching the law, thinking I would find something that would aid me in my defense of my clients. Forget it. The law is always against you. Remember that when you are assigned a case, that case arose as a result of a magistrate or a grand jury concluding that there is evidence of your client's guilt. Take it from there and don't think the law is going to help you. But remember this: the two sweetest words in the English language are these: "Not Guilty."

# 55

## The Wrap-Up

**A few years into retirement,** I was back at the Harvard Law School where it all began. It was the occasion of the two hundredth anniversary of the school's founding. It was also the fiftieth anniversary of my graduation. It was a gala event. Flags were flying, bands were playing, and the wine was flowing. The Supreme Court was there, at least the ones that had graduated from Harvard, and that was close to a majority of the court. The school had recently put to rest the minor flap that occurred when it was discovered that those shocks of wheat on the law school crest had not been harvested by the John Deere Company.

I was there out of curiosity to see if the school had changed since I had graduated. Was it still a place that brought back unpleasant memories? The celebration spanned four days, and I had paid to attend all four. I was substantially poorer as a result. I had signed up for all the seminars that touched on criminal law. The question of what I had done during the previous fifty years would occasionally come up. If I disclosed I had been a public defender, the conversation would come to a halt, and I would be treated as if I had some form of legal leprosy. Nobody said anything derogatory. They just moved a few chairs away. Most of my classmates had traditional careers in government, business, or law firms, and they actually made money, something I never did. Some of them made a lot of money as I found out when it was time to pass the hat at the class dinner on Saturday night.

The first day, I had an opportunity to attend some classes. I remembered that the trick when I was there was not to get called on and humiliated by the professor conducting the class. You sat in someone else's seat, hid behind a stack of books, or pretended it was not you when your name was called and the professor was looking right at you—or you just didn't go—my favorite.

As I was searching for the classroom I had in mind, I noticed what I assumed were students dressed in costumes and wondered what that was about. When I reached my destination, I discovered there was a costume party—something I didn't remember from my earlier days. But, yes, it was within a few weeks of Halloween, so why not? There was a game involved, and the way not to get called on in class was to have the best costume. If, for instance, you showed up dressed as an ordinary law student, you were at risk of being asked to answer some daunting question. Most of the students were disguised as animals of one kind or another, such that the room took on the aspect of a diorama of the Serengeti Plain. You would have thought there would be a few legal eagles, but I didn't see any.

The professor was explaining how to appeal to the United States Supreme Court, an important subject for the Harvards who expected to either be appearing there or presiding there. The professor was moving with speed as the time left for the class was drawing short, and he had a lot of ground to cover. The menagerie was no longer being called on and sat quietly waiting for the class to end. As he progressed, he had a verbal oddity in his dissertation. He kept saying "Are you with me?" before moving on. You could tell from the blank stares from a group of zebras that they weren't.

After morning classes, there was a luncheon spread for the returning alumni. I was seated at a table with graduates who were from foreign countries. Not a lot of conversation, but the food was out of sight. And then it was on to the main event, which was the "conversation" with the Supreme Court justices. That conversation consisted of softball questions from the newly appointed law school dean. It was reassuring to hear that the Harvards on the court still had a majority over the hated Yales. A great sigh of relief went up from the assembled. I was viewing all this through the prism of my forty-six years of practice as a public defender and was curious to find out if any of the judges had actually practiced. If any of them did, it was carefully hidden. They became suspect in my mind since they seemed to have genuinely enjoyed their experience as Harvard Law students. I knew that to be an impossibility since I had been there and seen the operation firsthand.

Perhaps in the rarified atmosphere where they work, the sun is always shining, and the past is a happy memory. Stories were recounted about the professors and little things that happened that were worth a laugh, and laugh the audience did. I noticed that the justices were heavy on the academic side—former professors. It seemed to me the only justice who had been a judge on cases where there were litigants and juries was the one who had retired. My experience told me a different story about the law and about practice. After all, I had been going to court virtually every day for most of forty-six years and handled thousands of criminal matters. The colloquium broke up, and I was out of there, but not until after a canapé or two but no wine. The next day was seminar day, all day. And as I drove home, I couldn't get this case out of my mind, and here it is in some detail. Perhaps it helps to explain why I have a different slant toward the practice of law.

# 56

## The Court Is Told Off

**The charges in that case** were assault with intent to rob unarmed and assault and battery, and I was the public defender assigned to represent the defendant. This happy event came about because my new client had just fired his previous lawyer, a staff attorney of the CPCS group. I had been the duty attorney for the day's cases and had returned for the afternoon session. Assignments initiate in the magistrate's session. The magistrate takes the arraignment—always a not guilty plea—and rubber stamps the government bail request, which in the superior court always has at least three zeros at the back end. An exception to this routine is when there is a request for the duty attorney in the judge's session next door. This almost always means one thing, and that is that an attorney is being fired. The case must be heard in the judge's session for the reason that only a judge can rule on the motion to have an attorney removed from a case. I reported to the judge's session, and sure enough, a hearing was in progress. The dissatisfied client was airing his grievances. The hearing concluded, and the current attorney was allowed to withdraw.

So now I'm on board with this new client about whom I know nothing except that I have been present at a portion of the hearing and had a chance to see my new client in action. I also know the charges because I have to file the NAC on which I am required to list them. My new client has been eyeing me anxiously. I, on the other hand, have been looking forward to my new assignment with eagerness; a prospective client who fires one of the Committee lawyers can't be all bad. I speak briefly with the discharged lawyer and attempt to get my hands on the case file. There's usually a parting comment of encouragement—something like "Good luck with this guy, he's a real jerk."

Now it was time to pay a quick visit to my new client before he is returned to his place of custody. The lock-up in the Suffolk Superior Court is on the mezzanine and accessed by a set of narrow stairs. The prisoners are held in groups in a number of different cells. To speak to a client, one either has to kneel and speak through an open slot about waist-high or one can speak through a small crack in the side of the door. The latter is preferable since one can remain standing and it's easier to take notes. I tell my client how glad I am to be his lawyer and what a great privilege it is to be representing him. It's good that I am talking through the side of the door because this client can't see me to gauge my level of sincerity. Also, I'm unable to tell if my prior counsel's assessment of my new client is correct, at least at first.

I survive my first test, which is not to get fired on first meeting, and maybe gain something which is in short supply, a little trust. I leave the courthouse but not before giving my new client my business card and telling him I will be out to see him soon.

Back at the office, I take a look at the file to learn what I already suspect, which is that the case is virtually defenseless, a not unusual occurrence. The police report and the grand jury testimony tell me all I need to know. The defendant approached the victim, who was walking onto his front porch, and demanded that he give him his "fucking money." He wasn't begging or panhandling—just give him the fucking money. When the victim didn't comply, the defendant punched him in the face and demanded, again, the "fucking money."

This was witnessed through an adjacent open window by a half dozen people or so getting ready for an evening meal. They exited onto the porch and chased the defendant away. The police were called, and after first bringing in some unfortunate who matched the description given over the air (no, no, he's not the one, all the witnesses agreed), the defendant was produced by the police and identified as the perpetrator. So a tough case. But this didn't mean that the case wouldn't go to trial.

The standard "not guilty" plea had been entered at the time of arraignment. Unless that plea is changed to guilty as a result of a plea bargain, the case will need to be tried. And that is something I needed to prepare for from the very beginning.

I also noted that this new client was being held in a maximum security prison, something highly unusual. Why was he being held there? Defendants waiting trial and held because unable to post bail were ordinarily at the county jail in Boston or, if they had previously served a state sentence, could be held in the prison in Concord, but only Concord.

Time passed, and it was time for a visit. I prepared for an interview with my client with a thorough review of the file. Copies of correspondence with the previous attorney shed some light on what the problem was with her. She had failed to prepare and file a motion to dismiss. It was clear that the reason the motion had not been filed was because the motion was baseless, frivolous—whatever one wants to call it. It was a little hard to understand, but the defendant had seized on some minor factual variances between the police report and the grand jury testimony, which, in his opinion, meant that the indictments were predicated on lies. An attempt to convince the defendant of the fruitlessness of his position resulted in her being fired.

I arrived at the maximum security facility, a forty-mile drive, and was greeted by the usual welcoming warning that once on prison property, my person, my car, and my belongings were subject to search by the authorities. I produced the required documents and was admitted. It was a prison I had been to many times before. I knew that the visiting room was just inside the main gate. My escort walked me past the visiting room and down a long corridor.

"So where was my client?" I inquired.

"He's in the SMU," I was told.

"And what," I inquired, "is the SMU?"

"The SMU is the Special Management Unit," came the answer.

The mystery was solved. My client was being specially managed because he had a propensity toward violence, I guessed. And I was on my way to a "contact" visit? Finally, I was taken to a small room accessed by a heavy steel door. I had never had any fears about seeing clients, but in this situation, I had a small amount of anxiety. My client was produced, and the enormous door was closed, and I was alone with my client, who was shackled and handcuffed. A guard kept an eye on the two of us through a small window. As it turned out, I didn't have to worry. I could tell that he was glad to see me because there was a lilt to the way in which he snarled at me. The discussion of the case didn't get far because he was stuck on his chief gripe, which was his prior lawyer's failure to manage a dismissal. He thought he had been greatly wronged because the motion to dismiss was an open and shut winner. He was steadfast in his claim that the grand jury testimony was all lies. It was hard to comprehend what he was talking about.

Very little was accomplished at this interview except that I got to know a little about my client. And just getting to know him—what kind of a person he was—was important. I knew that this was going to be a difficult representation, something to which I was no stranger.

This case demonstrates an important facet of the business. That is, no matter if one attended and somehow managed to graduate from Harvard Law School, as I did, the client knows more law than you ever thought of knowing, and it is useless to try to convince your client otherwise. Telling the client that some legal position that he or she has about the case is wrong guarantees dismissal or a complaint to the public defender organization or the Bar Association. Of course, there is always the possibility, particularly in my case, that my client does know more law than I do, so I am always circumspect in claiming that my client is wrong. My practice is to encourage my client to produce some case law, which often he is eager to do. That way, I can check and see if my client is right.

Back at the office, with my head still spinning, I cobbled together a motion to dismiss in which I tried to put in as much as I could understand of my client's position. I posted it to the court with a copy to my client. By return mail, even faster than I thought the postal authorities were capable, the motion came back endorsed, as was expected: denied. I forwarded a copy to the client.

Time passed, and I had no contact with my client. I needed to get a sense as to where the case might be headed. A plea deal seemed to be a natural outcome, but I had a rule to never discuss a possible plea with the Commonwealth unless specifically authorized by my client. I needed to hear from him before contacting the DA in the case. Another long drive to the prison. Another wait while I went through the process of being admitted to the prison. The wait was lengthy. A guard approached. My client, I was told, was refusing to see me. Was I crushed? Were my feelings hurt? Not exactly. At least I would be home early, and I would be saved possible recrimination for my failure on the motion. But it was going to be difficult to plot strategy for the defendant's case if it was going to be a trial.

At this point, most lawyers would have filed a motion to withdraw. I would tell the court that I could not represent this defendant because he would not cooperate with me. A lot of silly thoughts were involved, but I just couldn't bring myself to make that move. Besides, on another level, this case was beginning to get interesting. So I decided to do nothing and went home and forgot about it.

More time passed, and the trial date was approaching. I sent the defendant a letter suggesting we really needed to talk. The letter came back a few days later stamped "Refused, Return to Sender." If I had not yet been aware of it, I had a live one for a client. I waited, expecting to receive a copy of a motion to discharge me filed by the defendant. None came, and this meant I was still his lawyer. Trial time was advancing, and puzzlement was not a good description of what I was thinking. The DA was bombarding me with witness lists and motions of all kinds meant to sew up my client. The DA in the case had been assigned because, although she had little trial experience, apparently even the inexperienced couldn't lose this one in the view of the DA's office.

Every possible witness was on the witness list, all the police involved, all the civilian witnesses, as well as numerous medical personnel—a couple of dozen.

The trial date arrived, and still no contact from my client. The judge came out on the bench. The witnesses were present. The lawyers were there. It was time to produce the defendant, who had been brought in from the SMU. A couple of bailiffs were dispatched to bring the defendant down from the lock-up. After a wait, they returned with the news that the defendant refused to leave his cell. It was possible I might have to try this case with an empty chair for a client—defendant tried *in absentia*, as the Latin has it. I hadn't been required to do that yet, but there's always a first time. On learning of the defendant's refusal, the judge would have none of it and ordered that the defendant be brought in.

More than a few court officers, more like a posse, went off to retrieve the defendant. Soon the defendant appeared—was brought in. He and I exchanged salutations. The judge then went into a lengthy speech about the defendant's very important constitutional guarantees—right to counsel, right to a jury trial, his rights to confront all the witnesses and cross-examine them, and have the right to not testify and not have it held against him, and be cloaked with the presumption of innocence, such as it was. Everything was covered. Now didn't he want to be present to exercise all these rights guaranteed by our wonderful United States Constitution?

At the conclusion of this remarkable and persuasive speech by the judge, the defendant rose, and the courtroom grew quiet. While I imagined something like "Stars and Stripes Forever" being hummed in the background, the defendant had a suggestion for the court, and it was this: "Go fuck yourself."

What happened next happened very fast. In true Harvard tradition, I was able to sidestep the flying wedge of court personnel that landed on my client with such force as to spread-eagle him across the counsel table next to me. There was a brief struggle, after which whatever was left of my client was removed from the room, and decorum was resumed. The aftermath was that my client was deemed to be in need of a mental health evaluation and was committed to the state hospital for such; even though arguably, his outburst was the essence of sanity. What were all those rights going to do for him? What was I going to do for him? He was screwed, and he knew it. Why participate in a charade?

I won't say that this episode vaulted my client into my personal pantheon of favorites, but he certainly comes close. Eventually, since I was not considered qualified to represent clients in mental health matters, possibly for good reason, I left this case and never did find out how it ended.

My client's outburst was not quite on the same level as "Go west, young man"; "I chopped down the cherry tree"; or even "Give me liberty or give me death" but nearly. Needless to say, this case never made it into a topic in the Harvard Law curriculum. If it had, it might have gone this way: "Sir, what was the holding in the case of Commonwealth v. (name withheld)? Sir, it was held on appeal, following the leading case of Rex v. Whomever, Queen's Lunch (citation omitted), that 'Go Fuck Yourself' was not a plea recognized either at law or in equity, and the exceptions were overruled."

And I had a last thought. Brimming with my recently acquired knowledge of how to appeal to the Supreme Court I had learned from today's procedure class, I wondered if there were to be a way to get this case before the nine justices, where the great imponderables of the legal world are decided. I could be there wearing a frock coat or cutaway or whatever lawyers who appear there wear, my voice echoing off the marble columns thusly: "May it please the court: the question today is whether 'Go fuck yourself' is a proper plea in bar known at the common law or in equity." And what, I thought, was the relevance of Harvard Law to any of this? I'm still thinking that one over.

Years later, I saw this defendant in the lockup in the same court. I caught his eye for a moment and thought about calling him over and chatting with him for a moment. There was, however, a certain look in that eye that made me think he might have for me the same suggestion he had for the court those few years ago, so I thought better of it.

# 57

## Clinical Storytelling

**The next day, I attended** a seminar which consisted of a playlet entitled *Advocacy through Storytelling*, and I eagerly awaited the opening curtain. I knew two of the creators of this little passion play because I had seen them performing in court as part of the Harvard Law clinical studies program. I knew them to be among those who took the arm-patting, back-rubbing approach to succor the picked-upon unfortunates who happened to be caught up in the criminal justice system. And sure enough, that was what it was all about.

It was a little hard to follow, but it was a motion to dismiss an apparently trumped-up case against a beloved juvenile defendant. There was a particularly treacly scene where the up-against-it single mother is washing the kid's socks while he struggles with trying to differentiate cosine theta as part of his calculus class. Eventually, the stalwart Harvards win out, and the case is dismissed by the judge, who we are told, was a judge in real life. A general hug fest occurs at the end, and even the baddie DA beams enthusiastically now that justice has been done.

Remarkably, none of the cast members announced they had just won their case and were headed to Disneyland. All the Harvard grads in attendance applauded vigorously and marveled at the great work done by the Harvard clinicians. Undoubtedly, contributions poured in to enable the clinics to continue their great work.

After another of those lunches, the main event was for speakers of some note to talk generally about the criminal justice system. The speakers started off by decrying the large numbers of men and women caught up in the totality of the US penal system. Comparisons were made with other "civilized" nations, and the numbers were described as brutal. America has a much larger percentage of the population in prison, jails, or on probation supervision than these other nations, including the so-called repressive regimes. The assembled Harvards groaned and hung their heads in shame, and one might imagine thought about applications for Canadian citizenship. Our "broken" criminal justice system was pilloried by speaker after speaker.

I couldn't help reflecting, as I listened, that the system wasn't broken. They had it all wrong. Reality is a concept that is sometimes hard to grasp, and the reality of the criminal justice world is simple. The purpose of the system is to stick people in jail, and as such, the system is an unqualified success. The theory that has been the basis of the system is that people will be law-abiding if there is a penalty for lawbreaking. This idea has been behind the criminal justice system forever. Also, history has shown that a variety of approaches have never worked. Leniency, stiff penalties, programs, societal interventions—none of these have worked. So face it. A world in which there will be a certain amount of "criminal" activity will always be with us. I had a thought to raise my hand in the Q and A which followed and ask if people changed their behavior ever so slightly, might this result in a lowering of the incarceration rate? But this was Harvard, and I didn't want to get burned at the stake for a heretical question of that sort.

So is there a solution, assuming that our huge prison population is something that we would rather not live with? There is, and it is easily identified. It's the shift. What is needed are more lawyers and shiftier lawyers to help the accused get out from under. Instead of training lawyers in the commercial code and securities regulation, there should be courses in how to present criminal cases. Are there such courses? Of course not. Courses from experienced lawyers who know how to argue frivolous stories, how to stand, how to sit, how to tie the judges up in knots, how to charm the juries? Never.

The reason for this is that, in truth, Harvard Law hasn't the slightest interest in this pressing problem of our king-size prison population. What a marvelous thing it would be if Harvard took on a true social responsibility and its graduates descended en masse into the criminal courts of the nation. Fighting by shifty lawyers such as myself on helping the accused "beat the rap" is the true way to lower the prison population. Instead, what do we have? We have various pipe dreams aimed at ending what is referred to as the mass incarceration of our citizens. And how do these programs intend to succeed? Harvard has one that will work by "empowering" entire neighborhoods, although the methodology of empowerment is a little short on specifics. One can assume that this does not mean going to the ghetto and passing out guns and ammo. Anybody who has spent any length of time in the criminal courts must understand that defendants are not being put upon in the courts but just the opposite are doing things that will guarantee jail time. Probation is tried, suspended sentences are tried. Programs are tried, like those infuriating anger management programs. None of them work. Remember my client who trashed his sex board registration and was found not guilty?

Here are a few examples of how this goes. I had a client who was homeless. He was a level three sex offender. There was virtually no place he could live because he was zoned out of most areas of habitation. In the winter when it was cold, he would go to a store and steal a coat. If he got away with it, so be it, and he'd have the coat for warmth. If he got caught and went to jail, he wouldn't mind. It would be a place where he could get warm and get three squares.

Or how about this person whom I represented? A police officer who never arrests anybody is sitting in a marked police car outside a barroom. It is a sunny day, and it is noontime. He is the type who settles problems by trying to avoid arrests. "Did you steal that? Give it back." As he's sitting there, a man runs out of the barroom followed by a second man who, within a few feet of the car copiously marked "Police," pulls out a silver-plated revolver and shoots the fleeing first man. Our street cop who never arrests now has no choice. To make sure the shooting victim hustles back, pulls down his pants, and points out the bullet wound in his butt. Do you think our shooter is somehow daunted by the presence of the cop a few feet away? Of course not. It is this kind of behavior that is filling the prisons.

Or how about this one? I was in the municipal court, taking appointments on a very busy day. We were getting to the end of the day's chaos, and there were a few late arrests to be arraigned. I appeared for a young man who seemed to me to be a little familiar. It suddenly dawned on me that I had appeared for this man at the very beginning of the day. He had been charged with shoplifting and been released and now was back in court a few hours later charged with—you guessed it—shoplifting.

Do you think that the sex offender thought that rather than steal a coat and maybe go to jail, he should stay out in the street and risk frostbite? Do you think that the man who ran out of the bar and fired away in broad daylight thought for a moment, I better not do this because if I do, I won't be able to pay the rent and support my family and run for city council? Do you think the shoplifter thought he was lucky to have been released on bail and obeyed what he was warned, namely that he better not get in trouble or his bail order might be revoked? Of course not. We need to get real and stop the fantasy that those who wind up in prison are really saints in felons' clothing.

Generally, there are so many people in jail because of behavior that society continues to regard as criminal, and despite the many different approaches, it is a situation that continues.

So what is the solution? I have already suggested let's get the lawyers involved—real talented and shifty ones, not those who think that filing motions and reading cases will win—but things like knowing what a peck is and what's preposterous and, most of all, being able to try the loser cases. Give the criminal class a chance. Keep them out of jail. Everybody should get to know a con or two. I know a few who, given a chance, could straighten out a few of society's problems in a hell of a hurry.

# 58

## A Few Loose Ends

**It's Harvard Law School, and** some things just can't be fixed. I have written about the years I spent on the departed list until I was recognized not as a shade but as a living, walking being, and the idea that I was deceased had been put to rest. After all, I was invited as a flesh and blood graduate to all the festivities at my fiftieth reunion and was not challenged as a fraud. But I was heartened when my wife received a letter from the Harvard Law School Alumni Relations Director shortly after I had attended the reunion, which stated the following: "Over the years, the Law School has invited the widows and widowers of our graduates to return to Cambridge to reconnect...and enjoy a weekend of good cheer" and maybe make a donation. We had a good laugh over that one.

And finally, just when I thought I had at long last returned to civilian life, I had to bring BOBOO back to life. The occasion for this was that I received a threat I was going to be put in BOBO purgatory because I had not filed a registration statement for the past year. I was facing an "Administrative Suspension," whatever that is. Registrations had to be done for the three years after retirement. I called the BOBO hotline and suggested that I had not filed a statement for the last year because I had been retired for five years as they must have known from the letter I sent them at the time of my retirement. And I tried hard not to shout.

I was icily informed that didn't matter. The bean counters at BOBO need three consecutive registration statements, no matter the actual date of retirement. I was warned that as of 3:00 p.m. on a date certain, I would be "administratively suspended" from the practice that I was no longer engaged in if they did not receive that registration form. A new form was obtained and completed, and I made sure that I mailed it so it would miss the deadline. The SJC rule that mandated the three registrations was so that BOBO would be able to "locate" attorneys should they be complained of. *Locate* is a word that I somehow associate with looking for suspects in criminal cases. *Contact* might have been a kinder word to use. But it's the SJC, and finesse is not necessarily its strong suit. Papers sent, and I never heard from them.

To show that BOBOO was still on the beat, I enclosed a street map showing my current residence with an arrow demarking same. A notation was included that this was where I could be "located" most days unless I was at the beach or the ballpark. How was this received? Unknown since, administratively, I was never notified.

So it's done. It has a completeness to it, a sort of body of work of which I am most proud. I helped a lot of people through the process and managed to keep my sanity, mostly, while doing so. It's nice to think that five years after retirement, BOBO has not had to try and "locate" me to answer to some misdeed. And I don't miss the hours, which were brutal. My commute was fifty miles down one of the infamous feeder roads to Boston, and if I hadn't left home by 5:00

a.m., I was assured of being caught in a traffic jam. My route from where I parked to where I had my morning breakfast took me by the downtown police station. I paid prettily for my parking privileges and noted as I walked up the hill how the cops parked for free in an expanse marked for police vehicles only. And I took note of what they were driving. Far better than my high-mileage sedan.

I often thought that this gave me an edge later in the day when I was finally in court. I would be at the office by seven o'clock with time to prepare. By court time, I was more than ready for the day's cases, and the cops, the DAs, and the judges.

I have written about those days in my own kind of style. In spite of my frequent oblique remarks, I have to confess I nevertheless owe much to all the great people who worked in the court system and dealt with my shifty behavior. It's nice to remember that through it all, I was still referred to as Mr. Wood (or occasionally Mr. Woods), even though something else might have come to mind from a few with whom I locked horns over the years. Yet what really gave life to my career were the clients, messed or unmessed, who kept me on my toes and breathed life into everything I did.

There is not much I miss in retirement, except maybe those prison visits where I tried to give some unfortunate client who was up against it some hope that I was going to help him or her with their situation before the courts. Often I couldn't do much, but many times I could, and I keep with me a sense of pride in what I was able to accomplish. And so a debt of gratitude to those numerous clients, far too many to name or even try to count, who gave me a different and valuable perspective on life and a meaning to my career as a lawyer, a career at the beginning I never thought I would have.

It was an exciting and challenging time. Certainly an arduous time. It's all still with me, and I often reflect and try to make sense of what it all meant. The best I can probably say is that it gives me a feeling of accomplishment. I was extremely lucky in that I found a career that consumed me and took all my energies for a full forty-six years. And even those times when I took a few years off, I always felt the pull and had to go back—but not this time. It's finished, thankfully. I think of my father and how he made money, lots of money, but had no enthusiasm for his law practice, and I am even more grateful as to how things turned out.

I've often thought about the criminal justice world that I was involved in for such a span of time. I've thought about the advances that have been made in the rights of certain groups. But what about the criminal population which is so large and still growing? Shouldn't there be a Perp Pride day? Is there a scheduled march on Washington on behalf of the cons? Might it be called "Perps Are People Too"? Will starlets at the movie awards speak on behalf of the criminal element? I'm not holding my breath.

Punishment as a weapon in the criminal courts is alive and well, and as we move along ever so slowly forward—or backward, depending on how you look at it—in our politically correct world, you can be sure that sticking people in prison will not lose its luster as a solution to perceived wrongdoing. How many would attend that "perp" march on Washington? A million? Two million? For sure.

Age, health issues, and a general emotional exhaustion after so many years contributed to the decision to retire. And that last exhausting stretch was flat out for over twenty years. I spent the next months getting up late and reflecting on my many years of practice, mostly in the public cause. I had expected many phone calls about pending matters because I had retired with cases still ongoing that had been reassigned to other lawyers. I did receive a few but about older, long-settled cases. I have spent my retirement years in appreciation of all the fun I had and consider myself fortunate to have had the career that I had. It was all right up my alley—the craziness, the insanity, the weirdness to all of which I mightily contributed.

Anybody entering the legal world, I implore you to consider working as a public defender. You'll be truly working for your fellow men and women, and it will tax your energies and your resources like no other type of legal employment. So that's it. It's done!

# About the Author

**John Wood is a graduate** of Harvard College and Harvard Law School. He practiced criminal defense law in the District and Superior Courts of the Commonwealth of Massachusetts for forty-six years. He is currently retired.

www.ingramcontent.com/pod-product-compliance
Lightning Source LLC
LaVergne TN
LVHW090304210926
848480LV00001B/125

* 9 7 9 8 8 9 3 0 8 0 4 5 2 *